COTTAGE GARDEN FAVOURITES

CLIVE LANE

COTTAGE GARDEN FAVOURITES

*Annuals grown from seed
for summer-long beauty*

David & Charles

ACKNOWLEDGEMENTS

The author would like to express his sincere thanks to RON AND LIN HILL for the wonderful photographs they have taken for this book, and to the many kind people who allowed photographs to be taken of their gardens and cottages, including Les and Mike at the Barnhouse, for planting whole borders of annuals; Elmtree Dried Flowers, Frocester, near Stroud, for the use of their flower fields; and Luckington Manor, Wiltshire, where the Edwardian hot border was photographed.

Special thanks also to Anna Mumford of David & Charles, editors Jo Weeks and Sarah Widdicombe, Russell Lofkin, and to Pat Taylor and Anne Hamblin of the Cottage Garden Society.

All photographs by Ron and Lin Hill except pp 42, 53, 54 (left), 70–1, 80–1, 83, 145 by S & O Matthews. Artwork on pp 32–8 by Eva Melhuish and Maggie Raynor.

A DAVID & CHARLES BOOK

First published in the UK in 1997
First paperback edition 2004

This book was previously published by David & Charles as *Cottage Garden Annuals*.

A catalogue record for this book is available from the British Library.

ISBN 0 7153 1810 1 Paperback
ISBN 0 7153 0429 1 Hardback

Printed in Singapore by KHL Printing Co Pte Ltd for David & Charles
Brunel House   Newton Abbot   Devon

Visit our website at www.davidandcharles.co.uk

David & Charles books are available from all good bookshops; alternatively you can contact our Orderline on (0)1626 334555 or write to us at FREEPOST EX2110, David & Charles Direct, Newton Abbot, TQ12 4ZZ (no stamp required UK mainland).

CONTENTS

Foreword   7

Gardening with old-fashioned annuals   9

Ideas for using cottage garden annuals   13

Growing annuals from seed   32

A-Z OF COTTAGE GARDEN
    ANNUALS   41

Who's Who?   157

Seed merchants and societies   158

Further reading   158

Index   159

FOREWORD

'COTTAGE GARDEN.' The words evoke a chocolate-box picture of a thatched cottage, roses and hollyhocks around the door, a gnarled apple tree, flowers and vegetables mingled together in crowded and cheerful profusion, box hedges and wattle fencing, plus a clutch of Victorian children, a dozing cat, and perhaps a few hens pecking about in the sunshine. A rustic paradise indeed, and visually extremely pleasing. Victorian artists painted such scenes in vast numbers.

Much has changed over the last 150 years or so. Thatched cottages are much less common, and nowadays are more likely to belong to commuters to the nearest town than to families who have lived and worked in their village for generations. The thatch is now crowned with a television aerial, and telephone and power lines enter under the eaves – and a good thing too, doubtless would remark the nineteenth-century cottager, who did not enjoy the benefits of running water, indoor sanitation or electric lights.

What has changed least is the garden. The cottage garden style has never entirely fallen out of fashion and today is as popular, perhaps even more so, than ever. But while the overall appearance of cottage gardens has remained fairly constant, the contents have changed quite considerably. Instead of being planted among or alongside the flowers, vegetables are now more often found in their own specialized plot, while many species of flowers that we take for granted today are newcomers from overseas and were quite unknown in the cottage gardens of the last century. Nevertheless, the defining hallmark is still clear: the same close-planted exuberance and apparently artless informality.

Simply because the style is so popular, the aspiring cottage gardener (who may live on an estate or in a terraced, semi-detached or town house – the cottage is not obligatory) is not short of advice. Any bookshop can offer an abundance of books and magazines providing information on almost every aspect of cottage gardening: design, what to plant and where, plant associations, pests and problems, and so on. However, when it comes to advice on choosing plants, the emphasis is heavily on perennials and shrubs. These are, of course, essential, forming as it were the backbone and structure of the garden, but a relatively neglected aspect, and one which receives only a passing mention, is the role of annual plants in the cottage garden. This book sets out to bridge this gap.

Opposite:
ANNUALS PROVIDE COMPLEMENTARY SPLASHES OF COLOUR IN THIS MIXED BORDER

Although perennial plants are an essential component of the cottage garden, they are often slow to establish and require time to give of their best. By using annuals, a cottage garden can be created in one season. This book will be immensely helpful not only to the first-time gardener anxious to create a rapid splash of colour, but also to the more experienced gardener looking for new ideas and plants to fill bare patches, tubs and containers.

Annuals have, of course, always been planted (and self-sown) in cottage gardens. Some have been firm favourites for many years but many, for one reason or another, have gradually been disregarded and almost forgotten. Happily, one of the aims of this book is to rescue and reintroduce for today's gardeners some of the finest of the old-fashioned cottage garden annuals.

The author, Clive Lane, a passionate cottage gardener and author of the highly successful guide *The Cottage Gardener's Companion*, as well as a founder-member of the Cottage Garden Society and its Vice-Chairman for many years, has a particular interest in unusual and old-fashioned plants, and over the years he has built up an unrivalled collection of rare and interesting cottage garden curiosities. Here he provides fascinating profiles of a range of annuals, biennials and tender perennials, each giving a detailed description of the plant, its origin, history and folklore, habit of growth and culture, together with a selection of choice varieties suitable for a traditional garden.

Every cottage gardener, experienced or beginner, will find much in this book that will be of practical help; it is also a pleasure to read. Moreover, turning the pages is an inspiration in itself – the photographers, Ron and Lin Hill, are to be congratulated on the superb quality of their illustrations.

DOUGLAS TAYLOR
Chairman, The Cottage Garden Society

GARDENING
with
OLD-FASHIONED ANNUALS

OLD-FASHIONED ANNUALS BRING AN INSTANT SPLASH OF COLOUR TO THE GARDEN. THEIR ENTIRE LIFECYCLE – FROM SEED TO SEED – IS OVER AND DONE IN A SINGLE SEASON, AND A PAINTBOX COTTAGE GARDEN CAN BE CREATED FOR LITTLE MORE THAN THE COST OF A FEW PACKETS OF SEED AND A MINIMUM OF EFFORT.

COTTAGE GARDENING WITH ANNUALS IS BOTH COLOURFUL AND FUN – THEY SHOULD CERTAINLY NOT BE REGARDED AS THE CINDERELLAS OF THE GARDENING SCENE. THE PLANT PROFILES IN THIS BOOK WILL REACQUAINT EXPERIENCED GARDENERS WITH THE ANTIQUE ANNUALS – THOSE OLD FAVOURITES OF YESTERYEAR WHICH HAVE BEEN GROWN IN COTTAGE GARDENS FOR OVER A CENTURY – AND WILL INTRODUCE THESE VERSATILE PLANTS TO THE NEWCOMER, WHO UP UNTIL NOW MAY HAVE ASSOCIATED ANNUALS SOLELY WITH THE GARISH BEDDING DISPLAYS THAT ARE STILL A FAMILIAR SIGHT IN MANY MUNICIPAL PARKS AND GARDENS.

In days gone by, the growing and use of annual plants was surrounded by superstition and old wives' tales. Many annuals were said to have special powers, particularly in predicting the weather. The scarlet pimpernel (*Anagallis arvensis*) became known as the 'poor man's weatherglass', predicting fair weather if the flowers were open wide in the morning, but rain if they remained tightly closed. Similarly, if the leaves of calendulas or clover contracted, then a storm was imminent.

Medicinal powers were also ascribed to annual plants. For example, the old herbalists considered pot marigold (*Calendula officinalis*) a cure for all ills, providing a remedy for jaundice, toothache, pain caused by bee stings, warts and many more afflictions. On more of an emotional level, the sweet alyssum (*Lobularia maritima*) was said to have the power to suppress anger, hence the common name of 'madwort'. In today's turbulent world, a fortune is surely waiting to be made by someone able to prove the existence of this particular quality.

The profusion of colours, shapes and sizes available in annuals today is quite staggering, and if you choose varieties carefully you can have annuals in flower in your garden from late spring until autumn. There are plants suitable for a wide range of garden situations, some thriving best in open, sunny positions and others in semi-shade. Some prefer well-drained, sandy conditions while others are better suited to damp, loamy soils; a few will even thrive and flower prolifically on stony ground. Details of any specific cultivation requirements are given in each plant profile, while general guidelines on growing annuals in the garden are given on pages 32–40.

RAISING ANNUALS FROM SEED

When it comes to sowing seed of old-fashioned annuals, old wives' tales abound. While it is extremely unlikely that anyone continues the old tradition of dropping your trousers each spring to test the soil temperature by sitting on it – a damp and chilly experience presumably signalling a delay until a more comfortable sitting was achieved – there are still those who plan their sowings according to the phases of the moon. The trick, apparently, is to sow only with a waxing moon, as rain is supposedly more likely immediately following a new moon.

Today, however, straightforward practical advice can be given for the successful raising of annual plants from seed, and by following the guidelines given you will be able to create a kaleidoscope of annual colour without struggling to determine whether the moon is on the wax or wane – and will certainly be able to remain fully clothed throughout.

It is comparatively simple to collect seed from many of the annuals growing in your garden, ready to sow for the following year, and page 38 shows you how. In addition, many annuals will self-seed if they are allowed to die back naturally, releasing seed from their ripened pods to be carried off in the wind or fall wherever they choose. The natural, unaffected abandon produced by allowing plants to self seed in this way will give the garden that traditional cottagey look without your lifting a finger.

USING ANNUALS IN THE COTTAGE GARDEN

Annuals are particularly useful as fillers in the border when early flowers, especially those of bulbs, are over and the gaps are not easily filled by other types of plant. The annuals can be chosen for their flower form and

colour, their decorative foliage or even their fragrance – just think of sweet peas, stocks, mignonette and nicotianas – and you will find features on these and many other aspects of planning a display of annuals.

Annuals might also be grown in rows in a corner of the vegetable garden for cutting to use in arrangements through the summer months. Later, the 'everlasting' annuals can be dried to provide welcome colour indoors throughout the long winter. These plants are easy to grow and are decorative both in the garden and when used in floral arrangements. Some, such as honesty (*Lunaria annua*), love-in-a-mist (*Nigella damascena*) and paper moons (*Scabiosa stellata*), form somewhat curious, highly decorative seedpods, which are invaluable to the flower arranger for combining with dried grasses, perhaps spraying them with glittering paints to create stunning and long-lasting indoor displays.

UNDERSTANDING TERMINOLOGY

An annual is a plant that is sown, flowers, sets seed and dies all within one year or growing season. Annuals can be divided into two broad groups, hardy annuals and half-hardy annuals, but the distinction is somewhat artificial and is governed more by climatic conditions than any botanical difference. In warmer areas there can be considerable overlap between the two groups, with half-hardy annuals being grown as hardy annuals, while in bleaker climes hardy annuals may have to be treated as half hardy.

The term 'annual' is also very often loosely applied to certain tender perennials, which can only survive the winter outside in very mild climates but can be grown as annuals during the summer in other areas, and biennials, which take two years to complete their lifecycle, although these very often confound the gardener by hanging on to become short-lived perennials. Throughout this book, the general term 'annual' is used to encompass all these groups, while the precise terms 'hardy annual', 'half-hardy annual', 'tender perennial' and 'biennial' are used when referring to the status of specific plants.

Hardy annuals (HA): These can be sown in the open garden in early spring in the position where the plants are to flower. The seedlings and young plants will tolerate a certain amount of frost, and many will survive through relatively severe conditions. Some hardy annuals can be sown outside in the autumn, to produce sturdy young plants for early flowering the following spring. Hardy annuals lend themselves well to the cottage garden style, and many will seed themselves around haphazardly, giving a delightfully informal look to the garden.

Half-hardy annuals (HHA): While the seeds of half-hardy annuals are frost hardy, the plants themselves are not, although they will survive quite low temperatures. In frost-prone climates, therefore, seed of half-hardy annuals should only be sown outside in late spring, when there is little danger of severe weather killing off the seedlings as they germinate. However, half-hardy annuals sown outside rarely reach a reasonable flowering size until late in the year, and they are therefore normally sown in a heated greenhouse in early spring and planted out in the garden in early summer, when there is little danger of further frosts. As

A MIXED BED OF ANNUALS INCLUDING MOLUCCELLA, GYPSOPHILA, NICOTIANA AND NIGELLA

many of the hardy annuals pause for breath, the half-hardys take over, extending the flowering season of annuals in the cottage garden on through high summer until well into autumn.

Tender annuals (TA): These are annuals raised, grown and flowered in pots under glass. They can be planted out after the ground has warmed up and all danger of frost is past, but they seldom thrive out of doors in temperate climates and are probably best reserved for the greenhouse or conservatory.

Hardy biennials (HB): Biennials differ from annuals in that they require two growing seasons in which to complete their lifecycle: a period of warmth for growth, followed by cooler conditions to induce flowering. The plant germinates and makes growth in the first year, and then blooms and dies the following year. Seed of biennials is sown outside in late spring or early summer and the seedlings are pricked out into good, fertile soil when large enough to handle. The resulting strong, healthy plants are then transplanted to their final positions in early autumn, to flower the following spring or summer. Many biennials are cottage garden favourites; once introduced into the garden they will self-seed with abandon.

Tender perennials (TP): These perennials are from tropical parts of the world. They bloom in their first year from seed, but do not die after setting seed. They cannot survive cold winters, however, and are immediately killed by frost. They can be propagated easily by taking cuttings of non-flowering shoots in the

SCAEVOLA AEMULA: A TENDER PERENNIAL OFTEN GROWN AS AN ANNUAL

autumn and overwintering them in a frost-free greenhouse or on a sunny windowsill indoors. Tender perennials are particularly useful for growing in pots on a balcony or beside a path.

Varieties and cultivars: Seed catalogues often list a plant as a 'variety' or a 'cultivar'. A variety is a plant different in some way from the true species occurring in nature, while a cultivar (the term is an abbreviation for 'cultivated variety') is a variety developed by a plant breeder by deliberately crossing two different plants. Named varieties of old favourites are always much sought after by cottage gardeners and are guaranteed to add interest to the garden.

Hybrids: A hybrid is a new plant which is the result of the successful cross-pollination of two plants with different genetic traits. Hybrids are notable for their vigour, quickness to flower, and uniformity of habit, colour and size, as well as their resistance to disease: these qualities are highly appreciated by the cottage gardener. Seed of hybrids is invariably expensive, as its production is a skilled and labour-intensive process. Self-sown seedlings, or seed collected in the garden for growing the following year, will not come true and the results are often likely to disappoint.

Series: The term 'series' is used for those annual varieties in which the same type of plant is available in a range of different flower colours. Series are very common in petunias, impatiens, begonias, marigolds (*Calendula* and *Tagetes*) and several other popular cottage garden flowers. Whatever their colour, plants from the same series will be uniform in height, growth habit and flower size.

Mixtures: These are simply plants that are available in a mixture of flower colours.

Understanding the basic terminology and doing the right thing at the right time is half the battle in growing annuals, as cultivation presents few problems. Read through the practical advice and plant profiles in this book, study the features on planning displays for colour, fragrance, windowboxes and containers, shady situations and more, and then collect together the seeds you need to create a beautiful cottage garden in just one season.

IDEAS FOR USING COTTAGE GARDEN ANNUALS

ANNUALS, A HUGE AND INCREDIBLY DIVERSE CLASS OF PLANTS, CAN PLAY A VARIETY OF ROLES IN THE COTTAGE GARDEN. THEY CAN BRING INSTANT COLOUR TO A NEW GARDEN, QUICKLY COVER AN UNSIGHTLY AREA WITH A COLOURFUL SCREEN, PROVIDE FLOWERS FOR CUTTING OR DRYING FOR FLORAL ARRANGEMENTS AND BRING A BREATH OF THE COUNTRY TO A WINDY HIGH-RISE CITY BALCONY. A COTTAGE GARDEN CAN BE CREATED SOLELY FROM OLD-FASHIONED ANNUALS OR THEY CAN BE USED TO SUPPLEMENT A MORE MIXED PLANTING.

Painting with flowers

Traditionally, cottage gardens have always presented a jumbled profusion of unrelated colours. However, this should not be taken to mean that basic colour guidelines can be ignored totally when you are creating a cottage garden planting. This informal gardening style promises a pretty picture, but can easily end up as something of a mess if no thought at all is given to colour planning.

Choice of colour in the garden is, of course, very much a personal statement. One gardener's love of a riotous mix of bright colours such as red, orange and yellow may well be in complete contrast to that of the gardener next door, who uses colour more discreetly and whose careful choice of muted shades such as white, lavender, violet, pink and blue reflects a gentler, more subtle approach.

Of all plant characteristics, flower colour has the most immediate impact, and border plans are one way of deciding how to make the most of colour in the garden. Buying annuals in flower is a good way of ensuring that they will combine well together, but growing them from seed is less costly and much more satisfying. You can use the listings below to help you make a choice.

Success in combining colours may, however, occur accidentally: self-sown annual seedlings have an uncanny knack of popping up in just the right place, often resulting in pleasing – if unconventional – combinations which the gardener might never have entertained. Such occurrences can then spark off new ideas and provide a valuable lesson in colour gardening.

SOME COLOUR EFFECTS

In practice, there are no hard-and-fast rules for colour combinations and it is amazing just how many work well in the garden. However, there are some basic colour effects that are worth considering in order to make informed choices when ordering seeds for annual displays.

• Colour is more visually effective when used *en masse* in the border. Avoid placing small spots of colour – be bold and plant in large clumps.

• The use of blue, purple, green and white and combinations of these colours can make a garden look much larger. These 'cool' colours are also effective in sitting or rest areas, creating a peaceful, tranquil atmosphere.

• On summer evenings, as darkness descends on the garden, blues and purples deepen and become less obvious, but white and yellow flowers will retain their brightness, providing beacons of light here and there in the gathering gloom.

• Orange, yellow, red and maroon are the 'hot' colours. These will catch the eye first, and tend to make a garden look smaller.

• As well as their colour, the size of the individual flowers will affect the overall picture. Large, brightly coloured blooms will require fewer plants to make an impact than will small, delicate flowers in softer hues; a group of 2m (6ft) high bright yellow sunflowers will

*YELLOW, LILAC AND GREEN ARE VERY EFFECTIVE
AGAINST A RICH TERRACOTTA BACKGROUND*

quite overpower a small planting of low-growing bedding annuals.

• Cool blues and purples mix well with pale pink and soft yellow, while orange and gold work well with bronze and brown.

• A predominantly single-colour border is brightened up by the introduction of some white flowers. Plant them in drifts between bright colours, as one white flower introduced here and there will create a distinctly spotty effect.

• Neutral colours such as grey, or earth tones like brown, tan and olive, make good backgrounds against which to present other colours.

• In shady areas, or where there is a predominantly dark green background, consider lightening the effect using white flowers or plants with variegated foliage.

SOME ANNUALS FOR EARLY COLOUR

Many spring and early-summer performers come in cool, subtle colours which evoke a tranquil atmosphere. These colours are lacking in the high summer garden. Many of the traditional favourites provide early colour.

Antirrhinum majus (Snapdragon) – pink, yellow, reddish purple, lavender, red, white, bronze, multicolours.
Calendula officinalis (Pot marigold) – yellow, cream, orange, white, apricot.
Cheiranthus, Erysimum (Wallflower) yellow, red, orange, pink, purple.
Clarkia – lavender, yellow, pink, rose, red, white.
Consolida ambigua (Larkspur) – white, blue, lilac, rose, salmon, pink, carmine.
Eschscholzia californica (California poppy) – gold, orange, red, pink, white.
Iberis (Candytuft) – white, purple, pink, red, lavender.
Lathyrus odoratus (Sweet pea) – blue, purple, lavender, white, cream, pink, red.
Lobularia maritima (Sweet alyssum) – white, cream, pink, rose, violet, purple, lavender.
Matthiola incana (Stock) – white, cream, lavender, purple, pink, red, bicolours.
Myosotis alpestris (Forget-me-not) – blue, pink, white.
Nicotiana (Tobacco plant) – white, green, purple, pink, red.
Nigella damascena (Love-in-a-mist) – blue, purple, rose, pink, white.
Papaver (Poppy) – red, pink, orange, yellow, white, bicolours.
Pelargonium (Geranium) – red, pink, orange, violet, white, bicolours.
Petunia – blue, purple, pink, red, salmon, coral, white, bicolours.
Reseda odorata (Mignonette) – greenish white tinged with copper or yellow.
Schizanthus pinnatus – red, pink, purple, violet, yellow, white.
Tropaeolum majus (Nasturtium) – orange, red, cream, yellow, pink.

Viola (Pansy) – purple, blue, white, yellow, orange, bicolours.

SOME ANNUALS FOR LATE COLOUR

With late summer and early autumn come the vermilion-reds, strident oranges and brash yellows that draw the eye and create a lively atmosphere. Glimpsed through a tracery of green leaves, they glow like precious stones.

Amaranthus caudatus (Love-lies-bleeding) – blood-red, vibrant green.
Coreopsis tinctoria (Annual coreopsis) – orange, yellow, maroon, bronze, red, often with a contrasting band of colour surrounding the purplish brown centre.
Dahlia – every colour except blue.
Gaillardia pulchella (Blanket flower) – yellow, orange, red, bicolours.
Gazania rigens (Treasure flower) – scarlet, red, orange, gold, cream, pink, some with striped and zoned petals.
Helianthus annuus (Sunflower) – yellow, orange, creamy white, mahogany, bicolours.
Heliotropium arborescens (Cherry pie) – deep violet-blue, lavender.
Impatiens walleriana (Busy lizzie) – orange, rose, scarlet, pink, lavender, white, bicolours.
Ipomoea (Morning glory) – blue, red, white, violet-purple, chocolate, crimson, lavender.
Mirabilis jalapa (Marvel of Peru) – red, white, yellow, pink, different colours often appearing on the same plant.
Rudbeckia hirta (Gloriosa daisy) – golden yellow, mahogany-red, good bicolours.
Tagetes (Marigold) – yellow, orange, orange-red, whites.
Thunbergia alata (Black-eyed Susan) – yellow, orange, white with a dark eye.
Tithonia rotundifolia (Mexican sunflower) – orange with a yellow-orange centre.
Verbena × hybrida (Garden verbena) – bright red, purple, blue, white, pink, bicolours.
Zinnia elegans (Garden zinnia) – yellow, orange, red, pink, purple, white, bicolours.

Annuals for colourful foliage

Annual plants with bright foliage are useful for adding colour and texture to a display, and can be equally stunning as specimen plants. They have the added advantage of not requiring deadheading, their effect is longer lasting, and are often tolerant of shade. There are many annuals with wonderful foliage which will highlight any temporarily dull corner of the garden, and many are also effective when grown in pots and containers.

SOME PLANTING SUGGESTIONS

• Painted in shades of red, orange, rose, pink, chartreuse, copper, purple streaked with red, ivory ringed with green, or bright gold dashed here and there with green flecks, coleus foliage is as vibrant as any flower, and may well provide the brightest patch of colour in a shady garden.

• Some of the New Guinea busy lizzies have eyecatching variegated foliage. They are useful for bedding and make superb pot plants.

• Some recent newcomers among the ornamental cabbages and kales, *Brassica oleracea* cultivars, produce striking effects when grown as hardy annuals. Leaves in various shades of rose, pink or creamy white, are surrounded by an outer green layer. They are especially useful for late-summer and autumn display as they develop their most beautiful colours with the onset of cold weather, at just the time when everything else in the garden is fading into oblivion. They combine wonderfully with autumn- and winter-flowering pansies.

• *Kochia scoparia* var. *trichophylla* has feathery, soft green foliage in a dense, dome-shaped bush. 'Acapulco Silver', has light green leaves dusted with silver. These make excellent accent plants or temporary hedge.

• Rather more sombre in colour is *Perilla frutescens* with deeply cut, burgundy-coloured leaves with metallic overtones. It is attractive as an ornamental backdrop at the back of borders.

• Ruffled purple basil *Ocimum basilicum* 'Purple Ruffles', is particularly striking grown alongside pink or

SOME ANNUALS WITH STRIKING FOLIAGE

Abutilon hybridum variegata (Flowering maple) – yellow-splashed variegation.

Amaranthus caudatus (Love-lies-bleeding) – forms with rich bronze, or a blend of red, yellow and fresh green.

Ammobium alatum (Winged everlasting) – white and woolly.

Atriplex hortensis (Garden orach) – dark purple and gold.

Begonia semperflorens (Wax begonia) – dark bronze.

Brassica oleracea (Ornamental cabbage and kale) – rose, pink or creamy white.

Coleus blumei (Coleus) – green, yellow, buff, chartreuse, salmon, orange, red, purple and brown, often with several colours on each leaf.

Euphorbia marginata (Snow-on-the-mountain) – grey-green, striped and edged with white.

Impatiens New Guinea hybrids (New Guinea busy lizzie) – dark green, bronze or variegated.

Kochia scoparia var. *trichophylla* (Burning bush, Summer cypress) – soft green, feathery.

Ocimum basilicum 'Purple Ruffles' (Ruffled purple basil) – dark purple, frilled.

Pelargonium (Geranium) – some zonal and scented-leaved forms have variegated leaves.

Perilla frutescens (Beefsteak plant) – burgundy and metallic.

Tropaeolum majus 'Alaska' (Nasturtium) – blotched with pale cream in a variety of patterns.

pale yellow flowers. Try it with a *Calendula officinalis* variety such as 'Lemon Beauty', or with *Antirrhinum* Sawyers Old-fashioned Snapdragons Mixed.

• Several of the scented-leaved pelargoniums have variegated foliage and are very useful for growing in pots and containers. A further bonus is that when brushed or touched they release their aromatic sweetness in a variety of 'flavours'.

• Consider livening up the vegetable patch with some of the more colourful edible vegetables such as red, yellow and white Swiss chard; curly, crispy, red-leaved lettuce; purple-leaved and ruffled purple basil and purple and white broccoli. Combine these with some annual flowers and runner beans growing up poles to create a delightful potager.

THE EDWARDIAN HOT BED BORDER

Gardeners who crave bright colours need look no further than the Edwardian Hot Bed Border photographed at Luckington Manor, Wiltshire, for inspiration. The term refers to hot colours – *eye-catching plants in warm sunset colours such as reds, oranges and yellows.*

The annuals used to produce this exotic, tropical look require a warm sheltered spot with at least six hours of sunlight a day. Tithonias and zinnias are ideal candidates, along with cuphea, the highly ornamental canna lilies and the various decorative dahlias.

Other annuals and tender perennials with strong colours such as marigolds, helianthus, and scarlet poppies may be used but care should be taken with red, which can burn a hole in any colour scheme and is the most difficult colour to combine.

Fuchsias, double nasturtiums and the pretty Heliophila longifolia *with spikes of white-eyed, bright blue flowers help complete the picture, while* Perilla frutescens *and* Ricinus communis *(Castor-oil plant) provide contrast with their shiny dark metallic foliage.*

Annuals for shade

Most annuals are sun-loving plants, although a surprising number will tolerate partial shade or the dappled light beneath a high, thin canopy of deciduous trees, where leaves and branches filter the sunlight. Few plants of any kind will grow in very dense or day-long shade, but there are almost as many kinds of shade as there are gardens that are shady so, whatever shady sites you have, there is likely to be something that will grow there.

COPING WITH SHADE

Partial shade, where the area is in shadow for part of the day as the sun moves across the sky, is the easiest type to deal with; dense shade on the sunless side of a house is the most difficult.

A shady area of any type may be dry or moist; the conditions may also alter with the season, the plot being sunny in the spring but shady during the summer.

Where possible, locate beds for growing annuals to receive sun in the morning and only temporary shade for the rest of the day. Plants generally prefer the cooler morning sun to the scorching heat of the afternoon, and the early warmth will allow foliage that became moist during the night from rain or dew to dry out sooner, lessening the chance of diseases developing.

If the annual border is against a dark wall, you could consider painting the wall white to gain light reflection and lessen the effects of the shady conditions.

If you grow annuals in the shady parts of your garden, do not assume that they will require heavy feeding to compensate for the lack of light. Plants that receive *less* light actually require less fertilizer and water, unless they are competing with trees and shrubs for nutrients and moisture.

There is little point in planting sun-lovers in an area that is too shady for them as they will simply refuse to open their flowers. Keeping a record of which annuals work well in the shady parts of your garden is the best way to ensure success from year to year.

SOME PLANTING SUGGESTIONS

• The cool white spires of *Digitalis purpurea alba* and the unusual *D. grandiflora*, with its soft yellow flowers

FOXGLOVES ARE IDEAL IN A SHADY SITE, HERE WITH ROSE 'WILLIAM LOBB'

and neat foliage, are particularly well suited to growing in dappled shade beneath trees and are guaranteed to brighten up a shady corner.

• A tiny patio garden on the shady side of a house can be transformed into a miniature cottage garden by planting begonias, coleus, impatiens, and senecio in weathered clay pots and rustic containers. One simple but delightfully old-fashioned combination can be created by planting single-flowered, white tuberous begonias (*B.* × *tuberhybrida*), double-flowered, pink begonias (*Begonia semperflorens*) and blue browallias in a trough container.

• Violas or old-fashioned pansies and mimulus bloom reliably in partial shade. These plants prefer rich moist soil and are perfect by a stream or pool.

• Sprawling, bright orange nasturtiums and bushy blue browallias planted in half-barrels will brighten up a shady porch.

• Annuals with colourful foliage can be used to provide the brightest patch of colour in a shady garden. Coleus foliage brings an array of colours and texture to annual displays and is reliable in dense shade.

• Evening primrose (*Oenothera biennis*) with its scented, night-opening flowers is ideal for growing in partial shade. Along with foxgloves, it is ideal in a shadowy woodland site.

SOME ANNUALS FOR SHADE

Begonia semperflorens (Wax begonia)*
Begonia × *tuberhybrida* (Tuberous begonia)
Browallia speciosa
Cheiranthus, Erysimum (Wallflower)
Cleome spinosa (Spider flower)
Coleus blumei (Coleus)*
Consolida ambigua (Larkspur)
Cynoglossum amabile (Chinese forget-me-not)
Digitalis purpurea (Foxglove)
Impatiens walleriana (Busy lizzie)*
Lobelia erinus (Lobelia)
Lobularia maritima (Sweet alyssum)
Lunaria annua (Honesty)

Mimulus (Monkey flower)*
Myosotis alpestris (Forget-me-not)*
Nemophila menziesii (Baby-blue eyes)
Nicotiana (Tobacco plant)
Pelargonium (Geranium)
Schizanthus × *wisetoniensis* (Butterfly flower)
Senecio × *hybridus* (Cineraria)*
Thunbergia alata (Black-eyed Susan)
Torenia fournieri (Wishbone flower)*
Viola (Pansy)

**choose these for densely shaded sites*

Tall-growing annuals

Annuals growing to 1m (3ft) or more are the plants to use at the back of a border, in the middle of a bed, or for softening the effect of a large, high wall.

However, many of these tall-growing annuals bear large blooms which become too heavy for the plant to support without the help of a few well-placed stakes, especially during summer storms. Staking is perhaps the most neglected part of maintenance in the garden, but tall, rapidly growing annuals demand this attention, while others which become straggly and tend to flop will be greatly improved, giving the garden a much tidier appearance. Do not wait until the wind and rain have laid low your best plants – stake early.

In a mixed border, the use of a variety of heights and shapes makes the garden much more interesting. Place tall or spiky plants in the background, with rounded, intermediate-sized plants in the centre and the flat-growing, ground-hugging annuals at the front.

Some annuals, such as the Mexican sunflower (*Tithonia rotundifolia*) and sunflower (*Helianthus annuus*) cultivars combine great height with strong stems. These plants can be used to liven up a muted palette of relatively low-toned foliage or flowers, or to make a dramatic impact on their own. Suddenly appearing as a splash of bright colour beyond a picket gate, these beacons will draw visitors in, to view an exuberant medley of orange, yellow, scarlet, deep blue and pink – the hallmark of a paintbox cottage garden.

SOME PLANTING SUGGESTIONS

• Tall antirrhinums or salvias could be used as a background in a formal bed, with calendulas or pelargoniums in the middle, and a planting of lobelia or petunias in the front. Be careful to ensure that the arrangement does not look too busy, and plant individual types in groups of three or more to produce the best visual effect.

• An informal look can be achieved with a varied mix consisting of an airy mass of cleome, the striking crested flowers of celosia, the globes of gaillardia and daisy-shaped dahlias. Funnel-shaped petunias or salpiglossis, and flat, single begonias or impatiens complete the picture.

• The mahogany and velvety red sunflowers of the strain *Helianthus annuus* 'Autumn Beauty' and the fiery orange-scarlet Mexican sunflower (*Tithonia rotundifolia*) look stunning among the elegant dusky bronze filigreed leaves of the bronze variety of fennel (*Foeniculum vulgare*), which grows to a similar height. A perfect combination for the back of the border.

• Dill (*Anethum graveolens*), with its lacy yellow-green seedheads and ferny leaves to 90cm (36in) high, makes an unusual partner for bright pink cosmos and pastel-shaded poppies.

• With their dense flowers in a wide colour range, *Digitalis* Excelsior Hybrids are excellent behind medium-sized dahlias, in a border edged with low-growing nasturtiums.

TALL-GROWING ANNUALS

Alcea rosea (Hollyhock) 2–2.5m (6–8ft) or more

Amaranthus caudatus (Love-lies-bleeding) 60–120cm (2–4ft)

Antirrhinum majus (Snapdragon) 30–90cm (1–3ft)

Briza maxima 60–90cm (2–3ft)

Celosia argentea (Cockscomb) 30–90cm (1–3ft)

Clarkia 30–120cm (1–4ft)

Cleome spinosa (Spider flower) up to 1.5m (5ft)

Consolida ambigua (Larkspur) up to 1.2m (4ft)

Cosmos up to 2.2m (7ft)

Helianthus annuus (Sunflower) 0.6–4m (2–12ft)

Lavatera trimestris (Tree mallow) 0.9–2m (3–6ft)

Moluccella laevis (Bells of Ireland) 60–90cm (2–3ft)

Nicotiana (Tobacco plant) 30–120cm (1–4ft)

Tagetes erecta (Marigold) 15–120cm (6in–4ft)

Tithonia rotundifolia (Mexican sunflower) 0.9–1.5m (3–5ft)

Zinnia elegans (Garden zinnia) 15–90cm (6in–3ft)

THE EMPHASIS IS ON THE VERTICAL IN THIS COTTAGE BED WHICH INCLUDES SWEET PEAS, HOLLYHOCKS AND FLOWERING ONIONS

Annuals for containers

A garden is a garden, whether the plants are grown in the ground or enjoyed and observed at close visual range in pots on the balcony. Those of us who live in small town houses, or in flats without a garden, will often go to great lengths to produce effective displays using all sorts of containers and old-fashioned annuals are perfect for this. Window boxes, hanging baskets and some strange and wonderful containers can be pressed into service, ranging from granny's old copper urn or brass kettle to stylish ceramic pots and Ali Baba jars. All sorts of odd receptacles in which to grow plants can be picked up quite cheaply at car-boot sales or in junk shops. The possibilities are endless, depending more on ingenuity than the depth of one's pocket; the only requirement is to ensure that the containers can have holes drilled in the bottom for drainage purposes.

POTS AND TROUGHS

Where there is a garden, tubs and troughs, old chimney pots or even wheelbarrows can be used to decorate the outside of the house. For the more traditional gardener, the standard clay pot has much to recommend it. They are easy to use, inexpensive, and their colour harmonizes well with indoor or outdoor settings. Clay pots are available from most garden centres and range from 8–45cm (3–18in) in diameter. Filled with brightly coloured annuals, fragrant herbs, and trailing geraniums, containers provide instant colour and interest from early summer until the first severe frosts. These colourful displays on the patio or balcony are visible from indoors and on warm evenings the fragrance of the stocks, scented geraniums and sweet peas can waft through open windows.

Whatever its style, make sure to choose an appropriate size pot that is in proportion to the plant. Up to about 30cm (12in) they are ideal for growing geraniums. Pots that are too small easily topple over in the wind and plants in pots of less than 12cm (5in) will be susceptible to drying out in hot weather and will need to be watered several times a day.

Most annuals are ideal for growing in pots as they are shallow-rooted: however, those that are long-flowering, shorter varieties, ones with neat, compact habits, or that will cascade over the edges are the most satisfactory.

Planting: Before filling and planting, cover the drainage holes with mesh-nylon or metal gauze to keep out unwelcome soil pests like slugs, and woodlice. A layer of broken flowerpot pieces (crocks) comes next for drainage purposes. Then the container is ready to fill. It is advisable to raise containers off the ground, on bricks or pot feet, to aid drainage.

Use a lightweight, soil-less peat-based mix with perlite and/or vermiculite, specially designed for container gardening. Pre-blended potting mediums are sold in bags at all nurseries and garden centres and bulk supplies can usually be obtained at a discount from local suppliers. Never use garden soil: it is too heavy, and will check root growth. It may well also contain insects and diseases.

ANNUALS AND TENDER PERENNIALS FILL CONTAINERS QUICKLY WITH BOLD SPLASHES OF COLOUR

CONTAINERS CAN BE USED FOR A WIDE RANGE OF DISPLAYS FROM SUBTLE AND COLOUR-MATCHED TO VIBRANT AND CONTRASTING

Plant a little closer than you would in the open ground, and keep taller plants in the middle and shorter plants near the edge of the containers.

Large wooden containers fitted with castors or wheels can be moved around with ease, kept backstage while the plants are maturing and wheeled out into the limelight at flowering time.

Watering: The trickiest problem gardeners encounter when growing their antique annuals in containers and pots is keeping them watered and fed efficiently, especially in high summer. Annuals enjoy and thrive in a suntrap, but containers, especially small ones brimming over with plants, will need constant watering in hot sunshine, a tedious but essential chore if a wilting mess is to be avoided. Water-retaining capillary mats, impregnated with absorbent polymer are one solution to the problem. These can be put into tubs, pots, hanging baskets, in fact any container is suitable. Before the container is filled with compost the mat is watered so that it swells up; the roots then grow down into it and remove the water as they need it. Alternatively, there are water-retaining granules which, when wetted, form a sort of gel. This is added to compost before planting. Lining terracotta pots with polythene (leaving a few holes for drainage) or using pots with narrow mouths, are other water-saving techniques.

Constant watering will quickly wash out nutrients from the soil. Resin-coated, steady-release fertilizers, pushed into the compost, will release nutrient over the whole season, and are probably the best way of ensuring good growth.

WINDOW BOXES

The window box is merely another form of container, its shape and size designed for use on a window ledge or suspended below a window. There is something rather homely and friendly about the miniature gardens created in a window box, and certainly they decorate the house in a unique way.

Hanging: Purely from a balance and safety point of view, it is not wise to have window boxes much wider than the sills on which they will stand; it is so easy, when leaning out, to lean too far and push or topple the box off its perch. The size of the window will dictate the length of the box; however, several smaller ones are easier and safer to handle than one large one.

On balconies and roof gardens, larger, wider boxes can be used, and almost become raised beds.

Window boxes are available in all sorts of materials – wood, plastic, fibreglass and metal. The fibreglass ones very often often have a finish that makes them look like lead, while the plastic ones are generally more colourful.

When filled with soil, a window box, even a small one, is very heavy. Time spent fastening the box securely in place is time well spent. As a further safety precaution, it is wise to screw a strong screw-eye into the woodwork of the window frame on each side, and run very strong wire – which will hardly be noticeable – between the screw-eyes around the front of the box. Increase the impact of a window-box display by securing a second box to a ledge below the sill.

Planting: The window box must be put in its place empty, and then filled with soil. Apart from the risk of giving yourself a hernia by staggering around with a ready-filled box, it would also be extremely awkward to position. Ensure there are adequate drainage holes. Before filling it with potting compost cover each drainage hole with at least 2.5cm (1in) of broken crocks. If these are not available, then broken bricks, stones from the garden or weathered boiler clinker will serve the same purpose.

Fill the box to within 2.5cm (1in) of the rim and plant closely with brightly coloured annuals – this is not the place for pastels.

Watering: When watered, window boxes can drip dirty water down the walls of the house or onto window panes below. This can be avoided by standing the box on a piece of wood, metal or vinyl sheeting about 12cm (6in) wider than the window box, thus ensuring the surplus water falls well in front of the house walls.

HANGING BASKETS

The flowers in hanging baskets suspended from the walls or eaves can be looked up at or enjoyed at eye level, providing of course the baskets are not hung too high. Consider using heavy fishing line to suspend them because it is invisible from a distance: this gives the illusion that the plants are floating. Hanging baskets require a certain amount of care in their preparation, but are most attractive when filled with spreading or trailing annuals, or annuals with very compact habits, or a mixture of both.

Baskets can be wooden, wicker, wire, plastic or clay, and come in various sizes and shapes, and growing annuals in them is no different to growing them in containers. They are in effect aerial gardens in enlarged flowerpots or diminutive containers.

Planting: The first step is to line the basket with polythene, making a few holes for drainage to avoid creating a stagnant pool. Next put a lining of moss inside the polythene – with wire baskets put the moss lining outside to allow plants to be poked into the moss all the way around the sides and bottom of the basket to produce a full, rounded effect.

The basket is now ready for the compost and planting. Fill the centre of the basket with a soil-less mix, and place two or three plants in a 15cm (6in) basket, three or four to a 20cm (8in) basket.

Firm the potting soil around each plant and water gently. Any spare moss left over from lining the basket can be added between the top plants to act as a mulch.

Watering: Never let baskets dry out. Because root space is limited and all the surfaces are exposed to the drying effects of air, they need to be watered both in the morning and the evening, even if it does mean getting out a stepladder! The plants will soon droop if they need attention; however, if neglected regularly, they will lose their lustre and their will to live. Watering twice a day will leach out the nutrients from the soil so it is important to feed the baskets regularly.

ANNUALS GIVING AT LEAST 3 MONTHS OF BLOOM

Ageratum houstonianum (Floss flower)
Antirrhinum (Snapdragon)
Argyranthemum (Marguerite)
Begonia × tuberhybrida (Tuberous begonia)
Begonia × semperflorens (Wax begonia)*
Brachycome iberidifolia (Swan River daisy)
Browallia speciosa
Calendula officinalis (Pot marigold)
Convolvulus tricolor syn. *C. minor* (Annual convolvulus)
Heliotropium arborescens (Cherry pie)
Impatiens New Guinea Hybrids (New Guinea busy lizzie)*
Impatiens walleriana (Busy lizzie)*
Lobelia erinus (Lobelia)*

Lobularia maritima (Sweet alyssum)
Matthiola incana (Stock)
Mimulus (Monkey flower)*
Mirabilis jalapa (Four-o'clock flower)
Nicotiana (Flowering tobacco)
*Pelargonium**
Petunia × hybrida (Petunia)*
Portulaca grandiflora (Moss rose or sun rose)*
Salvia (Sage)*
Tagetes (Marigold)*
Thunbergia alata (Black-eyed Susan)*
Tropaeolum majus (Nasturtium)*
Verbena × hybrida (Garden verbena)*
Viola × wittrockiana (Pansy)*
Zinnia elegans (Garden zinnia)

*suitable for hanging baskets

Annuals for naturalizing

Some of the most beautiful flowers in the annual garden are wildflowers that will self seed, or 'naturalize'. Interspersed with cultivated plants in beds and borders, they give a 'natural' look to the garden and can also be used effectively to establish a mini-meadow.

A wildflower, in the strictest sense of the word, is a plant that is native to a particular area and is therefore well adapted to the prevailing conditions. Although most wildflower gardens contain perennial plants, many annuals can be used to create a wildflower area.

Other, non-native annual plants will also naturalize happily around the garden, self seeding in odd cracks and crevices, and creating colour combinations of their own – combinations that are often more effective than those planned carefully by the gardener.

CREATING AN AREA OF ANNUAL WILDFLOWERS

Wildflower meadows take several years to mature, but quick results can be achieved by using a cornfield mixture of annuals such as cornflowers, field poppies, corn marigolds, corn cockles and corn chamomile.

The mixture is best sown direct in the autumn, and all the species will flower in their first summer. A cornfield mixture without grasses will keep weeds down on an otherwise bare piece of soil, and will provide an almost instant splash of colour the following year with very little maintenance.

Cut back the area in late summer after the plants have set seed and cultivate the soil to simulate the action of a plough in the field. This will encourage the seeds to germinate, ready for flowering the following year. After a few years some of the flowers will disappear, and it will be time to clear the area and resow.

A mini-meadow of this kind is just the answer for a difficult area next to a shed, alongside a fence or even around a tree. It would also be perfect at the edge of a field or wood in a large country cottage garden.

SOME PLANTING SUGGESTIONS

• Foxgloves, sweet rocket, marigolds, pansies and violas, honesty and forget-me-nots are determined plants that come up year after year without any encouragement. Given the opportunity, they will quickly colonize a garden; often arriving uninvited, these artless annual flowers are welcomed by cottage gardeners, and despite their wandering ways are appreciated for their persistence, coming up everywhere to fill empty spaces in the border and give the garden its traditional cottagey hallmarks – profusion and variety.

• *Limnanthes douglasii*, the poached-egg plant, is quick-growing and its silver and gold saucer-shaped

THIS EXUBERANT DISPLAY IS ALMOST ENTIRELY NATURALIZED ANNUALS

flowers are delicately scented and beloved of bees. Every year it produces a thick carpet of seedlings ensuring that, once introduced to the garden, it is there to stay.

• The cup-and-saucer Canterbury bells (*Campanula medium*) have an old-world charm and will seed themselves wildly around the garden – but perhaps not quite as irresponsibly as the Welsh poppy (*Meconopsis cambrica*) which, if allowed, takes over the garden completely.

• *Impatiens roylei* has red stems, attractive foliage and bears a profusion of pendent, rose-pink or purple, helmet-shaped flowers in clusters. Given the right conditions, it becomes invasive so it is not suitable for small gardens.

• Honesty (*Lunaria annua*), with its rich deep purple or white flowers, may also become too much of a good thing. However, the seedlings are easily identified and can be removed or transplanted to another part of the garden as soon as they start to expand their territory.

• White sweet alyssum (*Lobularia maritima*), another persistent self seeder, will always find places in the garden to improve, but they are not invasive.

SOME ANNUALS FOR NATURALIZING

Agrostemma githago (Corn cockle) – soft lilac-pink, purple red.

Borago officinalis (Borage) – blue, white.

Calendula officinalis (Pot marigold) – orange, yellow, white, cream, apricot.

Campanula medium (Canterbury bell) – blue, rose-pink, white.

Centaurea (Cornflower) – blue, purple, pink, rose, white.

Cheiranthus, Erysimum (Wallflower) – yellow, orange, red, purple, burgundy, brown.

Clarkia – pink, rose, lavender, red, white.

Consolida ambigua (Larkspur) – lilac, pink, rose, salmon, carmine, blue, white.

Cosmos – red, pink, white.

Digitalis (Foxglove) – purple, white, pale yellow, yellowish-white, pink, brown.

Eschscholzia californica (California poppy) – gold, orange, red, pink, white.

Helianthus annuus (Sunflower) – yellow, orange, mahogany, bicolours.

Hesperis matronalis (Sweet rocket) – pale lilac, purple, violet, white.

Iberis umbellata (Candytuft) – white, pink, lavender.

Impatiens roylei – rose-pink, purple.

Limnanthes douglasii (Poached-egg plant) – white with a yellow centre.

Lunaria annua (Honesty) – purple, white.

Myosotis (Forget-me-not) – blue, pink, white.

Papaver (Poppy) – red, pink, orange, yellow, white, bicolours.

Tropaeolum majus (Nasturtium) – red, orange, yellow, cream, pink.

Viola (Pansy) – purple, blue, white, yellow, orange, red, bicolours.

Annuals for cutting

One reason for growing old-fashioned annuals is to provide colour in the garden in the shortest possible time. Another is a love of the past and the desire to grow the unusual. Rarely, however, is the objective a source of supply of flowers for cutting – woe betide the partner who dares to cut the pride and joy of the garden for a table decoration, or who picks bunches of heirloom annuals as a parting gift for visitors to the garden! Gaps here and there in the border caused by scissor-happy flower arrangers can also cause friction in the household, and will often spoil the look of the garden.

However, it is possible to enjoy annuals living out their natural span in the garden and at the same time provide armfuls of flowers for the house, simply by setting aside a small area specifically as an annual cutting garden. A corner of the vegetable patch is ideal; better still if this is near both the kitchen and a water tap. Here, seeds can be planted without the slightest thought being given to the overall design or possible clashing colour combinations – the sole aim is to provide masses of fresh cut flowers. The cutting area can also be used as a test ground for experimenting with different plant and colour arrangements for future use in the cottage garden proper.

With a little thought and planning, it is possible to provide cut flowers from annuals for most of the year. An autumn sowing outside, or plants raised from seed sown under glass early in the year, will provide early cutting material, and seed sown in the open in early spring will produce flowers well into late summer and autumn.

If the soil is in reasonably good heart there will be no need to add fertilizer, as this simply leads to lush growth and few flowers. However, poor, unworked soil will need to be improved by incorporating large quantities of garden compost.

For ease of cutting, consider planting in rows, and leave some space free for successive sowings and transplantings during the season. The beds should be about 1m (3ft) wide – any wider and it becomes difficult to reach across to cut the furthest stems. Raised beds are also an option and give easy access to the flowers. Be sure to plant the shorter varieties nearest to the path and the taller ones at the back.

Water regularly and thoroughly, especially if the plants appear to be wilting, and deadhead to encourage further flowers for cutting.

CUTTING FRESH FLOWERS

Always cut fresh flowers early in the morning, when moisture and sugar content are high, and the flowers are fully refreshed after the rigours of the previous day.

Take a bucket of tepid, not cold, water into the garden when cutting, and as you cut the flowers plunge the stems immediately into the water. Use scissors or a sharp knife, and cut the stems at an angle rather than

SWEET PEAS AND STOCKS ARE AMONG THE MANY ANNUALS SUITABLE FOR CUTTING

straight across – this ensures better water intake by exposing more of the stem end to water and preventing it from sitting flush on the bottom of the vase. Take more length than you think you might need, in order to have plenty of stem available for arranging.

Bring the flowers into the kitchen, and recut the stems under water to bring maximum moisture to the petals. Remove the bottom leaves, as foliage that is under water in the vase will begin to rot and restrict the water flow into the stems. Harden off the flowers by placing them in a cool, dark area for several hours before arranging them – this is called 'steeping' or 'conditioning'. If you are planning an arrangement for an important occasion or a party, cut the flowers several days ahead before the buds fully open and refrigerate them in water until you need them.

Once the flowers are arranged in their vase, change the water, or at least keep it topped up, every day. Add a floral preservative – a pinch of salt or lump or two of sugar is often used and is said to prevent the build-up of bacteria which cause the flowers to deteriorate quickly. Most floral arrangements also benefit from an

occasional spraying with clean water, particularly those displayed in heated rooms. It is advisable to remove all fading flowers daily, as the ethylene gas which these give off will cause the surrounding flowers to die faster. Ethylene is also produced by ripening fruit, and cut flowers placed near to fruit bowls may also 'go over' more quickly.

CUTTING TIPS

• When cutting flowers for an arrangement, choose a mix of shapes and sizes: use large and small, round and spiky flowers, with dainty blooms and sprays to use as fillers.
• Do not forget foliage. Adding a few leaves to an arrangement will make all the difference and help set off the flower colours.
• There is little point in cutting annual convolvulus for floral arrangements, as the flowers close at night and do not re-open if they have been cut.
• Avoid using fuchsia and impatiens flowers, as they drop after cutting.
• When cut, annuals such as poppies, dahlias and tithonias produce a milky fluid or sap that will clog stems of other flowers. Stop the flow by searing the very tip of the stems with a lighted match or candle flame.

SOME ANNUALS FOR CUTTING

VERTICAL OR SPIKY FLOWERS:
Alcea rosea (Hollyhock)
Antirrhinum majus (Snapdragon)
Celosia plumosa (Cockscomb)
Clarkia elegans (Clarkia)
Consolida ambigua (Larkspur)
Moluccella laevis (Bells of Ireland)
Salvia farinacea (Sage)
Verbena bonariensis (Tall verbena)

Scabiosa atropupurea (Sweet scabious)
Tagetes erecta (African marigold)
Tagetes patula (French marigold)
Verbena × hybrida (Garden verbena)
Zinnia elegans (Garden zinnia)

ROUND FLOWERS:
Calendula officinalis (Pot marigold)
Callistephus chinensis (China aster)
Centaurea cyanus (Cornflower)
Centaurea moschata (Sweet sultan)
Cosmos
Eschscholzia californica (California poppy)
Gomphrena globosa (Globe amaranth)
Nigella damascena (Love-in-a-mist)
Papaver (Poppy)
Pelargonium (Geranium)
Petunia × hybrida (Garden petunia)

FILLERS:
Ageratum houstonianum (Floss flower)
Avena sterilis (Animated oats)
Bellis perennis (Double daisy)
Briza maxima, B. minor (Quaking grass)
Gypsophila elegans (Baby's breath)
Lobularia maritima (Sweet alyssum)
Myosotis alpestris (Forget-me-not)

OTHERS TO TRY:
Cleome spinosa (Spider flower)
Heliotropium arborescens (Cherry pie)
Lathyrus odoratus (Sweet pea)

Annuals for drying

Putting the garden to bed in the autumn need not necessarily mean bidding farewell to all the garden flowers for another year. There are several ways of preserving their beauty to brighten up the dull winter months and many annuals are perfect for drying. Within the same season their brilliant colours can be enjoyed in the garden and the flowers harvested for drying.

AIR DRYING

The easiest annuals to dry are the so-called 'everlastings' and the annual ornamental grasses, which can all be air dried simply by hanging them upside down in small bunches in a warm, dark, airy attic, shed or basement. Annual flowers with floppy stems can be treated in the same way, stripped of their leaves and hung upside down from individual hooks or with several bunches suspended from one wire coathanger. Leave the flowers for two or three weeks until dry and store well away from any dampness until you are ready to use them.

Flowers with stiff stems, such as love-lies-bleeding (*Amaranthus caudatus*) and bells of Ireland (*Moluccella laevis*) will dry perfectly well simply stuck in a bottle.

USING SILICA GEL

Many-petalled annual flowers such as marigolds, zinnias and dahlias often dry best in silica gel. This is a drying agent that absorbs the moisture from flower petals so quickly that the dried floral colours are almost as fresh and bright as they were in life.

• First, find a cake tin, biscuit tin or other glass or metal sealable container and place a 5cm (2in) layer of silica gel in the bottom.
• Carefully place the flowers face up on the bed of silica gel, ensuring that they do not touch each other, and slowly sprinkle more silica gel over them until they are completely covered. Seal the container tightly and leave for two to six days.
• When ready, the flowers will feel crisp or papery to the touch. Blow or brush away the excess silica gel.

USING A MICROWAVE

It is possible to dry flowers in a microwave oven. Put a few blooms at a time in a small microwave dish. Place the dish in the microwave with a cup of water and use 50 percent power for 30 seconds to three minutes, depending on the size and thickness of the flowers and the wattage of the microwave. Results can be very variable, and you will need to experiment with the timing.

PRESSING FLOWERS

Pressing is another method of drying and preserving flowers. Flowers can be pressed in a special flower press, or simply between the pages of old telephone directories or heavy books – there is something rather

PLENTY OF ANNUALS MAKE AN ATTRACTIVE GARDEN DISPLAY AND CAN ALSO BE CUT FOR DRIED FLOWER ARRANGEMENTS

romantic in finding a pressed flower in an old book, placed there years, sometimes centuries, before and conjuring up images and memories of another age. The time required for drying will be between two and three weeks.

• Place the flowers between sheets of blotting paper or newspaper to avoid staining the pages of the book and then sit a brick or some other heavy object on top.

• With a flower press, the filled sheets of blotting paper or newspaper should be stacked in layers between boards and tightened down using the wing nuts.

ANNUALS FOR POT POURRI

• The leaves of the scented-leaved pelargoniums and lemon verbena are frequently used in the making of pot pourri.

• A cupful of dried zinnia or marigold petals added purely for colour and texture will improve the look of almost any pot pourri.

• An attractive colour combination is created by mixing the dried flowers of larkspurs, pot marigold and delphiniums.

• Mix annual herbs, such as basil, borage and lemon verbena, with a pot pourri for a refreshing fragrance.

SOME ANNUALS FOR AIR DRYING

Briza maxima, B. minor (Quaking grass) – ornamental grass with oval, pearly white spikelets.

Celosia cristata (Cockscomb) – crested flowerheads resembling roosters' combs or undersea coral.

Gomphrena globosa (Globe amaranth) – clover-like flowers in red, pink, purple, orange and white, keep their colour for a long time when dried.

Gypsophila elegans (Baby's breath) – dainty, star-like white or pink flowers.

Helichrysum bracteatum (Strawflower) – daisy-like flowers with stiff petals of red, orange, white or yellow, surrounding yellow-orange centres.

Hordeum jubatum (Squirrel-tail grass, Foxtail barley) – grass with pale green and silver featherlike flowers, turning brown with age.

Lagurus ovatus (Hare's-tail grass) – grass with fluffy pale green flowerheads like rabbit's tails.

Limonium sinuatum (Statice) – tiny, funnel-shaped blooms in clusters on stiff stems in white, yellow and apricot to red, deep blue, sky blue and purple.

Lunaria annua (Honesty) – old-fashioned biennial grown chiefly for the beauty of its moon-like seedpods (hence its Latin name) which, when dry and peeled, are much prized by flower arrangers.

Moluccella laevis (Bells of Ireland) – tiny, fragrant flowers encased in enormous green calyxes, like clappers in a bell.

Nigella damascena (Love-in-a-mist) – rounded cornflower-like flowers in blue or purple, rose-red or white, above ferny foliage.

Setaria italica (Foxtail millet) – ornamental grass with dense flower panicles.

Xeranthemum annuum (Immortelle) – white, woolly leaves and white, purple, magenta or pink flowers.

Annuals for fragrance

Annuals can bring more than colour to a garden. Many of the old-fashioned cottage garden annuals also carry the gift of fragrance, some being strongly scented, others just faintly aromatic. Either way, fragrance will add the finishing touch to any cottage garden.

It is a well-known fact that smells can trigger more memories than any of the other senses. The spicy scent of wallflowers on a warm spring morning, the delicious fragrance of sweet peas, or the rich clove-like scent of stocks on the evening air instantly catapult the mind back in time to the time when these flowers were last enjoyed, providing moments of pure nostalgia.

Scent is, however, one of the most elusive qualities in flowers and may vary from plant to plant of the same species, with the time of the day or night, and, of course, with personal preference – one gardener's favourite scent can often be a nauseating stench to another. A common example is the fresh, spicy aroma of crushed pelargonium leaves, which some gardeners love but others abhor, so if a visitor to your garden reacts unfavourably to a particular scent, simply steer them away quickly to another.

The brilliantly coloured annuals use their colours rather than their scent to attract pollinators and are rarely fragrant. Most of the strongly scented flowers are white or have very light colours. For example,

PETUNIAS HAVE A STRONG, SWEET SCENT

mignonette (*Reseda odorata*) has inconspicuous, dull brownish yellow flowers but is strongly fragrant on warm, sunny days. Night-scented stocks (*Matthiola bicornis*) have colourless, four-petalled flowers which are folded up and hang dejectedly on the stems like tiny bits of paper by day. Unfurling at dusk, however, the plant comes into its own, releasing its delicious scent to hang heavy on the warm evening air, bathing the garden in its heady fragrance.

EXPERIENCING FRAGRANCE

Garden flowers smell their best when the weather is warm and humid, and the scent increases after summer rain or a watering from a garden spray. Although the heat of the summer sun at noon will dull the scent of flowers, they will soon release their fragrance again as the afternoon draws on and the sun begins to set.

An evening stroll can be an almost intoxicating experience, attracting not only gardeners but many of the moths that are the butterflies of the night. Aromatic foliage plants, such as the scented-leaved pelargoniums, must be planted close to pathways or grown in pots, as they hold their fragrance to themselves unless brushed against or touched – some can really be quite stingy and refuse to release their fragrance until one of the leaves is actually crushed.

A well-placed seating area can take in all the sights and scents of the garden and is a perfect spot from which to observe the activities of the butterflies and other insects which are drawn to scented plants.

Sweet peas, stocks, sweet rocket and many of the other scented annuals are excellent for cutting to decorate a lunch or dinner table. Visitors to the garden rarely refuse the offer of a bouquet of fragrant annuals freshly picked from the garden, and nothing beats a sweetly scented sheaf of flowers as a gift when visiting friends.

SOME PLANTING SUGGESTIONS

• Combine both the pink- and white-flowered tobacco plant (*Nicotiana sylvestris* and *N. alata*) with various colours of sweet alyssum (*Lobularia maritumum*), blue, rose or white sweet scabious (*Scabiosa atropurpurea*), mignonette (*Reseda odorata*), petunias and stocks (*Matthiola incana*) for an impressive fragrant border.

• For evening fragrance include the white- or pink-flowered marvel of Peru (*Mirabilis jalapa*), evening primrose (*Oenothera biennis*), night-scented stock (*Matthiola bicornis*) and the white-flowered tobacco plants (*Nicotiana alata* and *N. sylvestris*).

• The weedy-looking flowers of mignonette (*Reseda odorata*) may look nothing to write home about, but their fragrance is another matter. Plant them beneath a window, by the back door or next to a garden seat.

SOME ANNUALS FOR FRAGRANCE

Cheiranthus, Erysimum (Wallflower) – richly scented single or double spring flowers.
Dianthus barbatus (Sweet William) – flowers with a strong, spicy clove fragrance, excellent for cutting.
Hesperis matronalis (Damask violet, dame's violet) – from the same family as the stock and wallflower, the white or pale lilac flowers have a similar clove-like fragrance.
Heliotropium arborescens (Cherry pie) – flowers with a powerful vanilla scent.
Lathyrus odoratus (Sweet pea) – sweet peas possess a powerful, sweet fragrance that once enjoyed is never forgotten. The blues and mauves or the old-fashioned varieties have the most fragrant blooms.
Lippia citriodora (Lemon verbena) – a delightful aromatic shrub with a rich lemon scent, released when the leaves are crushed (see A–Z section under Verbena).
Matthiola incana (Stock) – flowers with a spicy fragrance similar to that of the carnation.
Mirabilis jalapa (Marvel of Peru, four o'clock flower) – opening in late afternoon the flowers are fragrant and funnel-shaped.
Nicotiana alata, syn. *N. affinis*, (Tobacco plant, jasmine tobacco) – this has tubular white flowers with a sweet evening scent, equal in strength to that of the stocks.
Oenothera biennis (Evening primrose) – lovely clear, primrose-yellow blooms, which open at dusk to emit a delicious sweet perfume particularly attractive to moths.
Pelargonium species (Scented-leaved geraniums) – grown for their leaves which produce a delicious perfume when crushed.
Petunia × hybrida (Garden petunia) – the strong scent of these funnel-shaped flowers – particularly the deep blue shades – is not generally acknowledged.
Reseda odorata (Mignonette) – sweet-scented, small, brownish yellow flowers. Modern seed strains with variously coloured flowers lack its distinctive fragrance.

Annual climbers

Annual climbers raised easily from a packet of seed can add a new dimension to a cottage garden, and will literally cover a multitude of sins. Every garden has a blemish or two: unwanted bits and pieces, often piled up in a general dumping area at the bottom of the garden which never seems to be cleared away; an old garden shed; ugly boundary walls – all can be screened from view by using fast-growing annuals. These plants are also one of the quickest ways of bringing masses of colour to the garden, and are therefore an ideal prospect for the impatient gardener who is aiming for instant effect. As an added bonus, a number of annual climbers are not only beautiful to look at, but will also bring fragrance to the garden.

SITES FOR ANNUAL CLIMBERS

In today's smaller, overlooked urban gardens, eyesores are inevitable and privacy is generally at a premium. Screening will improve the look of the garden and turn a problem area into an unexpected and delightful fea-

ture. Trellis work need not be limited to just a single screen, but can be used to divide up the garden into separate areas of interest. It is also possible to make a trellis of brass hooks strung with heavy twine or fishing line – ideal for annual climbers.

Rustic pergolas and arches are another obvious support over which to grow climbing plants. Many of the climbers that are widely planted to grow over these structures will take some time to establish, and in the meantime annual climbers can be used to create quick, temporary summer colour without any risk of throttling the permanent residents waiting to make their mark.

Annual climbers can also be enjoyed on patios and balconies by growing them in large containers, with trellis attached to a wall or fence to provide support. This form of vertical planting has the further advantage that the display can be changed from year to year.

Colourful wigwams fashioned from bamboo poles, pea sticks or even strong twigs are a traditional feature of many cottage gardens, and are particularly effective where space is limited. A wigwam-shaped structure can be fitted into any small space, and when planted

THE CANARY CREEPER (TROPAEOLUM PEREGRINUM) IS LONG FLOWERING AND
MAKES A GOOD DENSE COVERING FOR TRELLIS OR PERGOLAS

with annual climbers will create an unusual feature in containers or borders, looking quite spectacular towering above other low-growing plants. Experiments can be made with different shapes – ovals, triangles and rectangles are all possible – but care should be taken not to bend each cane too much or it may snap. When the wigwam is fully clothed rain will have difficulty getting into the centre, so it is essential to water at least twice a week. Direct the water at the base of the plants and not on to the flowers and foliage.

SOME PLANTING SUGGESTIONS

• A mix-and-match of sweet peas and scarlet-flowered runner beans can be very effective grown in the vegetable patch or border. Guaranteed to give a rustic, cottagey look to the garden, they will quickly grow right to the top of a 1.5m (5ft) structure, making a pretty and compact display, and providing the gardener with both flowers for cutting and a crop of edible beans. Not all runner beans have scarlet flowers, however, and there are several unusual varieties which are well worth trying. Look out for white-flowered 'Desirée', pink-flowered 'Sunset' and red-and-white 'Painted Lady'. The purple-podded climbing French bean is pretty and delicious, and is well worth growing for its novelty value alone.

• Another attractive and complementary pairing is the prodigious cup-and-saucer vine (*Cobaea scandens*), with purple flowers and plenty of leaves, and the Chilean glory flower (*Eccremocarpus scaber*), with masses of small, tubular orange or yellow flowers. Both will give an excellent show from seed in the first year, although neither are fully hardy they are often seen growing in sheltered cottage gardens.

• Some of the more exotic annual climbers, such as *Rhodochiton atrosanguineum* and the balloon vine (*Cardiospermum halicacabum*) need a warm aspect and a long, sunny summer if they are to thrive, but many cottage gardeners consider them well worth trying for their unusual flowers or seed capsules.

• Less rampant than the balloon vine, black-eyed Susan (*Thunbergia alata*), with striking yellow, cream or orange flowers, with dark purple to black centres, from summer to autumn, can be planted to spill over the edge of containers, window boxes or hanging baskets.

SOME ANNUAL CLIMBERS FOR FLOWERS

Cobaea scandens (Cup-and-saucer vine, Mexican ivy, monastery bells) – large, bell-shaped flowers open yellow-green and mature to purple. *C. s.* 'Alba' is a pale green form. Reaching 3–6m (10–20ft), it is suitable for growing over an archway or trellis, for covering a fence or filling in gaps on a wall.

Eccremocarpus scaber (Chilean glory flower) – an unusual tender climber, usually treated as an annual, and producing spikes of bright orange, tubular flowers. Up to 6ft (2m) high, it is suitable for growing over trellis or a pergola or through a hedge or other climbers.

Lathyrus odoratus (Sweet pea) – few flowers smell as good as a sweet pea. Most varieties are climbers growing to 10ft (3m) and will clamber over arches, pergolas and all sorts of shrubs.

Lathyrus latifolius (Everlasting pea) – although perennial, this species can be grown as an annual. It produces pinky-purple flowers unfortunately with no scent; there is also a white-flowered form, *L. latifolius* 'Albus'. Height 1.5–2.5m (5–8ft).

Thunbergia alata (Black-eyed Susan) – tender, twining tropical perennial that is grown as an half-hardy annual and has yellow, cream, orange or white flowers, each with a purple to black eye. It will reach a height of 3m (10ft) in a good summer, and flowers for three or four months.

EXOTIC ANNUAL CLIMBERS

Cardiospermum halicacabum (Balloon vine, love-in-a-puff) – tiny, white flowers are followed in autumn by balloon-like, cream-coloured seed capsules. A warm, sheltered spot is essential. In ideal conditions the plant will grow to 3m (10ft), but more often only 90cm (36in).

Ipomoea (Morning glory) – exotic climbers giving a rich display of short-lived trumpet flowers in midsummer and

WHITE-FLOWERED THUNBERGIA ALATA

climbing up to 3m (10ft) in a season.

Rhodochiton atrosanguineum (Purple bell vine) – generally grown in the conservatory, but also well worth trying in a sheltered spot outside. It has tubular flowers with purple petals hanging beneath a large red calyx and will grow to 1.5m (5ft).

SOME ANNUAL CLIMBERS FOR TALL-GROWING FOLIAGE COVER

Humulus japonicus variegatus (Variegated hop) – a decorative and vigorous twining climber, grown mainly for its maple-like leaves. Quickly making 2m (6ft) of growth, it will provide dense cover and is ideal for covering eyesores.

Tropaeolum peregrinum (Canary creeper) – a star climber, with a profusion of fringed, canary-yellow flowers, until mid-autumn from an outdoor sowing. It provides the densest of cover and the longest flowering display of any of the annual climbers. Plants reach 1.5–2.5m (5–8ft) in height.

AN ANNUAL CLIMBER FOR LOW-GROWING FOLIAGE COVER

Tropaeolum majus (Nasturtium) – for covering old tree stumps, low walls or for use in hanging baskets and containers, the trailing nasturtiums are ideal.

GROWING ANNUALS FROM SEED

It is easy – and tempting for beginners – to buy trays of young bedding plants ready for planting out into the annual garden, but many gardeners prefer to start their own plants from seed. A surprisingly large number of annuals are difficult to obtain as plants or are only available from seed catalogues, and this is often the only way to get hold of both very new and very old species and varieties. In addition, growing from seed is generally more economical – it is also great fun.

Winter finds keen gardeners deeply immersed in the new season's seed catalogues, with order forms, 'want' lists and reference books strewn all around. This annual fix for weather-bound plantaholics is a universal experience, as popular today as when the firm of Robert Furber in Kensington, London, considered at the time to be England's most fashionable nursery, sent out the first book-form catalogue back in 1725.

Page after page of glossy pictures of new introductions, rediscovered treasures and old favourites lift the spirits and loosen the purse strings. Fired with enthusiasm and full of fresh ideas for an instant cottage garden, we invariably proceed to order more seed than can possibly be used in one season. As the orders are fulfilled, however, it is the out-of-stock items that gardeners regret most, rather than the mountain of seed which has been over-ordered. Ordering early will avoid many such disappointments, particularly if the seed is in short supply or great demand, or both. Some specialist societies may keep a waiting list for rare and unusual varieties, but for most it is a question of first come, first served.

STORING SEED

Packets of seed that arrive too early to plant should be stored in a glass jar on a refrigerator shelf. Do *not* use the freezer. If the refrigerator is out of bounds, find somewhere cool and dry to keep the packets until required. Never store seeds in a greenhouse or potting shed: the combination of heat and moisture will literally kill off seeds within six weeks.

Nowadays, some of the bigger seed merchants use foil packets that are vacuum sealed, but specialist societies and many of the smaller firms – usually the source of the most interesting seed – cannot afford such sophisticated packaging. However, if stored correctly, over-ordered seed even in open packets can still be kept for another year, and most will germinate after the second year of storage and beyond, although seed of some plants will lose vitality, especially if it is left lying about in the open – instead of around 80 or 90 per cent the germination rate will be down to 20 per cent or less.

To check the viability of stored seed, take 10 seeds and place them in a moistened paper towel. Place the paper towel in a plastic bag and leave it in a warm place. Consult the seed packet to see how many days are normally required for germination and start checking seeds after this time. If eight or more have germinated, the seeds are fine. If five to seven have germinated, sow more seed than you would normally. Fewer than five, and your results will be poor. Fewer than two – forget it.

PREPARING SEED FOR SOWING

Seed of some annuals requires special treatment before sowing if it is to germinate satisfactorily.

Stratification

Some seeds require chilling before they are sown in order to break their dormancy. Stratification, as the process is known, involves mixing the seeds with two to three times their volume of moistened sowing medium in a plastic bag and placing this in the refrigerator, not the freezer, for six to eight weeks. Ensure that the bag is sealed tightly and that it is labelled with the date and the name of the plant. After the recommended length of time (this is always stated on commercial seed packets), remove the bag from the refrigerator and plant the complete mixture as directed on the seed packet for sowing. Seed can also be stratified outdoors, provided the temperature is constantly below 5°C (40°F) for six to eight weeks.

The fact that some seed may benefit from this treatment does not necessarily mean that without it, it will not germinate eventually.

SOME SEEDS THAT NEED
STRATIFICATION
Moluccella laevis (Bells of Ireland)
Brassica oleracea (Ornamental cabbage)
Brassica oleracea acephala (Ornamental or flowering kale)
Viola × wittrockiana (Pansy)
Phlox drummondii (Annual phlox)
Verbena × hybrida (Garden verbena)

Soaking

Some seeds with very hard outer coats, such as sweet peas (*Lathyrus odoratus*), need special preparation before sowing. Soaking these seeds in hot, but not boiling, water prior softens the seed coat and hastens germination. Use a ratio of three parts water to one part seed. Place the seed in a shallow dish and pour water that has just gone off the boil over them. Most seed coats will be soft enough after 24 hours of soaking, however, if seeds do not swell, repeat the exercise.

Scarification

Scarification is also worth trying. This entails nicking or piercing the seed coat slightly, using a knife or a needle, to allow moisture to penetrate into the seed; a nail file can be very useful for seeds with particularly hard coats. Care should be taken not to cut too deeply, as this may damage the interior and prevent germination.

SOME SEEDS THAT NEED SOAKING
Ipomoea tricolor (Morning glory)
Lathyrus odoratus (Sweet pea)
Salvia splendens (Scarlet sage)

PREPARED SEED
Pelleted seed, where small seeds have been coated with clay to make them easier to handle, and seed tapes, where the paper tape itself is planted to avoid the need for the gardener to pay any attention to seed spacing or the proper planting depth, have made the growing of plants from seed more attractive to a new generation of gardeners. However, seed prepared in these ways is more expensive than standard loose seed, and old hands might argue that the additional cost of using these gimmicky products is of doubtful value when measured against the small amount of time and trouble saved by using them.

LIGHT LEVELS
Light levels can affect the germination of some seeds. The seeds of most cultivated plants germinate equally well in darkness or in light, but for a few seeds one or other will be a requirement for successful germination.

The length of exposure and the type of light can influence germination. In the garden there is little chance of altering either, but by adjusting the sowing depth it is possible to ensure that the seeds are in darkness or light.

SOME SEEDS THAT NEED LIGHT TO GERMINATE
Antirrhinum majus (Snapdragon)
Begonia semperflorens (Begonia)
Coleus × hybridus (Coleus)
Helichrysum bracteatum (Strawflower)
Impatiens hybrids (Impatiens/Busy lizzie)
Lobularia maritima (Sweet alyssum)
Matthiola incana (Stock)
Moluccella laevis (Bells of Ireland)
Nicotiana (Tobacco plant)
Petunia × hybrida (Petunia)
Tithonia rotundifolia (Mexican sunflower)

SOME SEEDS THAT NEED DARKNESS TO GERMINATE
Calendula officinalis (Pot marigold)
Consolida ambigua (Larkspur)
Lathyrus odoratus (Sweet pea)

Nigella damascena (Love-in-a-mist)
Papaver rhoeas (Poppy)
Schizanthus × wisetonensis (Butterfly flower)
Tropaeolum majus (Nasturtium)
Verbena × hybrida (Verbena)

TIMING
Seed can be sown at almost any time of the year, providing adequate conditions of light and temperature can be maintained. In fact, some very satisfying results can be obtained by sowing at the most unlikely times. However, general guidelines can be given for the different types of annuals and biennials.

Hardy annuals
Hardy annuals are usually sown outside when the sun is gaining strength, and the soil has started to warm up after winter and is easily workable – that is, not frozen or heavy with moisture. Seeds that are sown in unfavourable conditions will have a very poor germination rate or may even fail to germinate at all.

A number of hardy annuals can be sown outside in late summer or early autumn from freshly collected seed, to provide sturdy young plants for early flowering the following spring. The disadvantage is that it is very easy to forget about them after sowing and then hoe them out when tidying up the garden for winter! Bad weather can also take its toll. One technique worth trying is to sow the annuals thinly in rows about 10–15cm (4–6in) apart on any reasonably well-drained spare piece of soil and cover with a cloche until late winter. Guard against slugs, and then move the plants to their permanent positions in early spring.

Half-hardy annuals
Half-hardy annuals, and perennials that are treated as half-hardy annuals, are sown under glass eight to ten weeks before the last expected frost. Slow-growing plants such as begonias should be sown as early as possible, while fast growers like French marigolds can be started much later on. Transplant the seedlings into the garden after all risk of frost is past.

There are many half-hardy annuals that are worth trying from a late outdoor sowing, but these will not usually reach a reasonable flowering size until quite late in the year, except perhaps in favourable seasons and mild areas. Plants with fine seeds (both hardy and half-hardy) should always be started indoors, as they are easily washed away by rain and will have a difficult time competing with weeds when young.

SOME SEEDS WHICH MAY BE SOWN IN AUTUMN
Agrostemma githago (Corn cockle)
Calendula officinalis (Pot marigold)
Centaurea cyanus (Cornflower)
Clarkia elegans (Clarkia)
Consolida ambigua (Larkspur)
Eschscholzia californica (California poppy)
Iberis umbellata (Candytuft)
Limnanthes douglasii (Poached-egg plant)
Nigella damascena (Love-in-a-mist)
Scabious atropurpurea (Sweet scabious)

Hardy biennials
Seed of all biennials should be sown outside in late spring, following the general guidelines for sowing annuals *in situ* below. Sow the seeds thinly in drills 15–22cm (6–9in) apart and ensure that the soil is kept adequately moist during germination and seedling growth. Prick out the seedlings into good, fertile soil as soon as they are large enough to handle, and transplant the resulting sturdy plants to their flowering positions in early autumn.

SOWING ANNUALS *IN SITU*
Sowing seeds directly into the garden is by far and away the simplest method of growing annuals. Once the ground is warm and the planting bed is properly prepared it is quite amazing how quickly they spring up and grow to flowering size.

For sowing annuals in their flowering position outside, the choice of site is important, as most are sun-lovers. The plot should certainly receive sun for most of the day, and you should avoid exposed situations where taller plants may be buffeted by strong winds and rain. A few annuals, such as stocks and nicotianas, are more tolerant of semi-shade or sunless situations.

Time spent preparing the ground for sowing will be time well spent. A good soil is not essential, but it does help if it is weed free. Dig over the soil a week or two before sowing to give new weeds a chance to surface and be rooted out. Make sure that the ground is damp before sowing.

To avoid identification problems later on, it is advisable to label sowings carefully. Alternatively, sow a few seeds of each variety in labelled pots, which can then be used as a reference collection that can be taken along to the border to resolve any doubts. It is also useful to keep back some seed for later sowings and emergencies.

To test if the soil is ready for sowing, pick up a handful and squeeze. If it stays together in a ball it is too wet to work, as its structure will be ruined; wait a few more days and try again. If the soil crumbles, however, it is ready.

1 Rake away rough stones and weeds, and then work the surface of the soil to a fine, crumbly tilth. If the soil is very sandy, add compost, peat or composted bark, mixing this in with the surface soil to hold the moisture and help the plants to grow.
2 Using the edge of a hoe or rake, make a reasonably straight furrow of the

appropriate depth for the seeds you are sowing. Even if you are sowing annuals informally in small drifts it is still best to sow in rows within these, as weeding will be much easier.
3 Unless the ground is moist, water the drill thoroughly before sowing, but refrain from sowing in a puddle. Watering after sowing may wash out

the seeds or at least uncover them, and on some soils may form a 'cap' on the surface that will hinder germination.
4 Scatter the seeds thinly in the furrows and cover them lightly with soil. Thinning out seedlings can be more time-consuming and tedious than the sowing itself, and carefully spaced seeds will make thinning much easier. Firm the soil well with the flat of the hoe or the edge of a board.

THINNING

1 When the seedlings are 5–8cm (2–3in) tall, or have developed two or three sets of true leaves, it is time to thin them out. Choose a cloudy day, and if necessary spread the operation over a couple of weeks. Water the soil first to make it easier to remove unwanted seedlings.

2 Pull up the weakest seedlings carefully before they crowd their neighbours. Leave 5–15cm (2–6in) between those remaining, according to their ultimate size, and ensure that they are not disturbed as you remove the rest.
3 When the seedlings have grown enough so that they begin to touch, again remove the weakest, leaving the remainder at the required final distance apart. Seedlings which are removed at this stage can be used in another part of the garden or shared among friends and neighbours.

SOWING LARGE AREAS

Instead of sowing annuals in small drifts or rows, you may wish to plant a large area of the garden with sweeps of colour.

1 Prepare the soil as before and mark out the sowing area informally with flowing sweeps of sprinkled lime or lengths of string.
2 For each sector, tip half the seed to be sown into one hand. Cup your hand slightly and move it across the area, tapping your wrist with the other hand. Repeat with the remaining seed, this time moving back across the area to return to the original starting place. Avoid sowing in windy weather, as the seed can easily be blown away. Label each sowing area to help identify the young seedlings and distinguish them from weeds.
3 Firm the soil gently over the newly sown seeds with the flat of the hoe or the edge of a board, taking care not to bury them too deeply. Most annual seeds will germinate when just pressed into the soil.
4 To discourage birds from taking the seed, attach brightly coloured empty seed packets to small sticks and place them in the middle of each sowing. Cotton thread stretched between sticks to cover the sowing area is another good deterrent. For a more informal, cottagey look, you could scatter ('broadcast') the seed over the prepared soil in a random manner.

SOWING UNDER GLASS

When sowing annuals under glass, always use containers that have been cleaned thoroughly to avoid the risk of spreading disease to the seedlings.

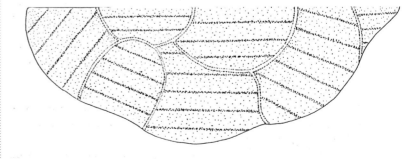

MARKING OUT SOWING AREAS ON A LARGE BORDER

Plastic plant pots and seed trays are much easier to wash and for this reason are more popular than clay pots. The latter will also need to be soaked in water before use, as a dry pot may absorb moisture from the compost. For most purposes and types of seed, a 9cm (3½in) pot will be quite adequate for raising the numbers of seedlings required by the average gardener.

Biodegradable pots of moulded peat and wood fibre are best for growing single plants (put in three seeds and thin out to one seedling) and for those that resent transplanting, as the whole thing can be inserted into the soil, avoiding root disturbance. Always sow seed in a sterilized loam- or peat-based seed compost. Never be tempted to use a potting compost: the higher nutrient level could well inhibit germination or damage the seedlings.

Gardeners frequently encounter problems when starting annuals from seed because the compost is too cold. Many plants will germinate at temperatures below 10°C (50°F), but most annuals do much better when provided with gentle bottom heat, which is more important than air temperature in encouraging strong growth. A heated pad is the simplest way to turn an unheated propagator (seed tray and clear plastic cover) into a heated one. This is a heating element in the form of

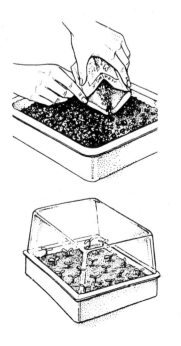

a metal plate. It is placed in the bottom of the seed tray and covered with compost.

1 Measure out the amount of compost needed to fill the pot or seed tray and wet it thoroughly. Fill the containers to within about 1.5cm (½in) of the top to allow for free circulation of air. Press down the compost lightly with your fingers, and spray with a fungicide containing benomyl. Allow the pots or trays to drain for about two hours, and then proceed with sowing.

2 It is sometimes easier to tip the seed from the packet into a folded piece of paper and then gently tap out the seeds from the paper with a finger. Sow the seed thinly and evenly; individual seed packets will advise how deep to plant the seeds and whether light is required for germination. A moistened matchstick is useful for positioning small seeds, while very fine seed is best mixed with dry silver sand in order to distribute it evenly. If seed has been obtained from a specialist nursery or garden society without sowing instructions, leave fine seeds leave uncovered and just settle them in with a light spray of water; otherwise, cover the seeds with layer of fine compost as deep as the diameter of the seed.

3 Spray the surface with a fungicide again before placing the pot or tray in a clean plastic bag, ensuring that it is pulled taut over the top and does not dip on to the compost, and secure with plastic-coated wire. This obviates the need to water the seeds again until after germination, and prevents the compost from drying out – a common cause of failure. Label each pot or tray clearly with the name of the plant and the date of sowing, and place in a warm, well-lit spot; a greenhouse is ideal but a sunny windowsill can work equally well. If the air temperature in the chosen area is less than 16°C (60°C) provide bottom heat.

4 Protect the pots or trays from strong sunlight. If the greenhouse is not shaded, cover the pots or trays with newspaper or brown wrapping paper. Remove the paper as soon as the

seeds begin to germinate, as they will now need light to prevent the seedlings from becoming leggy.

5 Give the seedlings a few more days and then remove the plastic cover. Check the compost every day; when it starts to dry out, you will need to water. Always use tepid, not cold, water for watering young seedlings. If the seeds sown were very fine or dust-like, stand the pot or tray in a bowl containing 2–3cm (1in) of water and let it soak up gradually through the compost. For larger seeds, use a fine-rosed watering can or the fine mist from a sprayer.

DAMPING OFF

The fungus disease called damping off is probably the number one enemy of the seed raiser. Young seedlings may appear healthy, but the disease will attack them at, or just below, compost level, causing them suddenly to wilt, collapse and die. However, it can be virtually eliminated if a sterile, peat- or loam-based seed compost is used. Prevention can also be helped by the following good practices:

• Make sure all equipment is clean.
• Treat the sowing medium with a fungicide containing benomyl, as above.
• Prick out seedlings before they become overcrowded.
• Do not overwater.
• Provide growing seedlings with fresh air but do not stand them in draughts.

PRICKING OUT

The first leaves you will see after germination are the 'cotyledons', or seed leaves. As soon as the first true leaves – which look completely different to the seed leaves – have unfolded, you will need to 'prick out' the seedlings into larger, or even individual, containers. This will prevent overcrowding, which would cause competition for light, moisture and nutrients, and might even lead to damping off.

1 With extreme care, take hold of a seedling by a seed leaf (which will soon drop off in any case) – not a true

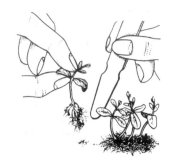

leaf or the stem, as this could easily damage the vital food and water-carrying vessels.

2 Using a dibber or pencil, make a hole in the compost in the new container ready to receive the seedling. Push the dibber or pencil into the compost next to the seedling, then lift seedling and compost together using the dibber or pencil, and place it gently into the new hole.

3 Close up the hole firmly using the dibber or pencil, so that the roots of the seedling are in close contact with the surrounding compost.

Invariably there will be more seedlings than can be accommodated. Select individuals with an assortment of sizes – paradoxically, it is often the small and weak-looking seedlings that eventually produce the best flowers with the most interesting colours. This is particularly true when you are dealing with mixtures or varieties, where any reversion to the parent species is often associated with the strongest seedlings.

HARDENING OFF

When risk of severe weather is past and when seedlings are strong and sturdy, you will need to harden them off to accustom them to garden conditions, before planting them outdoors. Start hardening off a week or two before transplanting. Move the pots and trays outside during the day and place them in a shady, protected spot or cold frame. Bring them back inside at night. Each day expose the young plants to a little more sun, and towards the end of the week leave them out all night.

When seedlings have been hardened off, it is easy to forget how much water they require. Suddenly these tiny

plants are out in the open air, where soil and leaf evaporation occur at a much faster rate than when they were under cover. Ensure that they receive plenty of water, but do not use a fertilizer at this early stage of growth.

SEEDS OF SUCCESS

The important guidelines to ensure good germination for seed sown under glass are:

• Use a soil-less seed compost.
• Do not cover the seeds too deeply: fine seeds should be left uncovered, and larger seeds should be sown no deeper than twice their diameter.
• Keep the growing medium just moist. Do not overwater, but never allow the compost to dry out completely.
• Use a mister or a fine-rose watering can to water tiny seedlings, or water from below.
• Keep seeds out of direct sunlight until germination is complete.

PLANTING OUT

Once they have been hardened off, the seedlings will be ready for transplanting into the garden.

If possible, choose a dull or cloudy day, and water the soil a few hours before planting. If it is fine and sunny, plant early in the morning or late in the afternoon, and try to work quickly. Watering the young plants thoroughly before transplanting will make it easier to remove them from their containers without disturbing the delicate root systems. Keep the plants in the shade until you can deal with them, and do not allow the roots dry out.

Before planting out, check the seed packet to see how far apart the plants should be spaced. Never be tempted to crowd seedlings – they will probably look quite lost in a sea of brown earth at first, but they will soon spread out and fill the gaps.

Seedlings that were pricked out into individual pots may be set out in the planting area still in their pots to try out different configurations. To achieve the biggest visual impact with annuals in a small garden or area, place them in odd-numbered groups (five, seven, nine

or more). In a larger garden, plant them in drifts. More formal plantings will require the use of a metre rule (yardstick) or measuring tape to lay out precise planting patterns.

1 Remove the plant from its container. If a seedling grown in an individual pot does not fall out readily, tap the bottom and sides of the container with the handle of a trowel to loosen it, or lay the pot on its side and press on it, while rolling it back and forth a few times. Remove any damaged stems or leaves.

Annuals that have been grown individually in peat pots can be planted out still in their pots, which will gradually rot. Ensure that the top edge of the pot is set below the soil level, and break the pots in a few places to help the roots penetrate into the soil more easily.

If the young plants have been grown in plastic 'strips', which is often the case with purchased seedlings, break open the strip and ease out the plants carefully.

Seedlings in multi-plant containers need to be turned out of the container and separated before planting. Water the plants well beforehand. Some roots are bound to be broken off in the process; pinch out the top growth on the plant to help keep a balance between stem and leaf and root areas.

2 Fill a watering can with tepid water, then dig the planting hole larger than the plant's rootball and fill it with water. When the water has soaked through, add more, then place the plant in the hole, pressing the soil down firmly and leaving a slight depression around the stem to trap water. Care must be taken to set the plants at the same depth or slightly deeper than they were in the seed tray so that their roots can spread into the soil – planting too deep will cause many annuals to rot at the crown, while those planted too shallow wiii dry out quickly.

WATERING

After transplanting, water the seedlings

extremely carefully until they have recovered from the shock. Thereafter, water daily for about a week until the plants are well established and show signs of new growth. Gradually reduce watering to a thorough soaking once a week to encourage strong, deep roots.

TRANSPLANTING TIPS

The steps to successful transplanting of young plants into the garden can be summarized as follows:

• Water the soil and the plants a few hours before planting out.
• Plant out the seedlings to the correct depth and distance apart.
• Ensure that the planting hole is larger than the rootball, and fill the bottom of the hole with water before planting.
• Firm the soil around the plant, leaving a slight depression around the stem to trap water.
• Always water young seedlings with tepid water.

AFTERCARE

As a rule, annuals do not require specially cultivated or artificially enriched soil – in fact too rich a soil will simply encourage leafy growth at the expense of flowers. However, this does not mean that by simply punching a hole in solid clay and sowing seed or by sowing in very poor, dry soil means you can expect all annuals to thrive and cheerfully bloom all summer.

SOIL TYPE

In soils that have very good drainage, such as sandy soil, nutrients and trace elements are leached away very quickly. Improve the soil by adding plenty of compost, including old livestock manure and shredded leaves. Clay soil drains slowly, feels sticky to the touch, easily becomes waterlogged and is slow to dry out, and when it does dry it becomes rock-hard. To lighten its texture, add plenty of organic matter and improve drainage by adding builder's sand. Loam, the ideal garden soil we all strive for, is a combination of sand and/or clay and contains plenty of organic material. Loam provides a good home for bacteria and worms which are constantly at

work, feeding on fallen leaves and dead vegetable matter, aerating and improving the texture of the soil.

WATERING

It is not always easy to gauge exactly when plants require water – so much depends on the soil conditions and the weather. If you are lucky enough to get a soaking rain every week or so then additional watering is quite unnecessary. Remember, however, that gardens with sandy soil and plants subjected to bright sun and wind lose a lot of water that needs to be replenished. Containers, especially the small ones, dry out very quickly in hot weather and may well need watering twice a day.

When plants are watered infrequently but thoroughly, they will develop large and deep root networks. Waving a hose around the garden or frequent light waterings causes the development of shallow root systems, just below the soil surface. This means poorly-anchored plants which are subject to toppling in heavy wind or rain and become a wilting mess in drier weather unless they are watered daily.

A good way to tell when to water is to poke your finger 5–7cm (2–3in) into the soil – if it feels dry, then it is time to water. There is little point in taking a pinch from the surface, you really need to know what it is like down where the roots are. When you do water, water deeply, supplying enough water to penetrate the soil to a depth of at least 15cm (6in).

How often to water during a drought is largely determined by the soil type. On average, a good loamy soil would require watering once every ten days or so, whereas a sandy soil drains faster and will need to be watered every week. Clay soil which retains moisture better, needs to be irrigated only every two weeks.

FERTILIZERS

If well-rotted compost or manure is added to the garden yearly it will not be necessary to use chemical fertilizers. If not, work in a slow-release granular fertilizer into the soil in spring or

autumn. For an added boost, use a liquid fertilizer when transplanting.

PINCHING OUT

To encourage plants to make bushier growth, remove the growth bud at the end of the main stem when the plant is in the rapid growth stage that precedes first flower bud formation. The best tool you can use for this is your thumb and forefinger. Known as pinching back, this redirects the energy of young plants into sending out more side shoots instead of growing taller; many plants will double in width after they have been pinched back. Plants grown from seeds sown directly in the garden should be pinched back when they reach 7–10cm (3–4in) tall. Any plant that has become too leggy or too tall will benefit from being pinched back to make it more compact.

STAKING

Do not wait until the wind and rain have laid low choice annuals; stake the plants in good time to allow them to look their best. Those plants that produce tall, single spikes will require individual staking. Push a wooden or bamboo stake into the ground 5–7cm (2–3in) from the plant and tie the stem loosely to this, every 15cm (6in) along its length; a final tie should be made just below the flower bud cluster. Only a few varieties need this treatment, it takes just a few minutes and your effort will be well rewarded. For plants with a spreading habit, pushing much-branched pieces of brushwood into the ground beside them to form a network of twigs through which they can grow and lean on for support will make them look much tidier, and it also helps to prolong the flowering period.

SINGLE STAKING

• Ensure that the stake is firmly anchored in the soil.
• Loosely tie each stem to this central stake, at 15cm (6in) intervals.
• Make a final tie just below the flower bud cluster.

PEA- OR BRUSHWOOD STAKING

• Brush thicket gives better support if

the tops are bent over and interwoven.
• Don't worry if it looks a tangle, the plant stems will soon conceal it.

SUCCESS WITH STAKING
• Metal stakes are more expensive than bamboo or brushwood, but they are easier to use and last for years.
• Corrals using four or more stakes are best for large clumps of plants.
• Link stakes with string or yarn, cross-woven between them. Several tiers of string may be needed for tall plants: space tiers 10–15cm (4–6in) apart.

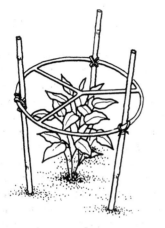

DEADHEADING
Deadheading flowers promptly once they have faded keeps the garden looking neat and tidy and can prolong the flowering season. The removal of dead flowers and seedpods as they form encourages repeat flowering in some species and prevents dieback in the stems. Large-flowered annuals, such as the zinnias, are easy to deadhead: simply pinch off or cut flowers back to the next branch. It is easier with smaller-flowered plants such as alyssum and verbena just to trim the flowerheads off with pruning shears. Never remove more than a third of the plant and always follow up with a feeding. This can be quite a relaxing job on a sunny day when it is a pleasure to be outside.

SOME ANNUALS WHICH NEED REGULAR DEADHEADING
Ageratum houstonianum (Floss flower)
Lobularia maritimum (Sweet alyssum)
Antirrhinum majus (Snapdragon)
Calendula officinalis (Pot marigold)
Callistephus chinensis (China aster)

Convolvulus tricolor syn. *C. minor* (Annual convolvulus)
Cosmos bipinatus (Cosmos)
Dahlia (Bedding dahlia)
Digitalis purpurea (Foxglove) remove central spike
Eschscholzia californica (California poppy)
Helichrysum bracteatum (Strawflower)
Iberis umbellata (Candytuft)
Lathyrus odoratus (Sweet pea)
Lobularia maritimum (Sweet alyssum)
Phlox drummondii (Annual phlox)
Scabiosa atropurpurea (Sweet scabious)
Verbena × hybrida (Garden verbena)
Viola × wittrockiana (Pansy)

SEED COLLECTING
Collecting and growing your own seeds is great fun, especially for an informal cottage garden, but should you require a particular plant of a certain colour then the only sure way to get it is by buying seeds from a reputable seedsman. The results from collected seed will vary widely. Flower colour, for instance, may be different, particularly if there was cross-pollination between the parent plant and other nearby plants of the same kind but different colours – white foxgloves grown near purple foxgloves will result in some seedlings having white flowers and some with purple ones.

When collecting seeds from the garden for the following year it is worth bearing in mind that seed of F1 hybrids (cross-pollinated by seedsmen) are rarely worth the trouble as they will not reproduce new plants like the parent but revert to look like their respective grandparents instead.

Seedpods vary in design with some pods holding the seeds tenaciously, others spilling, or sprinkling them out a few at a time, and a few catapulting or flinging their seed in every direction as soon as it is ripe.

ANNUALS THAT DROP THEIR SEEDS
These are the annuals that have seedpods which, when ripe, open their tops and allow the seeds to drop out like pepper from a pepper-pot. To harvest, shake the newly ripe seedheads over a plate.

Calendula officinalis (Pot marigold)
Consolida ambigua (Larkspur)
Dianthus barbatus (Sweet William)
Nicotiana (Flowering tobacco)
Papaver (Poppy)
Petunia × hybrida (Petunia)

ANNUALS WITH CATAPULTING SEEDPODS
To catch the seed of annuals which catapult or spray seeds, place a small paper bag over the seedhead (after they have been pollinated, but before they dry out) and secure. Never use plastic bags, as destructive moulds will develop.

Cleome spinosa (Spider flower)
Impatiens roylei (Policeman's helmet)
Lathyrus odoratus (Sweet pea)
Viola × wittrockiana (Pansy)

ANNUALS WITH SEEDS WHICH NEED TO BE EXTRACTED
Some seedheads remain tightly packed to maturity and need to be torn apart by hand when they are well dried in order to release the seeds.

Alcea rosea (Hollyhock)
Ipomoea tricolor (Morning glory)
Scabiosa atropurpurea (Sweet scabious)
Tagetes (Marigold)
Zinnia (Garden zinnias)

ANNUALS WITH SEEDPODS WHICH NEED PROTECTION
These are the annuals with seedheads that are particularly appealing to birds and animals. The trick is to get in before the competition! Protect the seedheads by covering them with brown paper bags as they near maturity, and then pick promptly.

After harvesting the seed, separate from the pods and spread them out in a dry place away from the sun. Allow them to dry out for about two weeks and then store them in airtight containers in a cool dry place until planting time.

Cosmos bipinnatus (Cosmos)
Helianthus annuus (Sunflower)
Lathyrus odoratus (Sweet pea)

PESTS AND DISEASES

Unfortunately there are others that enjoy a beautiful garden as much as any gardener – pests and diseases. Even at night the garden is not all peace and harmony, as the fading light can signal the arrival of some most unattractive visitors, such as slugs and snails, who can munch their way through surprising amounts of greenery in just one night. However, not all insects are pests, and many, such as ladybirds and hoverflies, are positively beneficial in keeping down insect pest populations.

Be vigilant, and deal with problems promptly, but avoid becoming the classic paranoid gardener: the occasional nibbled or disfigured leaf is not the end of the world and, especially in a cottage-style garden, will go unnoticed amid the profusion of plants and flowers.

PREVENTION

As in many things, when dealing with problems in the garden prevention is a lot easier – and less harmful – than cure.

Tidying up: The first line of defence is a tidy garden. When weeding and pruning, for example, clear away the weeds, prunings and other debris, adding all suitable material to the compost heap. Never leave diseased or decaying plant material lying around just anywhere – rotting plants can be a source of infection, and some actually attract pests to the garden. Boxes, old flower pots and other garden bits and pieces are a breeding ground for slugs and earwigs, so make sure that all such equipment is stored away in the garden shed.

Keep plants strong: A strong-growing plant is more likely to withstand pest or disease attack than a weak specimen. You should reject lanky bedding plants, whether purchased or grown yourself from seed, and throw away old seeds which have been kept well past their sow-by date.

Make sure that the plants are suited to the site, and follow the advice for sowing, planting and cultivation given earlier.

Cultivation: Hoe any bare soil regularly to remove weed seedlings and expose insects and disease-causing organisms to the sun, thereby lessening their chances of surviving in the garden. Spray plants with water from time to time dislodge insect pests and remove suffocating dust.

Be observant: Take advantage of periodic walks in the garden to check on the health of your plants. The observant gardener may often be able to identify the first sign of serious trouble and take prompt action, whereas delay could result in a disease or pest destroying plants and wreaking havoc in the garden.

Under glass: The humid atmosphere of a greenhouse is a paradise for pests and diseases. Control is frequently difficult, so prevention here really is much better than cure.

Ensure that the greenhouse is adequately ventilated: dry air encourages pests and poor growth, while saturated air encourages diseases. Avoid sudden fluctuations in temperature, and water regularly in the morning: evening watering leaves foliage wet at night inviting disease and a mid-morning watering will dry out too quickly. Remove any dead leaves and plants immediately.

PESTS

Slugs and snails: These are major pests in the garden. Gliding about at night on trails of slime they can chew holes in almost any plant without being observed. The problem will be far worse in damp conditions and young seedlings and recent transplants are a particular delicacy.

Slug and snail killers are available in many forms, but poisoned baits should be avoided if there are pets or small children in the household. It is far better, although more tedious, to take a torch into the garden at night and sprinkle a few grains of salt on to the molluscs' tender bodies. Alternatively, drop

them into a can of soapy or salty water. If you expose the slugs and snails during the day, birds will also keep down the numbers and are worth encouraging into the garden for this reason.

Beer traps – jars full of stale beer sunk into the ground – are a classic lure for slugs. While there can be no doubt that slugs do indeed find the beer irresistible and fall into the traps and drown, the party will also attract 'gatecrashers' in the form of beneficial insects, who will perish as well. In addition, slugs from all over the neighbourhood tend to join in, so that the garden may end up with a bigger slug problem than it had before.

Aphids, red spider mites, whiteflies and scale insects: These are all pests which like to gather on the undersides of leaves and on the tender young growth at the tips of stems and in leaf axils. Pot marigold, nasturtium, sweet pea, busy lizzie, heliotrope and morning glory (*Ipomoea*) are all martyrs to these pests, which can often be dislodged by aiming a hose directly at the plants, but failing this, they can be controlled with applications of insecticidal soap and sprays. Avoid overcrowding plants and make sure you have good drainage throughout the garden: stagnant water is a breeding ground for insects.

Caterpillars: Large, irregular holes in the leaves of ornamental or flowering cabbage, petunias and nicotianas are usually the first sings of the presence of caterpillars in the garden. Butterflies and moths, very much a part of the cottage garden, are welcomed and encouraged. Infestations of caterpillars are therefore not surprising, but they can be controlled by picking off and destroying if necessary. Where damage is widespread use an insect spray or pest and disease duster.

Earwigs and ants: The degree of attack from these two insects varies from season to season. Earwigs, with their pincer-like rear appendages, feed at night on soft leaf and flower tissue, and are particularly fond of dahlias. Leave a rolled, moist newspaper in the garden at night and the earwigs will hide in it in the morning. They can then be disposed of in a bucket of water.

Although not a serious garden pest, ants can steal seeds and disturb the soil around plant roots, and they may also carry greenfly from one plant to another. If you really want to control them, dust along the ant runs and crevices with an anti-ant duster.

DISEASES

Viruses: Diseases caused by viruses and mycoplasma, often transmitted by aphids and leafhoppers, will cause stunting and distortion of plants, and mottling and striping of the leaves and flowers of many annuals. There is really no cure and infected plants should be destroyed. Keep sap-sucking insects under control.

Mildew: This general menace in the garden is worst in hot, dry weather. Powdery mildew, which coats leaves and flower buds, especially on dahlias and zinnias late in the year, is difficult to control once established. Mulch in spring and water during dry periods in summer

to prevent it from appearing. There is some chance of successful treatment if the plants are sprayed regularly with pest and disease duster from the first sign of infection, but mildewed plants are best pulled up and burned.

Rust: This is a common problem with antirrhinums and hollyhocks. Raised orange, brown or black pustules usually appear first on the undersides of leaves. If an infestation occurs, destroy infected plants or remove affected leaves.

One way of preventing rust is to give the planting area a good winter clean-up. Clear away remains of infected plants and leaves and remove all gardening debris. During the growing season, avoid overhead watering, and water early in the morning so that any splashed foliage can dry quickly.

Using sprays: A wide range of insecticides and fungicides is available at the garden centre for protecting plants against pests and diseases. Few products, however, will control diseases due to viruses, bacteria and mycoplasma.

Organic insecticides, derived from plants such as pyrethrum or derris, are quickly broken down into harmless substances and are considered much safer both for the user and the environment than inorganic chemical insecticides. However, care should be taken when handling any chemical – even organic products can be quite toxic when applied.

Sprays are usually either 'protectant' or 'systemic'. Protectants will keep pests and disease organisms away from uninfected parts of the plant, while systemics move through the plant and are absorbed by the sap, killing fungi inside the plant and pests, such as aphids, which feed on the sap.

Contact insecticides only kill pests that are actually hit by the spray or which eat sprayed leaves. It is therefore important to spray or dust the plants thoroughly, paying special attention to the undersides of the leaves, where pests tend to congregate.

If a spray has to be used, those listed are among the least harmful to both gardener and environment, including beneficial insects and organisms.

Insect spray (Derris-quassia)
- Controls greenfly, blackfly, red spider mite and small caterpillars.
- Dilute 5ml (1tsp) in 1 litre (2 pints) of water and apply through a sprayer at the first sign of trouble.
- Useful for treating large areas.
- Safe to bees, but keep well away from ponds.

Pest pistol (Horticultural soap)
- Controls greenfly, whitefly, blackfly, red spider mite and scale insect.
- Purchase a ready-to-use spray and apply at the first sign of trouble.
- Useful for treating small areas.
- Can be used on fruit and vegetables.
- Safe to ladybirds.

Pest and disease duster (Derris-sulphur)
- Controls greenfly, blackfly, red spider mite, small caterpillars and mildew.
- Purchase a ready-to-use puffer.
- Apply when infestation begins to build up, and repeat as necessary.
- Safe to bees, but keep well away from ponds.

HOLLYHOCKS CAN BE PRONE TO RUST

A–Z of
COTTAGE GARDEN
ANNUALS

Abutilon × hybridum

Abutilon × hybridum, or flowering maples, are tender perennials which are easily grown as outdoor half-hardy annuals. They are popular as houseplants but also make an unusual and striking addition to garden beds and borders in semi-shady areas. With very soft, light green, maple-like leaves, a bushy habit, and exotic-looking, bell-shaped flowers to 6cm (2½in) wide, in many different shades of orange, salmon, yellow, white and maroon, they are also very effective in containers and window boxes as the bottom branches, heavy with flowers, will cascade over the edges.

Abutilons often lose their lower leaves and look distinctly leggy in dry conditions. Their bare knees, however, can be completely hidden if planted in the middle or the back of the border.

CULTIVATION

Start seeds indoors ten weeks before the last frost, potting them individually into peat pots when the first true leaves appear. Seeds will germinate in 21–28 days at 21–27°C (70–81°F). Plant out, pot and all, into moist, fertile soil, rich in organic matter, when the outside temperature exceeds 10°C (50°F); space them 30cm (12in) apart. They prefer protection from strong afternoon sunlight and must be kept well-watered for best results.

ABUTILON × HYBRIDUM VARIEGATA

A layer of mulch around the base of each plant will help prevent moisture from evaporating and the lower leaves from falling off. In the first year, plants grown from seed will reach 60cm (24in). They can be brought indoors from the garden in late summer to overwinter as houseplants, and replanted back in the garden the following summer.

COTTAGE GARDEN VARIETIES

• *Abutilon × hybridum maximum* 'Benarys Giant'
Easy from seed, Benarys Giant has large chalice-shaped flowers in lovely shades of orange, salmon and maroon, produced in profusion during the summer months. Height 60cm (24in).
• *Abutilon × hybridum variegata*
This cultivar has variegated leaves that are splashed with yellow. Quite a show-stopper. Height 60cm (24in).

Ageratum houstonianum

Ageratum houstonianum (syn. *A. mexicanum*), known as the floss flower, is a reliable old half-hardy favourite for summer and autumn colour. Mound-shaped plants, blooming non-stop from early summer until the frosts, produce clusters of tiny, fluffy, true-blue flowers (as well as a handful of pink or white varieties) like powderpuffs. The leaves are dark green, hairy, ovate and toothed.

Most cultivars form dwarf mounds 10–20cm (4–8in) high and twice as wide, but a few can reach 38cm (15in) in height. Few annuals beat ageratum for a showy edging to the border, for bedding out and for container planting. The taller varieties are more open in growth and are excellent as cut flowers, lasting a long time in water.

Deadheading the small flowers as they fade and turn brown will prevent the plant looking messy and at the same time prolong the flowering period. In the autumn small plants can be dug up and brought indoors as houseplants.

CULTIVATION

Seeds will germinate in 5–10 days at 16–21°C (61–70°F) but take 6–10 weeks to reach transplant size. Press the seeds lightly into a planting medium and do not cover them as they need light to germinate. Transplant the seedlings into separate pots when the first true leaves appear and grow them on in a sunny window. Plant outside after the last frost 15–20cm (6–8in) apart, in sun or light shade. Pinch back after planting to promote bushiness.

Ageratums are not particularly fussy about soil, although they do better when it is rich, moist and well-drained. Keep them well-watered in dry conditions and fertilize monthly with a water-soluble plant food.

COTTAGE GARDEN VARIETIES

• *Ageratum houstonianum* 'Bavaria'
A new variety, claimed to be the first bicoloured ageratum, with large, deep blue flowers with pure white centres borne on plants of a dwarf, compact habit. Height 25cm (10in).
• *Ageratum houstonianum* 'Blue Banquet'
A tall-growing blue variety which is recommended for bedding and for cutting. Height 50cm (20in).
• *Ageratum houstonianum* 'Blue Mink'
A compact plant bearing clusters of Wedgwood-blue flowers. Perfect for bedding displays, window boxes and tubs. Height 23cm (9in).
• *Ageratum houstonianum* 'Pink Powderpuffs'
This is a dwarf, free- and long-flowering variety, hiding the foliage under a mass of rose-pink blooms for most of the summer. The colouring holds well and does not fade with the sun. Height 15cm (6in).

Agrostemma githago

Agrostemma, from the Greek meaning garland of the fields, once a weed of cornfields, is the native corn cockle. This graceful, slender hardy annual, growing 60–90cm (24–36in) high, with large, satin, soft lilac-rose flowers, 5cm (2in) across, produced freely all summer, is without doubt a cottage garden plant *par excellence*. With their long narrow leaves on elegant stems, the flowers are also useful for cutting.

In spite of their slender habit, the plants stand up well to wind and wet. The hairy silver-grey stems sway gently backwards and forwards in the breeze without breaking. It is probably at its best grown in clumps in the middle or back of a border and will sow itself generously around the garden.

CULTIVATION

Sow it *in situ* when the ground can be worked in early spring. Germination takes 12 days and plants should be thinned out to 30cm (12in) apart. The plant is not fussy about soil but prefers a position in full sun or light shade.

COTTAGE GARDEN VARIETIES

• *Agrostemma githago* 'Milas'
Named after a small town in Turkey where it was discovered, 'Milas' bears soft lilac-pink flowers and has shorter stems than the true wild form. Height 60cm (24in).

AGROSTEMMA GITHAGO with CALENDULA

• *Agrostemma githago* 'Purple Queen'
First introduced over 30 years ago, this fine plant bears large and attractive purple-red flowers which make a good companion for 'Milas'. Height 60–90cm (24–36in).

Alcea rosea

Alcea rosea, syn. *Althaea rosea*, is the stately hollyhock. With its lobed, rough-textured leaves and spires of rounded, ruffled flowers, it was for many years a feature of every cottage garden – almost as natural to the garden as thatch to the cottage. Towering against whitewashed walls, almost reaching the eaves, the old-fashioned hollyhocks were as pretty as a picture.

The hollyhock has a fascinating garden history – Pliny described it as 'a rose growing on stalks like the mallow'. In addition, *Althaea*, the generic name derived from the Greek *althaia*, meaning a healing medium, indicates the plant's once widespread medicinal use.

Long believed to be a native to China, but never actually found growing wild, the hollyhock is probably a natural hybrid between *A. setosa* from Turkey and *A. pallida* from Eastern Europe and Crete. The Anglo-Saxon word for a mallow is *hoc*, while the religious connotation of 'holy' – holy mallow – suggests that seeds may well have been brought back home by the crusaders from countries over which they fought the Turks.

In his *New Herbal* of 1551, William Turner referred to the plant, which was widely grown at the time, as 'our common holyoke'. It was also known as the jagged mallow. Writing about the plant some 50 years later, Gerard mentioned that it was sown in gardens almost everywhere in his day and called it 'the tame or garden mallow…since it is a magnificent relative to our common wild mallow'. Parkinson described many varieties which he grew, including both single and double forms in many colours, and one 'of a darke red like blake blould'.

English herbalists of the sixteenth and seventeenth centuries added the dried and powdered roots of the hollyhock to wine to prevent miscarriages, to kill worms in children and to prevent blood clots. Flowers boiled in wine and water, to which honey had been added, were used as a gargle. Culpeper, whose advice was always taken very seriously in his day, prescribed the root to treat 'incontinence of urine, immoderate menses, bleeding wounds, spitting of blood, the bloody flux and other fluxes of the belly' – not the most romantic image of hollyhocks ever portrayed!

Hollyhocks continued to be fashionable during the eighteenth century, and some much-admired plants with variegated or striped flowers, now lost to cultivation, were raised by Lord Burlington in his London garden. By the middle of the nineteenth century the plant had been taken up as a florists' flower, rivalling the dahlia in the number of hybrids available, with lavish prizes presented for the best new varieties.

One of the champions of the great age of the hollyhock was Mr W. Chater, who during the 1840s and 1850s grew a whole acre of hollyhocks in his Essex nursery garden. Named varieties of his exhibition strain included 'Model of Perfection', white with a chocolate ground; 'Commander-in-Chief', towering 3m (10ft) high; 'Attraction', elegantly veined puce and silver; 'Black Prince', sable-black; 'Pallida', lilac; and 'Magnum Bonum', rich glossy maroon.

Just as the fashion for growing hollyhocks was declining naturally at the end of the nineteenth century, tragedy overcame the plant. Rust disease struck, wiping out nearly all the hybrids and decimating whole nurseries virtually overnight. Interest in hollyhocks plummeted, and has never revived to anything like the levels of 100 years ago. Almost none of the enormous number of named varieties grown then are available, although seed strains from the firm of Chater are still to be found: 'Chater's Double', with peony-like flowers in a wide range of colours, including yellows, scarlets and maroons, is offered by several seed merchants.

Attempts were made during the last century to grow hollyhocks as a commercial crop. Three hundred acres of land in North Wales were planted with hollyhocks with the sole intention of converting the fibres of the stalks into thread, in the same way as for hemp or flax. The idea was perhaps not as unlikely as it sounds, bearing in mind that the cotton plant, *Gossypium hirsutum*, is a relative. In the event, the venture was a flop – but what a gorgeous sight it must have been!

Hollyhocks are relatively short-lived perennials, but because of continued problems with rust disease they are usually grown as biennials or annuals. The stems can tower up to 3m (10ft) in height and the instantly recognizable mallow-like flowers, 10–12cm (4–5in) across, open from the bottom of the spire upwards from mid- to late summer. The plant is a veritable magnet for bees, which frequently become intoxicated as they over-indulge in its rich nectar.

Today, plant breeders have succeeded in producing hollyhocks with fluted, double and powderpuff flowers in a wide range of colours. They have also introduced various short-growing kinds that do not need staking, but these lack the old-world charm of the stately traditional types.

Place hollyhocks at the back of a border in groups of a single colour or in mixed clumps. Better still, give them a spot of their own beside a weathered building or fence, or use them as an accent at a doorway.

CULTIVATION

Sow seed under glass in late winter, or in a shady border outside during early spring. Seed must be sown thinly and covered lightly. Since the plants have long tap roots, the seedlings should be transplanted to their permanent position as soon as four leaves have formed. If this is not possible, pot up the plants individually until they can be planted out. Bearing in mind the eventual size and height of the plants, they should be planted at least 1m (3ft) apart each way. Modern strains will often bloom in the first year from seed, but old-timers will not put on a show until their second summer.

Cuttings of fine specimens can be taken from young shoots, which arise from the base of the flower stems in spring, and should be inserted singly in small pots. Collect ripe seed for future use, always selecting from the best colour forms; dispose of inferior plants after flowering.

Hollyhocks require a sunny position and enjoy a rich soil and regular watering. Give them plenty of room and drive a heavy stake 1.5–2m (5–6ft) tall into the ground behind the centre of the clump, tying the individual spikes to it. The plant's large leaves will conceal the evidence! Vigilance and fungicide will keep rust disease at bay.

COTTAGE GARDEN VARIETIES

Many catalogues continue to list *Alcea* as *Althaea*.

• *Alcea rosea* 'Chater's Double Apricot'
Sumptuous apricot flowers, which look almost like double begonias, are produced all the way up the stems of this wonderful garden plant, which is also good for cutting. Other colours are available. Height 1.5–2m (5–6ft).

• *Alcea rosea* Majorette Mixed
This mixture produces dwarf, semi-double laced blooms, up to 10cm (4in) across, in glorious pastel colours including pink, crimson, apricot, lavender, lemon and white, bringing a mass of colour to the garden. Height 60–75cm (24–30in).

• *Alcea rosea* Mr Fothergill's Giant Single Mixed
A delightful old-fashioned strain. Large, simple cup-shaped flowers are festooned along the stems in a glorious range of colours from white to deep carmine. Height 2–2.5m (6–8ft) plus.

• *Alcea rosea* var. *nigra*
A most unusual strain of hollyhock, with single flowers in an exceptionally dark shade of maroon that is almost black. This unique and impressive colour is guaranteed to provoke comment from visitors to the garden. Height 1.5–2m (5–6ft).

• *Alcea rugosa*, syn. *Alcea ficifolia*
This is the fig-leaved hollyhock, introduced from Siberia at the end of the sixteenth century and bearing long spikes of clear lemon-yellow flowers with a darker centre. A branching plant with multiple stems, it is less susceptible to rust than *A. rosea*. Height 2m (6ft).

ALCEA ROSEA

Amaranthus

You call it love-lies-bleeding so you may,
Though the red flower, not prostrate only droops,
As we have seen it here from day to day,
From month to month, life passing not away.

WILLIAM WORDSWORTH

Amaranthus caudatus has been known since 1665 by the quaint and poetic name of 'love-lies-bleeding', partly because of the drooping, rich blood-red flowers which hang in cord-like formations, often touching the ground and suggesting a flow of blood, and partly because some confusion appears to have arisen at one time between *amar* and the French *amor*, whereby the everlasting flower became associated with love. The French, of course, made no such mistake, although their name for *A. caudatus* was even more bizarre: *discipline des religieuses* – the nuns' whipping-rope!

Gerard grew *A. caudatus*, and both he and Parkinson called it the 'great purple flower-gentle'. It was planted in the parterres of sixteenth- and seventeenth-century gardens, and during the nineteenth century was frequently used as a lawn specimen, often reaching a height of 1.2–1.5m (4–5ft) on a rich diet of one-fifth fresh horse manure added to the compost, and a daily watering of pigeon-dung water!

It is because the tasselled flowers became associated with this formal Victorian style of planting that amaranthus has fallen from favour in recent years. Although the plants are great fun, the modern cottage gardener will need more than a little imagination in order to position these heavy-looking specimens discreetly in a small garden, but they can be enjoyed grown in pots to decorate a sunny patio, paths or steps, and are very effective as background plants for a display of multicoloured annuals.

The dark purple and green forms of *A. caudatus* are both excellent for cutting, as they last well in water. The flowers may also be dried, but they should not be hung upside down: instead, stand the stems upright in a weighted bottle and air dry for winter decoration.

A. tricolor, possibly a form of *A. gangeticus*, was one of the first tropical plants to be introduced to Britain, arriving from India in the sixteenth century, and the Elizabethans were fascinated by the multi-coloured foliage which gave it the common name of 'Joseph's coat'. Gerard waxed lyrical about it: 'It farre exceedeth my skill to describe the beautie and excellencie of this rare plant called Floramor; and I think the pensil of the most curious painter will be at a stay, when he shall come to set it downe in his lively colours…for in a few words, everie leafe resembleth in colour the most faire and beautifull feather of a Parat'.

The plant proved something of a challenge to grow, and in 1770 William Hanbury, writer, clergyman and distinguished gardener, warned that 'many a Gardener has been ambitious of excelling his brother in showing them in the greatest perfection but many a Gardener after repeated trials has failed in his attempts'.

The Victorians were soon to learn the secret of success: the plants were started early in the greenhouse and were then planted out in grand Victorian bedding displays. There are several forms with considerable variation in foliage colouring, combining bronze, gold, orange and scarlet, to striking autumnal effect. North American author Hermon Bourne wrote about the species in *Flores Poetici (The Florist's Manual)* published in Boston in 1833. He noticed how after a shower of rain or in the early morning 'the plants appear to stand sparkling in dew-drops, or rain-drops, like a cluster of rubies or crimson coral, bedropt with thousand sparkling gems or diamonds bright'.

CULTIVATION

Although described as perfectly hardy, it is perhaps wiser to regard amaranthus as half-hardy and sow seeds under glass in early spring. As soon as the seedlings show their second leaves, pot them up individually. Harden off the young plants ready for planting out in late spring, where they will flower from midsummer to the first frost. Position at least 30cm (12in) apart in full sun or partial shade, and enrich poor soil with a top-dressing of well-rotted manure.

Although *A. tricolor* will adapt to most soils, leaf coloration is even more pronounced when the plant is grown in poor soil, albeit at the expense of smaller plants. The drooping purple flowers are of little value and are best removed.

COTTAGE GARDEN VARIETIES

• *Amaranthus caudatus* var. *atropurpureus*
A variety with slightly deeper and richer purple flow-

ers than the species. Height 90–120cm (36–48in).

• *Amaranthus caudatus* var. *viridis*

This is the green form of love-lies-bleeding, much in demand by flower arrangers, with vibrant lime-green flower tassels. Height 90cm (36in).

• *Amaranthus tricolor* 'Splendens Perfecta'

This plants presents an explosion of coloured foliage – a simultaneous blend of rich red, yellow and green leaves. Height 60cm (24in).

Ammobium alatum

The charming half-hardy annual *Ammobium alatum* is classed as an everlasting flower since the blooms can be cut and dried for winter decoration. *Ammobium* is from the Greek meaning to grow in sand; the common name, winged everlastings, refers to the stems, which are stiff, branched, and have raised ridges or wings.

The leaves are pale green with white woolly hairs and the silvery-white flowers with yellow centres are borne continuously from early summer through until the autumn.

Much prized by flower arrangers for dried arrangements, the flowers should be cut when they are past bud stage but not fully open, then hung upside down in a dry room. Plants of winged everlastings will often self sow.

CULTIVATION

Sow seeds outdoors 5mm (¼in) deep as soon as the soil has warmed up. Plant in full sun, and thin the seedlings 25–38cm (10–15in) apart. For early flowering start indoors six weeks before the last frost and transplant outdoors after all danger of frost has passed.

COTTAGE GARDEN VARIETIES

• *Ammobium alatum* 'Bikini'

A new variety with sturdy-stemmed sprays of many yellow-centred, silver-white flowers each 2cm (¾in) across. It thrives in full sun or partial shade and is excellent for bedding, cutting or drying. Height 30–40cm (12–16in).

• *Ammobium alatum* 'Grandiflorum'

This cultivar has white flowers with yellow centres. Up to 5cm (2in) wide, they are much larger than the common species. Height 60–90cm (24–36in).

AMARANTHUS CAUDATUS (top) and AMMOBIUM ALATUM 'BIKINI'

Antirrhinum majus

Antirrhinum majus is usually grown as an annual or biennial, but would probably be disqualified for being in the wrong class if entered as such at a flower show as, strictly speaking, it is perennial. It has showy, tubular flowers, each up to 4cm (1½in) long, and with a light, spicy fragrance. They are borne in spikes that bloom from bottom to top; during the course of the season a single plant may well produce seven or eight flower spikes. The foliage is medium green, lance-shaped and somewhat sticky.

'Snapdragon', 'dog's-mouth', 'toad's-mouth', 'lion's-snap' and bunny rabbits are all traditional rustic names for the old-fashioned antirrhinums, and it is little wonder that they are a favourite with children, who delight in pressing the sides of the flowers to make the mouth gape and the stigma appear as a tongue, then watching the snapping together of the lips as the pressure is released. Patient bumble bees (honey bees are not heavy enough) have also perfected the trick of pressing open the lips to gain admittance, revelling within as the flowerhead snaps tightly around them once entry has been gained.

Native to south-western Europe and Sicily, antirrhinums have long been grown in gardens, naturalizing themselves on old walls and in sunny corners of cottage plots. Gerard and Parkinson both grew white, purple and yellow varieties, although Gerard noted that 'The yellowe kinde groweth not common, except in the gardens of curious Herbarists'. Parkinson actually included the anthirrhinum in the chapter of his book devoted to plants that were regarded at the time as English flowers, not apparently to be confused with 'outlandish' foreign novelties such as the tulip and auricula! In his *Eden, or a Compleat Body of Gardening* of 1757, John Hill wrote: 'We treat here of a Plant which, though not a Native of our Country, bears the free Air perfectly well in it, and sows itself freely like a wild Weed', and went on to say that 'The Gardener will smile to hear us speak of instructing him in the culture of a Plant, that will live on an old Wall, and propagate itself from year to year without his Care'.

Considering the virtues that many less decorative herbs were supposed to possess, and the fact that the plant had been grown throughout Europe since the sixteenth century, it is surprising to find that the old herbal-

DOUBLE-FLOWERED ANTHIRRINUM *(above) and (inset)* A. BRIGHTON ROCK MIXED

ists were unable to attribute any valuable medicinal properties to the antirrhinum. Gerard did, however, quote Dioscorides as saying 'that the herbe being hanged about one preserveth a man from being bewitched,' and William Turner, also quoting from the classics, added 'that some men have supposed that the use of thys herbe should helpe men to obtayne prayse and worship. But all these are but dreames of sorcerers'.

During the eighteenth century antirrhinums were considered slightly vulgar, and an historian of that time suggested that they should therefore not occupy a place in the parterre among choice flowers, but should be mixed with the shrubs in the background. The Victorians had no such hang-ups about the plants, and in fact they were taken up enthusiastically by the florists in the middle of the nineteenth century. Antirrhinums with rose-pink stripes on a white ground like carnations, and named, sterile, double-flowered varieties which were propagated by cuttings, were all popular prizewinners at Victorian flower shows. By the late 1880s flowers were available with orange stripes,

 rose-pink speckles on white, crimson mottling on yellow and even in cream with a violet belt behind the snout. Plants were grown to enormous heights and reports of specimens reaching 2.2m (7ft) high and 1.5m (5ft) across were not uncommon. These enormous, showy bushes were in sharp contrast to the dwarf strains used then and now as bedding plants, and must have been a quite remarkable sight when in full flower.

A combination of neglect and a fungus disease that causes rust has deprived today's cottage gardeners of these wonderful plants, although it is still possible to obtain seed strains that are not too dissimilar and which are a far cry from the short-growing bedding varieties used so uniformly in bedding displays. There is, in fact, considerable variation in height within the three height ranges offered by seed merchants.

Vigorous, tall varieties, which grow to 90cm (36in), will probably need staking, but are very useful for filling gaps in the mixed border. Intermediate varieties, reaching about 45cm (18in) in height, are the most popular, as they produce stems long enough for cutting but not tall enough to require staking. Finally, the cushion-like dwarf strains, which grow to 20cm (8in), make

compact little bushes and are frequently grown in pots or as edging plants, and in the rock garden. There are also forms with double flowers and some have ruffled blooms, and an increasing number of rust-resistant varieties are becoming available.

CULTIVATION

Modern antirrhinums are more tender than the old-timers, and it is advisable to start seeds under glass six to eight weeks before planting out. Plant out leaving enough space between plants for good air circulation. The plants will, however, tolerate slight frost and can be put out in the garden early. Good results can also be obtained from a sowing made in late summer in a cold frame, the plants being overwintered there and then planted out in late spring.

Good drainage is important for antirrhinums as they will not thrive in waterlogged conditions, and a position in full sun or light shade is preferable. Deadhead as the flowers fade to encourage continued bloom.

COTTAGE GARDEN VARIETIES
• *Antirrhinum majus* 'Appleblossom'
This variety has tall spikes of lovely, delicate white blooms with soft pink markings on the throat. Height 90cm (36in).
• *Antirrhinum majus* Brighton Rock Mixed
Grown and reselected from varieties last seen at the end of the nineteenth century, this has blotched and striped bright bicolour flowers. Height 45cm (18in).
• *Antirrhinum majus* 'Miniature Magic Carpet'
This delightful miniature 'snap' has a trailing habit and bears flowers in lots of different colours. It is ideal for a rock garden or small beds. Height 15cm (6in).
• *Antirrhinum majus* 'Night & Day'
The dark green foliage of this very striking and beautiful variety provides a backcloth to the spikes of dark, velvety crimson flowers with a sharply contrasting silvery white throat. Height 45cm (18in).
• *Antirrhinum majus* Sawyers Old-Fashioned Snapdragons Mixed
This is a very hardy, colourful mixture, developed from original plants found growing on old walls on a farm in Suffolk. Height 30cm (12in).
• *Antirrhinum majus* 'White Wonder'
A beautiful old cottage garden favourite, this variety has yellow-throated, pure white flowers. Height 45cm (18in).

Argyranthemum

Classified until fairly recently under *Chrysanthemum*, argyranthemums are tender perennials, not hardy enough to winter outside in frost-prone climates, although they are easy to propagate from cuttings and grow as annuals. Their chrysanthemum-like single or double flowers in rose, pink, yellow, apricot, or white, provide a long season of display from late spring until late autumn. Even when out of flower, the fine foliage provides an excellent foil for other plants.

Few plants have inspired such an explosion of interest during the last few years as these. The once-humble 'marguerite' is now scaling the horticultural social ladder and is available in a kaleidoscope of colours, with both single or double flowers, and considerable foliage variations. Gardeners could be forgiven for thinking that this plant of the 1990s is a newcomer to the gardening scene, especially with its spanking new name, but in his *Encyclopedia of Plants* of 1840, the writer and landscape painter, J.C. Loudon (1783–1843) mentioned one species that he said was introduced to cultivation in 1777, which more than qualifies the plant as an antique.

Argyranthemums were popular plants at the turn of the century but almost disappeared during the period of the two World Wars, as wartime restrictions on glasshouse heating fuel and the drastic reductions in manpower took their toll. However, in recent years the remoter parts of Madeira and the Canary Islands have become a particular magnet for discerning plantsmen, and these are the sources of most of the recent new introductions which are there today and here tomorrow.

The pink-flowered *A.* 'Las Freiras', discovered by Roy Cheek who formed the National Collection of Argyranthemums at Cannington College, Somerset, is a typical example of such recent introductions. Found growing by a cottage on the outskirts of a village in Curral das Freiras ('valley of the nuns') in Madeira in 1991, the plant – probably a hybrid between two native species, *A. haemontomma* and *A. dissectum* – has a long flowering period, strongly branched stems and deeply incised leaves. Because of the high altitude of its collection site, 'Las Freiras' may well be hardier than other pink cultivars to date.

Argyranthemums have spread throughout the world and are now grown as far afield as the Far East, New Zealand, Australia and Canada. However, it appears that the same or similar plants frequently masquerade under different names in several countries, which makes positive identification difficult. The popular double-flowered, anemone-centred pink *A.* 'Vancouver', introduced from the Botanic Gardens of British Columbia in Vancouver in 1993 by Brian Halliwell, then Assistant Curator at Kew, acquired its name as a result of a misleading label. Apparently, in the course of handling the plant the word 'from' was lost from the label, which originally read 'from Vancouver'. 'Vancouver' stuck, and it now appears in catalogues under this name.

A. frutescens is the shrubby, rather tender 'Paris daisy', introduced to Europe from the Canary Islands in the late sixteenth century and widely grown in Holland and France for the flower markets. The long stems made it ideal for cutting and bunches were sold in quantity in Paris, hence the popular common name. Another was 'French marguerite', commemorating Marguerite de Valois (whose marriage in 1572 to Henri of Navarre was the signal for the Massacre of St Bartholomew), who apparently grew these plants in her garden at Issy, near Paris. The plant was introduced to England in 1699, and because it was not hardy it was grown in pots and tubs which were stood outside on terraces and in parterres for the summer. Throughout the eighteenth and nineteenth centuries the marguerite was also very popular in towns and cities, not only as a pot plant but also for window boxes.

A. frutescens has the longest flowering season of all the species, and the much-branched flower stems ensure several flowers on each at any one time. Today, the plant is still used extensively as summer bedding, in groups in the border, and is as popular as ever for growing in urns, troughs or tubs. Restaurants and cafés wishing to 'go continental' use well-trained and groomed plants to grace the entrances to their establishments, ensuring a continuous flowering of white daisies month in, month out.

Argyranthemums can be enjoyed from late spring until late autumn. As they are so easy to propagate from cuttings, it seems hardly worth the effort of trying to get them through a winter outside (by applying a deep mulch of straw or leaves around the base of the plants before the onset of the first frosts), as there is a less than even chance of their surviving, and intense cold will certainly finish them off. Use plants as summer bedding, or grow them in pots and containers which can be brought inside during the winter.

CULTIVATION

Argyranthemums are ideally suited to growing as annuals. Nodal cuttings, taken from non-flowering shoots in late summer or early autumn, and overwintered in a frost-free greenhouse or on a sunny windowsill indoors, can be planted out in late spring after all danger of frost has passed and enjoyed throughout the summer and into autumn. Choose a sunny position and well-drained soil and plant 30cm (12in) apart.

Standard plants are easy to train. Pot up rooted cuttings individually in spring and provide each with a thin cane. Tie the main stem to the cane and pinch out all the sideshoots. As the pot fills with roots, transfer the plant to a larger one and replace the thin cane with one which is taller and stronger. Remove all flower buds and continue to pinch out any sideshoots which may develop. It is probably best to keep the plant in a greenhouse until a stem of at least 90cm (36in) has been produced, a height at which sideshoots can be allowed to develop. This process will take between 18 months and two years.

COTTAGE GARDEN VARIETIES

• *Argyranthemum* 'Double Yellow', syn. *A.* 'Hopley's Double Yellow'
The anemone centre of this cultivar is primrose-yellow and the rays cream to white. The plant is inclined to sprawl. Height 40–70cm (16–28in).

• *Argyranthemum frutescens* subsp. *canariae*
The gaps between the petals on this exceptionally floriferous plant create a very elegant-looking single, white daisy flower. Height 20–40cm (8–16in).

• *Argyranthemum* 'Jamaica Primrose'
This vigorous, bushy plant produces a good succession of single, primrose-yellow flowers and will grow almost as wide as it is tall. Height 90cm (36in) or more.

• *Argyranthemum* 'Mary Wootton'
This lovely pale pink, anemone-centred cultivar was named after Miss New Zealand 1948. The plant does tend to become leggy and will need support in exposed places. Height 90cm (36in).

• *Argyranthemum* 'Pink Australian'
With a deeper centre and domed outline, the light pink flowerheads of this cultivar make an attractive contrast to other forms. It also has fairly broad, greyish green leaves. Height 20–40cm (8–16in).

• *Argyranthemum* 'Pink Pom'
This cultivar from New Zealand is very similar to *A.* 'Vancouver' with anemone-centred, rose-pink florets. Height 90cm (36in).

• *Argyranthemum* 'Snowstorm', syn. *A.* 'Jamaica Snowstorm'
This cultivar has glaucous grey-green foliage and forms an open cushion of foliage, on which the single white daisies are liberally borne in continuous succession. Height 20–40cm (8–16in).

THIS SINGLE WHITE ARGYRANTHEMUM IS MARVELLOUS IN A SUMMER BORDER

Atriplex hortensis

Known as mountain spinach or garden orach, *Atriplex hortensis* is a hardy or half-hardy annual, grown for its ornamental leaves, which can be used in salads as well as for foliage displays in the garden. Although nothing to write home about (the flowers are insignificant), this plant does make an attractive foliage dot specimen, particularly the crimson-red-leaved forms, which glow with a stained-glass window effect as the late afternoon sun shines through the leaves.

Since the plants can grow to 2m (6ft) high, they are also excellent as quick hedges for a cottage garden border. *A. hortensis* is tough, and winds and rain do not seem to spoil the leaves. Once it has been grown in the garden it will reappear every year.

CULTIVATION

Atriplex are best sown outdoors in early spring where the plants are to mature. They thrive in good, well-drained soil, in full sun and should be thinned to 30cm (12in) apart.

COTTAGE GARDEN VARIETIES

• *Atriplex hortensis* var. *purpurea*
A variety with dark purple leaves. Height 1–2m (3–6ft).

ATRIPLEX HORTENSIS VAR. *PURPUREA*

• *Atriplex hortensis* 'Copper Plume'
Deep red flower spikes with ornamental matching foliage. Height 1–1.5m (3–5ft).
• *Atriplex hortensis* 'Green Plume'
Vivid green foliage and vivid green flowers. Height 1–1.5m (3–5ft).
• *Atriplex hortensis* 'Red Plume'
Beautiful wine-red flower spikes with ornamental matching foliage. Height 1–1.5m (3–5ft).

Begonia

The tuberous begonias, *Begonia × tuberhybrida*, are tender perennials, grown as annuals. They come in a wide variety of flower types, both upright and pendulous, and can be single, ruffled, fully-double or camellia-form. The colours can be single or accented with a contrasting edge, and in white, pink, rose, red, orange and yellow.

Very adaptable, performing well in all kinds of weather, they have a long flowering period and are suitable for many uses. They are particularly valued as showy plants for semi-shady locations, and are also prized as pot plants; the pendulous varieties are ideal for containers and hanging baskets.

Begonia semperflorens, or wax begonias, also sometimes called fibrous begonias because of the texture of their roots, have neat mounds of waxy, bronzy red or green semi-succulent, broad foliage, with the small, single or double flowers that are white, pink, rose or red growing so close together they often cover the foliage. They are superb plants for window boxes, hanging baskets, beds and borders. The green-leaved varieties usually perform better in full sun than those with bronze leaves.

These begonias can be lifted in the autumn and potted up as houseplants, where they will bloom indefinitely on a sunny windowsill.

CULTIVATION

Propagation may be by seed, tubers, or cuttings – most of the large-flowered tuberous begonias are sold as named-variety tubers. When starting from seed, care should be taken when opening the packet as begonia seeds are very small indeed. Ensure that the planting medium is moist and ready when you open the seed packet. Sow seeds on the top and cover them with clear

BEGONIA × TUBERHYBRIDA

plastic or a glass pane to keep from drying out until the plants appear. They need light and heat to germinate: growing lights and bottom heat of 21°C (70°F). Seedlings have extremely fine root systems and quickly deplete the nutrients in the seed compost, so give a weak solution of liquid fertilizer weekly in the early days, before transplanting, to prevent them from starving. Plant out into rich, well-drained soil high in organic matter, preferably in a site with midday and afternoon shade, otherwise the foliage may well scorch on hot days.

Smaller-flowered tuberous begonias can usually support their own growth; however, the large-flowered varieties easily become top heavy and will almost certainly need staking. Powdery mildew can be a problem, especially if they are grown where there is not enough air movement around leaves and stems. At the first signs of a white powder on the leaves, spray with a fungicide.

Growing wax begonias from seed is a challenge, even for experts. In order to have reasonable-sized plants for the garden, seed should be started in midwinter. They germinate in 2–3 weeks at 21–27°C (70–81°F) and should be kept above 10°C (50°F) at night. Seeds are very small, dusty and difficult to handle: many gardeners mix them with fine sand to enable them to sow evenly on the surface of the planting medium. On no account must seedlings be planted out until it is certain that the nights will not go below 10°C (50°F). Soil should be rich and well-drained, with shade from the afternoon sun, but avoid deep shade, which will make the plants grow leggy and set fewer flowers.

COTTAGE GARDEN VARIETIES

BEGONIA × TUBERHYBRIDA

• *Begonia* 'Illumination'

A gorgeous new F1 hybrid begonia for hanging baskets and window boxes, with cascades of lovely, large double blossoms in shades of pink. Height 22cm (9in).

• *Begonia* 'Illumination Orange'

This F1 hybrid colour selection produces a blazing cascade of flaming orange all summer. Height 22cm (9in).

• *Begonia* 'Nonstop'

An F1 hybrid early flowering variety producing 7cm (3in) fully double blooms in a wide range of eye-catching colours including apricot, bright red, yellow and pink nestling against glossy green foliage. These vigorous plants are excellent for summer bedding, pots and containers. Height 22cm (9in).

• *Begonia* 'Pin-Up'

A wonderful, new award-winning variety with an abundance of single, showy flowers, 13cm (5in) across, of a pure white with a bold picotee rim. Invaluable for containers. Height 20–30cm (8–12in).

BEGONIA SEMPERFLORENS MIXED CULTIVARS

BEGONIA SEMPERFLORENS

• *Begonia semperflorens* 'Cocktail'

A sun-resistant, dwarf, dark bronze-leaved variety with flowers in a formula mixture of many colours. Height 13cm (5in).

• *Begonia semperflorens* 'Whisky'

A lovely variety with shining, dark bronze foliage contrasting nicely with the abundance of pure white flowers produced for many months. Height 20cm (8in).

• *Begonia semperflorens* White with Rose Edge

A Japanese green-leaved strain with a dwarf mounded habit and rapid growth. It has white flowers with a pretty picotee rose-coloured edge. Height 35cm (14in).

Bellis perennis

Though technically perennial, *Bellis perennis* is more often than not grown as a hardy biennial or an annual. The present garden forms with double flowers are derived from the common daisy beloved by poets from the time when the Anglo-Saxons spelt it *daeges eage* or 'day's eye' because the flowers open with the dawn.

In cottage gardens the large fully-double strains are often seen edging low borders and pathways. They are easily grown from seed and are excellent plants for spring bedding, either by themselves or as groundcover for bulbs and other taller-growing plants. The leaves are strap-shaped, widening towards the end, and form a basal tuft above which the double daisy-like flowers are freely borne in colours from white to shades of pink and red. The petals may be flat or quilled.

The curious *B. prolifera*, better known to cottage gardeners by the name of hen-and-chicken daisy, and the real old timers such as 'Dresden China', 'Rob Roy' and 'The Pearl' are grown as perennials and propagated by division in spring or autumn.

CULTIVATION

Sow seed thinly in a cold frame or nursery bed in early spring. Prick out in the open and plant 15cm (6in) apart, in their flowering positions in autumn. All double daisies are completely hardy, but resent dry conditions in summer. They require a good fertile, well-drained garden soil, and can be exposed to the sun or be in partial shade.

MIXED DOUBLE DAISIES

COTTAGE GARDEN VARIETIES

• *Bellis perennis* 'Bright Carpet'

A delightful, compact variety bearing myriad medium-sized, very double blooms, in shades of pink, red and white. Height 10–15cm (4–6in).

• *Bellis perennis* 'Goliath'

The enormous double blooms of red, pink and white are surrounded by a rosette of bright green leaves. Height 15cm (6in).

• *Bellis perennis* 'Pomponette'

Small, button-like double flowers with quilled petals in delicate shades of red, pink and white. Height 15cm (6in).

• *Bellis perennis* Spring Star Mixed

A superior strain with large, fully double blooms of pompom flower type. This bears considerably more flowers than many existing varieties and the blooms in shades of red and rose, together with white, are held above tight rosettes or foliage. Height 15cm (6in).

Borago officinalis

Borage is one of the oldest and most decorative of the annual herbs. Equally at home in the herb garden or cottage border, although perhaps self seeding too freely for the owners of more sophisticated gardens, the flowers open from pink buds to an intense sky-blue, with five pointed petals arranged like a star. Both the attractive greenish grey leaves and the stems are covered with bristly, purplish grey hairs that glisten in the sun.

Even in Roman times, borage had the reputation of being a cheerful, encouraging plant; it was mentioned in herbals as early as 1265 and was cultivated for its cordial properties, being added to drinks to 'make a man merry and joyful'. Centuries later, Gerard wrote that 'the leaves and floures of Borrage put into wine make men and women glad and merry, driving away all sadnesse, dulnesse and melancholie' – whether the wine had rather more to do with this merriment than the borage is debatable.

Many seventeenth-century books extolled the virtues of 'Burrage and Bugloss'. The juice was extracted from the leaves and made into a syrup with sugar or honey to expel melancholy and sadness, clarify the blood and comfort the heart. It was an antidote to poisonous bites and stings, was said to cure yellow jaundice, and was used to bathe tired and sore eyes.

A decoction of borage and yellow fumitory (*Corydalis lutea*) was prescribed to cleanse the blood and treat ringworm, while a refreshing tonic tea made from borage leaves was given to young ladies and the lovelorn to cure swooning and unrequited love.

In the kitchen, borage was used as a pot herb. Chopped leaves were added to thick broth (pottage) before serving; seedling leaves were also used in salads and were in great demand before the introduction of lettuce. The peeled stems of borage have a cucumber-like flavour and these too were used in salads, with the flowers added for decoration. Flowers were also pickled in wine vinegar and have long been candied in the same way as violets.

Although no longer regarded as a herb for the kitchen, borage has continued to be used in beverages to this day. The flowers and leaves have long been found to bring a cooling taste to drinks – hence its nickname of 'cool-tankard' – due to the presence of potassium nitrate, which is often found in the blue flowers

BORAGO OFFICINALIS

situ at two-week intervals in spring and early summer will provide young leaves and flowers throughout the summer months. A sowing made in midsummer in a sheltered spot will provide seedlings that will pass the winter in rosette form, making especially fine flowering plants by early spring of the following year.

Seed is set freely in most summers and should be collected for future use, although once established borage will self seed with abandon.

Brachycome iberidifolia

Brachycome iberidifolia is a hardy Australian annual known as the Swan River daisy. The flowers have fragrant white, rose, pink or lilac petals, surrounding golden centres, and bloom for six weeks or more in summer and early autumn if deadheaded regularly; the foliage is dark green, fine and lacy.

With their gentle, soft hues, the flowers combine well with warmer-coloured annuals like zinnias and marigolds, and are excellent for massing in mixed beds and borders. The plants' bushy, mounded habit, make

of the family Boraginaceae. Borage itself frequently appears as a constituent of the crown of fruits and herbs which invariably garnishes a glass of Pimms or a gin sling, while the flowers can be frozen in ice cubes to give added interest and flavour to a long, cool summer drink and are often floated on a claret cup.

Borage is an excellent bee plant, producing large quantities of nectar secreted at the base of the ovary. As well as the classic blue-flowered species, there is an uncommon form with white flowers, and a rare pink form for connoisseurs. The Rev William Hanbury, writing in 1771, mentioned a borage with variegated leaves, but this would appear to have been lost to cultivation – or is perhaps just waiting to be rediscovered.

CULTIVATION

Borage is something of a sprawler and grows 45–75cm (18–30in) tall. Like most herbs, it prefers a dry, well-drained, sunny position, but will also grow and flower in partial shade.

The plant has a relatively short flowering season of about three weeks, but a succession of sowings *in*

BRACHYCOME IBERIDIFOLIA

them suitable for growing in hanging baskets, containers and window boxes. Flowers may be cut for indoor arrangements.

CULTIVATION

Swan River daisies can be sown directly in the garden. Cover the seed lightly, and thin the plants 12–15cm (5–6in) apart. Pinch the tips out to induce bushiness. They like a position in full sun in average, moist garden soil. As the plants are fragile, place short, brushy twigs among them to keep them from being beaten down by the weather.

COTTAGE GARDEN VARIETIES

• *Brachycome iberidifolia* 'Blue Star'
A neat, compact new form, ideal for bedding, edging, and containers. The blue flowers have elegantly quilled petals. Height 22–30cm (9–12in).

• *Brachycome iberidifolia* 'Brachy Blue'
An improved award-winning variety, bred, among other things, to stand upright, unlike some Swan River daisies which have a tendency towards drunken, floppy behaviour. 'Brachy Blue' produces neat, compact

plants covered with a profusion of blue flowers over a long period of time. Height 22cm (9in).

• *Brachycome iberidifolia* 'Splendour'
This is a profuse and long-flowering annual, each plant producing well over 100 blue to purple ('Purple Splendour') or white ('White Splendour') ebony-eyed flowers. Height 22–30cm (9–12in).

Brassica oleracea

Some recent newcomers among the ornamental cabbages and kales produce striking effects when grown as hardy annuals for late-summer and autumn display. The centres (in the kales heavily fringed), in various shades of rose, pink or creamy white, are surrounded by an outer green layer, giving the appearance of enormous old-fashioned roses. These fancy-leaved cousins of our familiar vegetables develop their most beautiful colours with the onset of cold weather in autumn, at just the time when everything else in the cottage garden is fading into oblivion. Although edible, the leaves are bitter, and when cooked, they turn an unappetizing grey.

BRASSICA OLERACEA

CULTIVATION

Start seed in early summer 6–8 weeks before transplanting outdoors. They germinate in about ten days at 18°C (64°F). Ornamental cabbage seeds need light to aid germination. Conversely, cover kale seeds with 5mm (¼in) of soil. Transplant into the garden (38–45cm/15–18in apart) or display containers in late summer. When planted out in spring, ornamental cabbage and kale form looser heads and tend to bolt quickly as the weather warms.

COTTAGE GARDEN VARIETIES
• *Brassica oleracea* Dynasty Series
Ornamental cabbage in pink, red or white with semi-waved leaves. Grows up to 38cm (15in) across. Height 30cm (12in).
• *Brassica oleracea* Nagoya Mixed
Ornamental kale F1 hybrid with numerous heavily fringed red or white leaves neatly surrounded by an outer green layer. Height up to 45cm (18in).

Browallia speciosa

Although this frost-tender genus is native to tropical America, it commemorates a Swedish bishop and botanist, John Browall. Two species are generally offered in seed catalogues and *Browallia speciosa* is the most commonly grown: as an annual or greenhouse perennial. It is a sprawling, vigorous plant with brilliant blue, violet, or white flowers up to 5cm (2in) across, related to, and resembling, small petunias. Blue-flowering types have a contrasting white eye or throat. The leaves are lance-shaped and bright green.

Browallias are perfect for bedding and excellent for containers and hanging baskets as their mound-shaped habit ensures that they cascade over the sides. They may also be grown in pots as houseplants.

Because the flowers take longer than most annuals to develop, their season is short, often delaying their appearance until late summer or early autumn particularly in poor summers.

CULTIVATION

Start seeds indoors 6–8 weeks before planting out. Do not cover as they need light to germinate. Browallias can withstand light frosts, so move the plants into the garden two weeks before the last expected spring frost. Space 22–30cm (9–12in) apart. They grow well in shady locations. Never overfeed or overwater (or you will have all leaves and no flowers), and keep the soil cool and moist with a summer mulch.

COTTAGE GARDEN VARIETIES

• *Browallia speciosa* 'White Troll'
A particularly fine dwarf, compact variety with masses of pure white flowers. Height 20–25cm (8–10in).
• *Browallia speciosa* 'Blue Bells'
A variety with violet-blue flowers that turn lavender-blue. Requires no pinching to stay bushy. Height 30–38cm (12–15in).
• *Browallia speciosa* 'Jingle Bells'
Comes in shades of blue, white and lavender. Height 30–38cm (12–15in).

Calendula officinalis

Calendula officinalis is the marigold most commonly seen growing in old cottage gardens. A sow-and-forget hardy annual, once introduced to the garden it will self seed with the persistence of a weed, although in this case the seedlings are rather more welcome for the cheerful colour they lend to the cottage garden scene.

The botanical name hails from the Latin *Calendae*, meaning the first day of the month, which alludes to the plant's almost continuous flowering through the season.

CALENDULA OFFICINALIS 'FIESTA GITANA'

Gerard noted that 'the Marigold is called Calendula: it is to be seene in floure in the Calends almost of every moneth: it is also called Chrysanthemum, of his golden colour'. In Chaucer's time, the plant was known as 'gold-flower', 'sunnes bride' and 'sunnes hearbe', while in Shakespeare's play *Cymbeline* it was the 'winking Mary-bud'. Greatly valued at one time as a pot-herb – hence the popular name of 'pot marigold' – the flowers were, and still are, used in the kitchen for flavouring soups and stews.

Pot marigold was once thought to possess wondrous medical virtues and was grown in every medieval garden, where plants bloomed from spring to snow fall. It was used by herbalists as a remedy for sore teeth and as a comforter of the heart and spirits. Calendula tincture and cream are excellent soothing ointments, and are still used today for treating cuts and grazes.

Growing 30–60cm (12–24in) high and forming a bushy plant bearing single, orange-coloured, daisy-like flowers freely throughout the summer, *Calendula officinalis* is considered a rather coarse and unattractive plant by some gardeners, who prefer instead to sow the many improved varieties available in softer colours ranging from white through cream, lemon and apricot, to yellow. The true pot marigold will, however, always find a home in the cottage garden, brightening up a dull corner here and there, and filling odd gaps in the border – a truly cheerful plant from the past.

C. o. 'Prolifera', the 'hen-and-chickens marigold', is a most unusual form in which the normal marigold flower is surrounded by secondary flowers, arranged sun-and-planet style with their stalks springing from just beneath the petals of the parent bloom. Grown in gardens since the sixteenth century, this is a marigold

POT MARIGOLDS with ARGYRANTHEMUM

which no gardener would be sniffy about and, coming true from seed, it is a most attractive flower in its own right.

CULTIVATION

All calendulas thrive best in a well-drained, fertile soil in full sun. Sow *in situ* outside in both spring and autumn and thin severely to 30cm (12in) or more apart. The two sowings will provide a long flowering season, and early thinning will result in sturdy, bushy plants and flowers in abundance. Removing faded flowers and seedheads will ensure that the plants flower continuously until the first frosts.

Calendulas tend to be prey to blackfly in late summer; affected plants should be pulled up and destroyed.

COTTAGE GARDEN VARIETIES

• *Calendula officinalis* 'Art Shades'

A very popular strain in uncommon shades of apricot, flame, pale orange, primrose and cream. The flowers are large, graceful and well frilled. Height 60cm (24in).

• *Calendula officinalis* Fiesta Gitana

A lovely, compact, dwarf marigold producing double flowers in a richly coloured mixture. Height 30cm (12in).

• *Calendula officinalis* 'Golden Princess'

An eyecatching variety with double, quill-petalled, bright golden flowers with a prominent black centres. Height 30–60cm (12–24in).

• *Calendula officinalis* 'Radio'

A deep orange variety with beautifully quilled petals. The blooms are globular in shape, and do not show the centre until a very advanced stage. This old, tried, tested and ever-popular variety has been sown in gardens since the early 1930s. Height 45–50cm (18–20in).

Callistephus chinensis

Callistephus chinensis is the botanical name of the China or annual asters and means 'beautiful crown', an apt description of these lovely single to fluffy double daisy-like flowers, among the most popular and colourful of the old-fashioned annuals. As the colloquial name implies, the plants are native to China and when seeds were first sent to the royal garden of Paris in 1728 – reputedly by the French Jesuit missionary Father d'Incarville, who introduced many Chinese plants to Europe (the incarvillea is named in his honour) – the single China asters with flowers of red or white, which the French called *La Reine Marguerite*, caused something of a sensation. On a visit to France in 1770, Sir Horace Walpole was clearly impressed by the popularity of the plant, and noted that 'in the garden of Marshall de Biron at Paris, consisting of fourteen acres, every walk is buttoned on each side by lines of flowerpots, which succeed in their seasons. When I saw it, there were nine thousand pots of Asters, or La Reine Marguerite'.

Seed of the red and white single varieties was sent from Paris to the Chelsea Physic Garden in London in 1731, and was followed by the single purple and the doubles a few years later. Mr James Justice, an enterprising Scots gardener, raised plants from imported seed in the autumn and overwintered the plants in a cold frame,

proudly announcing that 'I had from these Plants as fine ripe seed, in September, as any which came from abroad, from which, in anno 1749, I raised many extraordinarily beautiful seminal varieties of Pink, deep Carnation, blue, white and purple Colours; and one in particular, with a striped blue and white flower'. Also known as 'fair ladies' stars', the China asters were grown in American gardens from 1740 onwards.

The plants became enormously popular during the mid-nineteenth century, with seedsmen falling over themselves to offer new and striking variations each year. One catalogue of 1867 listed a 'hedgehog' type, describing it as very curious, with long, quilled petals that were sharply pointed. The new flat-petalled Comet strain was described by *The Gardener's Chronicle* in December 1887 as resembling 'very closely that of a large-flowered Japanese Chrysanthemum. The petals are long and somewhat twisted or wavy or curled'.

In Germany, where the quilled varieties were first produced, China asters were known as 'death-flowers'. It is strange to think of this cheerful flower being associated with death, but the story is told that Elizabeth, Empress of Austria, on finding her room in a Swiss hotel decorated with China asters, complained to her attendant that the flowers gave her a feeling of foreboding. Her premonition proved correct, and the following day she was found murdered by an Italian anarchist. Incidentally, Francis Ferdinand, whose assassination sparked off the First World War, was her great-nephew.

After years of hybridization and selection, China asters are now available in many outstanding flower forms: peony-flowered, with incurved flowers; ostrich plumes, with feathery petals; Comet, with double flowers with loosely arranged rays or petals; anemone-flowered, with flat florets around a quilled centre; chrysanthemum-flowered, with large, fully double flowers; pompon, with small, fully double flowers; Lilliput, a dwarf group; and Giant and Mammoth strains. The single-flowered varieties, with a prominent daisy-like centre, are also still much in demand. The tall forms are useful for cutting and very popular with flower arrangers, while the dwarf, rather squat varieties can be used as edging or container plants and may also be grown indoors, where they will bloom quite happily on a sunny windowsill.

China asters come in a wide range of colours

including white, creamy yellow, pink, red, blue and lavender or purple, often with a yellow centre. They bloom for about a month but, unlike with most other annuals, deadheading will not induce further flowering. To extend the flowering season and to achieve continuous blooming, sow seed at two-week intervals in the spring, or plant early, mid-season and late varieties.

A massed planting in the border will provide a spectacular sight and armfuls of cut flowers, but do resist sticking in odd plants here and there, as they will look stiff, awkward and distinctly out of place.

CULTIVATION

China asters are half-hardy annuals and all types share similar cultural requirements. They are usually raised from seed sown in early spring in gentle heat, pricked out into boxes of compost and finally planted out 20–24cm (8–10in) apart, in late spring or early summer. Grow them in full sun, and enrich the soil with well-rotted manure, compost or leaf mould before planting.

The plants are shallow rooted and will benefit from a mulch to help retain moisture in the soil. Once the flower buds begin to swell, feeding with a weak solution of natural manure will also prove beneficial.

Asters are not the easiest of annuals to grow, since they resent transplanting and are susceptible to fusarium wilt, which causes both young and old plants to turn yellow and wilt. Avoid the disease by sowing wilt-resistant seed, and when planting out be careful not to bury the crowns too deeply. It is also inadvisable to plant China asters in the same bed year after year, or to grow them in heavy clay soil which tends to become waterlogged.

COTTAGE GARDEN VARIETIES

• *Callistephus chinensis* Colour Carpet Mixed
With a spread of 30cm (12in), this dwarf mixture is ideal in beds and borders and also as edging. The double tightly knit blooms on neat mound-shaped plants come in a range of bright colours such as scarlet, red, pink,

MIXED CHINA ASTERS with AMARANTHUS

purple, white and lavender. Height 15–23cm (6–9in).

• *Callistephus chinensis* Duchess Series

The flowers of these asters are large and fully double, resembling incurving chrysanthemums in amethyst, ruby-red, deep purple, deep pink, pale rose and creamy white. The plants are vigorous, erect and branch from the base, providing excellent cut flowers as well as a grand display in the garden. Height 60cm (24in).

• *Callistephus chinensis* Giant Princess Aster Special Mixed

An excellent mixture of mid-season asters with huge, long-stemmed flowers in a brilliant array of bright colours from scarlet-reds to purples and blues and golden yellow. Height 60cm (24in).

• *Callistephus chinensis* Ostrich Plume Series

The name just about says it all! These asters, with early flowers in a range of colours including white, carmine, purple and greyish blues, are ideal for bedding and cutting. Height 60cm (24in).

• *Callistephus chinensis* Pompon Series

Eyecatching and different, plants of this series have almost spherical flowers and a mass of petals, the outer half being scarlet and the inner pure white. Height 50cm (20in).

• *Callistephus chinensis* Quadrille Formula Mixed

A mixture of giant ray asters bearing large flowers, up to 15cm (6in) across, with long, needle-shaped petals and strong stems for cutting. Flower colours include blue, purple, red and white. Height 60cm (24in).

Campanula medium

Canterbury bells is a hardy biennial but will flower the same year from seed sown under glass in late winter and planted out in early spring. This old-world charmer is fairly tall with roughly the top two-thirds covered with blue, lavender, pink, rose or white, bell-shaped flowers. Because of their height Canterbury bells make excellent accent or back of the border plants. The variety *Campanula medium* var. *calycanthema*, called the cup-and-saucer Canterbury bells, has double bells, one inside the other.

CULTIVATION

To grow as a biennial, sow seeds outdoors in midsummer. Thin and space out 30cm (12in) apart during the following spring in a deep, moist loam or humus-enriched soil. Shade the roots from hot sun with other plants or mulch.

COTTAGE GARDEN VARIETIES

• *Campanula medium*

It is available in the following colours, sold separately, blue, rose-pink, white. All are single flowers. Height 60–90cm (24–36in).

• *Campanula medium* var. *calycanthema* 'Ringing Bells'

This popular cup-and-saucer variety is a delightful free-flowering dwarf strain, ideal for bedding, with cup and saucers in lovely shades of blue, rose, white and lilac. Height 35cm (14in).

Cardiospermum halicacabum

Like *Rhodochiton atrosanguineum* one of the more exotic climbers, *Cardiospermum halicacabum*, the balloon vine, needs a warm aspect, well-drained but moisture-retentive soil and a long, sunny summer if it is to thrive outside, but is well worth a try for its unusual seed capsules.

Also known as love-in-a-puff, this tender climbing perennial, treated as a half-hardy annual, produces very small, insignificant, four-petalled white flowers; its main feature is the balloon-like, cream-coloured seed capsules, up to 4cm (1½in) across, that follow the flowers. When mature, these balloons float on the plant like dozens of different-sized light green bubbles, and are so strong that they must be squeezed to break them. As the seed capsules do not appear until the autumn, a sheltered spot is essential. In ideal conditions the plant will grow to 3m (10ft), but many gardeners will have to be satisfied with plants no taller than 90cm (36in). A plant for the more adventurous cottage gardener.

CULTIVATION

Sowing times can be critical, and they seem to do best when started indoors.

Seed should be sown in early spring under glass in a sterilized loam- or peat-based seed compost. By late spring the plants will be ready to plant out in average soil and full sun. Space plants 30–35cm (12–14in) apart to use as a screen. The plant is also suitable for growing in a conservatory or greenhouse.

Celosia argentea

The name *Celosia* comes from the Greek word *burned*, alluding to the brilliant red blossoms, and a fleeting glance at these unusual plants with elaborate crested flowerheads, resembling roosters' combs or undersea coral, reveals that they are aptly named. Two types of these half-hardy annuals are usually available, *Celosia argentea cristata*, with tight flower-heads, and *C. a. plumosa*, with feathery plumes; the former are often mistakenly offered as the latter.

The plants are best massed together or planted near other brightly coloured annuals such as marigolds or zinnias. Both do well growing in pots on a terrace or in any good rich garden soil, and they dry beautifully for winter decoration.

CULTIVATION

Start seed indoors four weeks before the last frost, using individual peat pots as the plants do not transplant well. Plant them out in early summer in a rich, well-drained soil in full sun allowing 30–45cm (12–18in) between plants.

COTTAGE GARDEN VARIETIES

• *Celosia argentea cristata* (Cockscomb)
This has velvety-textured, round, ridged flowers that resemble a brain or the comb of a rooster. In bright shades of crimson, rose, pink, yellow, cream, apricot, orange, gold and salmon. Height: dwarf 13–15cm (5–6in), tall 90cm (36in).
• *Celosia argentea cristata* 'Coral Garden'
A dwarf mixture with fantastically crested flowerheads in a range of almost unreal colours. Height: 30cm (12in).
• *Celosia argentea cristata* Jewel Box Mixed
Large comb-shaped blooms in a rich blend of blood-red, gold, yellow, pink and salmon shades. Ideal for bedding and containers. Height: 15cm (6in).
• *Celosia argentea plumosa* (Prince of Wales Feathers)
Produces long, feathery flower stalks, resembling ostrich plumes. In bright shades of crimson, rose, pink, yellow, cream, apricot, orange, gold and salmon. Height: dwarf 13–15cm (5–6in), tall 90cm (36in).
• *Celosia argentea plumosa* 'Century Mixed'
Very attractive tall feathery plumes in a mixture of vivid yellow, orange, red, crimson and purple. Height: 60–90cm (24–36in).

CAMPANULA MEDIUM (top) and
CELOSIA ARGENTEA PLUMOSA

• *Celosia argentea plumosa* 'Flamingo Feather'
A lovely new variety with pointed, feather-duster blooms, bicoloured rose at the top fading to pale pink and white at the base and produced over a long period. Height: 1–1.2m (3–4ft).

Centaurea

It was the old Greek doctor Dioscorides who named the cornflower family after Chiron the centaur. It was believed that one of the plants had cured a poisoned-arrow wound in the centaur's foot. *Centaurea* is, in fact, a rather large and diverse genus, with several species that are very attractive hardy annuals, invaluable for growing in mixed borders and for cutting.

The annual cornflower, *C. cyanus*, was in Parkinson's day a common wildflower 'furnishing, or rather pestering, the Corne-fields'. Also known as 'bluet' or 'blew-bottle', it is hardly surprising that this lovely cornfield weed, with innumerable smallish round bright blue heads of flowers held above the rather sparse, long and narrow grey-green leaves, had become so unpopular, as it blunted reaping-hooks to such an extent that, according to Gerard, it was known as 'hurt-sickle' because 'it hindereth and annoieth the reapers by dulling and turning the edges of their sickles in reaping of corne'. He also suggested that the plant might be useful for inflammation of the eyes, and in Saxony herbalists prescribed beer in which cornflowers had been boiled to cure jaundice.

Farming methods have come a long way since the days of reaping hooks, and it would be a rare sight indeed for cornflowers to be seen pestering cornfields today, or indeed surviving anywhere as a common wildflower, but the romantic image of the cornfield peppered with bright blue cornflowers for as far as the eye can see still inspires cottage gardeners to grow this lovely plant.

CENTAUREA CYANUS

Plants taken from the wild were grown in Tudor gardens, and Parkinson recorded varieties in many colours: 'wholly blew, or white, or blush, or of a sad or light purple, or of a light or dead red, or of an over-worne purple colour, or else mixed of these colours'. All these and more are available today, along with dwarf and king-size varieties, but the intense blue of the true wild form is of a shade all too scarce among garden plants and no mixed border of annuals is complete without them. In addition, birds are attracted to the seedheads.

Parkinson's 'stranger of much beautie' is none other than the musk-scented *C. moschata*, the 'sweet sultan' or 'sultan's flower', a plant originally from Persia which Parkinson in 1629 claimed 'had but lately come from Constantinople where, because (as it is said) the Great Turke, as we call him, saw it abroade,

C. MOSCHATA

liked it, and wore it himselfe'. *C. moschata* is a bushy plant 60cm (24in) high with fragrant, fluffy flowerheads, 5–8cm (2–3in) across, in shades of purple, lilac, yellow and white. Flowering from midsummer until mid-autumn, the flowers give off a musk-like scent, diffusing a whiff of the exotic East on the air. A fast-growing annual, it has lance-shaped, toothed, bright grey-green leaves scattered along the branching stems and can be recommended for its cutting and border qualities.

The giant sweet sultans, varieties of *C. imperialis*, are generally agreed to be offspring of *C. moschata*. These are striking garden annuals, although at 90cm (36in) tall they do look somewhat overgrown. They have a similar colour range to *C. moschata*.

CULTIVATION

Few annuals are easier to grow than *C. cyanus*, but as the plants do not transplant well seed should be sown *in situ*, either in the autumn for late-spring flowering (particularly if the plants are required for cutting), or as soon as the ground can be worked in the spring. Two or more sowings at two-week intervals will provide a continuous display and prolong the season. A sunny position in a well-drained soil suits the cornflower well. They should be thinned to 20–24cm (8–10in) apart.

Tall varieties which are effective in the back or middle of a border should be staked early, while dwarf forms can be grown in pots and containers as well as in the border.

Although *C. moschata* and its varieties deeply resent transplanting and it is usually recommended that seed is sown *in situ*, this can sometimes be a bit of a hit-or-miss exercise, resulting in plants which are hardly worth looking at. However, seedlings raised in a frame, transferred to small pots as soon as possible, and planted out in mid-spring in soil which has been well limed will pay dividends. A few twiggy sticks will support the plants and prevent wind damage. They are also best spaced 20–24cm (8–10in) apart.

While *C. moschata* and its relative *C. imperialis* should be planted in full sun, they are at their best in cool weather. Flowering slows down in very hot conditions, and resumes as the temperature falls in the autumn.

COTTAGE GARDEN VARIETIES

• *Centaurea cyanus* 'Black Ball'
This unusual cornflower has flowers in a lovely rich, milk-chocolate hue, which on cloudy days can look almost black. Height 75cm (30in).
• *Centaurea cyanus* Choice Mixed
A mixture containing many different shades of blue, mauve, violet, salmon-pink and pure white. Excellent for cutting. Height 1m (40in).
• *Centaurea cyanus* Frosty Mixed
A mixture of blue, maroon, azure, pink and crimson blooms with white or pastel contrasts at the petal tips. Height 75cm (30in).
• *Centaurea cyanus* Polka Dot
A good mixture of double-flowered, dwarf varieties in shades of blue, pink, carmine and white, which can be used at the front of the border or in containers. Height 40cm (16in).
• *Centaurea cyanus* 'Snow Man'
A lovely pure, clear white variety which makes an excellent cut flower. Height 90cm (36in).
• *Centaurea moschata* 'Dairy Maid'
Not the usual form found in mixtures, but a larger-flowered sweet sultan with rich yellow flowers and a lovely fragrance. Height 45–60cm (18–24in).
• *Centaurea moschata* 'The Bride'
A very fragrant, pure white variety of the sweet sultan, which is perfect for cutting and also a lovely garden plant. Height 40–60cm (16–24in).

Cheiranthus

The wallflower in its ordinary form hardly needs introducing to cottage gardeners, as it is by far and away the most popular of all spring bedding plants. The bushy, erect plants bear single brown, blood-red, mauve or mustard-yellow flowers; these fill the air with a spicy fragrance – harbingers of warmer weather to come. The old-fashioned double-flowered forms, on the other hand, may not be as well known. Special seed strains with a high percentage of double flowers are now more widely available, although named and particularly fine doubles are always propagated by cuttings.

Long before the wallflower enjoyed its enormous popularity and reputation as a cottage garden plant *par excellence*, it was to be found growing wild. Attaching itself to the ruins of old walls on desolate castles and abbeys, the plant enlivened the crumbling stones, as much a part of the romance and atmosphere of the place as the clinging ivy, screeching owl or gliding spectre. An unattributed Victorian verse sets the scene:

The Wall-flower – the Wall-flower, how beautiful it
blooms;
It gleams above the ruined tower, like sunlight over tombs;
It sheds a halo or repose around the wrecks of time;
To beauty give the flaming rose, the Wall-flower sublime.
Flower of the solitary place! grey ruins golden crown!
Thou lendest melancholy grace to haunts of old renown:
Thou mantlest o'er the battlement, by strife or storm
decayed;
And fillest up each envious rent time's canker-tooth hath
made.

In the Middle Ages the flower was carried in the hand at festivals, hence its botanical name *Cheiranthus*, which means 'hand-flower'. The powerful clove-like scent of the wallflower and stock are so similar that the wallflower was known to Gerard as the 'yellow stock-gillyflower'. Parkinson referred to it as the 'wall-gilloflower' and said that 'the sweetness of the flowers causeth them to be used in nosegays and to deck up houses'.

Single forms, usually yellow or brown-red but sometimes with the two colours striped together, have been grown in gardens since Elizabethan times. White and scarlet varieties appeared in the eighteenth and nineteenth centuries, and varieties with both silver- and gold-variegated leaves were also very popular at the time. Plants of a rich mulberry colour called 'The Negress' were the hit of 1852, and changed hands for huge prices.

Double-flowered forms have been in existence since the sixteenth century. They became very fashionable in Georgian and Victorian gardens, and gardeners at the time had access to many seed strains that yielded good percentages of double-flowered plants. Sowing the seed at the full moon was believed to yield a better proportion of doubles, and choice plants raised from seed were propagated by cuttings and named.

A much sought-after variety during the nineteenth century was 'Chameleon'. The petals at first appeared bright yellow, gradually became paler until they were nearly blanched white, and then took on a purple tint, so that flowers of three different hues appeared on the plants at the same time. Another fine old variety with lilac flowers was known as 'Old Cottage'; some of the old named doubles are still grown in cottage gardens today, and are much prized by collectors.

Modern-day garden wallflowers are particularly good value. They come in a wide range of colours and sizes for different parts of the garden, and you will find around 500 seeds in the average packet. Tall varieties, sometimes called 'standard' varieties in seed catalogues, are often seen interplanted with tulips or used to hide unsightly gaps on shrubs that are going bare at the base. They are a good choice for growing alongside paths and lawns, where the scent can be appreciated fully – red and yellow colours are the most fragrant. Dwarf varieties are better able to cope with exposed positions than the taller ones and are the best for planting in tubs, window boxes or small raised beds near the patio. The erysimums, which wander between *Cheiranthus* and *Erysimum* in seed catalogues, are more suitable for the rock garden, although they are also quite at home in the border.

CULTIVATION

Sow seed for wallflowers to be used as bedding plants in a shady seed bed in early summer. As soon as the seedlings have formed their third leaf, transplant them to a nursery bed, and then plant them out in their flowering quarters in the autumn. Plant in moist soil with good drainage. Seed can also be sown in the crevices of an old stone wall, where the plants will thrive without any attention.

Space tall varieties 12–15in (30–38cm) apart and dwarf types 6–10in (15–20cm) apart. When mixing bulbs with wallflowers, ensure that the bulbs are planted afterwards to avoid damaging them and to get the spacing right.

MIXED WALLFLOWERS

Double wallflowers that have been propagated by cuttings appreciate a well-drained, sandy soil containing a little decayed manure and an open, sunny situation. To propagate named varieties, remove the blooms after flowering and leave the plants where they are; they will quickly form an abundance of shoots from the base, which can be removed when they are about 8cm (3in) long. Take off the lower leaves and insert the cuttings in boxes of sandy compost. Protect the boxes from the sun and expect the cuttings to root in about four weeks. Pot them up and grow on in a cold frame until they are ready to plant out in early spring.

Seed of double-flowered strains should be sown outside in early spring for flowers the following spring.

COTTAGE GARDEN VARIETIES

• *Cheiranthus × allionii*
The jolly orange flowers of the Siberian wallflower radiate warmth and fragrance. A very popular spring bedding plant, it blooms slightly later than other wallflowers, bridging the gap between spring and summer colour. Although listed under *Cheiranthus*, the plant is in fact an erysimum, grown since 1847. Height 38–45cm (15–18in).

• *Cheiranthus cheirii* 'Cloth of Gold'
A very popular variety with large, deep yellow flowers and a heady fragrance. Perfect in large clumps or planted with tulips. Height 45cm (18in).

• *Cheiranthus cheirii* Double-flowered Tall Branching Mixed
This special strain produces a surprisingly high percentage of double flowers. The cheerful, many-petalled blooms come in a wide range of colours and offer today's cottage gardeners the chance of raising their own 'Chameleon'.

• *Cheiranthus cheirii* My Fair Lady Mixed
A selection of soft colours including lemon, cream, gold, apricot, purple, salmon, rose and mahogany. A cheerful mixture which Eliza no doubt would have called 'loverly'. Height 30cm (12in).

• *Cheiranthus cheirii* Tom Thumb Mixed
A particularly fine strain of dwarf red, mauve and mustard-yellow wallflowers which are ideal for small beds, edging, growing among bulbs and for pots and window boxes. With some protection from severe frost, they can be in flower in the greenhouse from the end of autumn until spring. Height 15–23cm (6–9in).

• *Erysimum* 'Bowles' Mauve', syn. *Cheiranthus* 'Bowles' Mauve'
A superb single-flowered variety, forming a vigorous bushlet of upright habit. The plant has glaucous foliage and large spikes of rich mauve-purple flowers in early summer and at times throughout the year. Although perennial, it tends to become leggy and is best replaced every other year. Not fully hardy in very cold areas. Height 60–90cm (24–36in).

• *Erysimum* 'Constant Cheer', syn. *Cheiranthus* 'Constant Cheer'
This wallflower produces compact mounds of dark green foliage and showy heads of single, dusky red and purple flowers. Height 60cm (24in).

NAMED DOUBLES

• *Erysimum cheiri* 'Harpur Crewe', syn. *Cheiranthus cheirii* 'Harpur Crewe'
An outstanding bushy, sweetly scented, golden yellow, double-flowered wallflower, possibly Elizabethan. The plant was rediscovered in the last century growing in a Hampshire kitchen garden by the Rev Henry Harpur Crewe, whose own garden was said to contain one of the richest collections of hardy plants in Europe. Such a visitor to the Hampshire garden was most fortuitous, as he was certainly well qualified to recognize the wallflower as special and to ensure its survival. Height 60cm (24in).

• *Erysimum cheiri* 'Miss Massey', syn. *Cheiranthus cheirii* 'Miss Massey'
A very lovely, deep and warm yellow, double-flowered wallflower with a strong constitution, although it is wise to overwinter a few plants under glass. A similar large double yellow was grown in the seventeenth and eighteenth centuries. Excellent for a conservatory. Height 60–75cm (24–30in).

• *Erysimum cheiri* 'Old Bloody Warrior', syn. *Cheiranthus cheirii* 'Old Bloody Warrior'
A dark blood-red, heavily perfumed, double-flowered wallflower which has somehow survived the centuries, despite its well-deserved reputation for being difficult. Margery Fish, whose inspirational books on cottage gardening were based on her own experiences at East Lambrook Manor, Somerset, wrote in *Cottage Garden Flowers* of her struggle to keep 'Old Bloody Warrior' going and suggested reversing the first two words of his name! Cuttings must be taken each year. Height 60cm (24in).

DOUBLE-FLOWERED CLARKIA

Clarkia

This genus includes four or five species of hardy annuals, two of which, *Clarkia pulchella* and *C. elegans*, are the parents of the numerous varieties grown in gardens today. Annual clarkias have ruffled flowers in many colours, including white, cream, yellow, rose, pink and salmon. These are produced on wiry stems up to 90cm (36in) long, making them perfect for cutting.

C. pulchella was first discovered by Captain Meriwether Lewis who, along with Captain William Clarke, took part in the Lewis and Clarke expedition in 1804 to explore the Pacific coast of America, an area almost unknown at that time. The plant is reported to have been found growing by the Kooskoosky and Clarke rivers and, fortunately for gardeners, was named after the latter! It was not until David Douglas was sent to collect plants in North America by the (not yet Royal) Horticultural Society in 1823 that the clarkia, previously only known as a herbarium specimen, was introduced to gardens. Douglas, a Scot, had a string of successful introductions to his credit, among them many of our best-known garden plants, including *Ribes sanguineum*, the flowering currant; *Garrya elliptica*; *Lupinus polyphyllus*, parent of the garden lupins; many species of penstemon; and a whole range of Californian annuals including eschscholzias, godetias and nemophilas. In a letter to Sir William Hooker, Director of Kew Gardens, referring to the large number of species of conifer – including the Douglas fir – which he had introduced, he quipped 'You will begin to think that I manufacture Pines at my pleasure'. It was David Douglas who discovered the musk plant, probably more famous today for having lost its scent than for ever having had it. Unfortunately, his plant-collecting days came to a tragic end in 1834 when, botanizing in Hawaii, he fell into a pit dug to trap wild cattle, and was found there gored to death by a young bull which had also been caught.

C. elegans is the most popular species of clarkia, a cottage garden favourite and popular hardy annual, with 60cm (24in) spires of frilled blossoms in many colours, providing a wonderful display all summer long.

The colours range from white through the various pinks, scarlets, crimsons and orange shades to purple, with large double or semi-double flowers on reddish stems bearing fairly broad leaves.

C. *pulchella* and its varieties differ from C. *elegans* mainly in the shape of the white, lavender or carmine flowers, which have slightly broader petals but even so are not as showy. They are smaller plants, excellent for edges and borders.

Clarkias can be used to create elegant and beautiful floral arrangements, but the flowers will only last if all the leaves are stripped off.

CULTIVATION

Seed of C. *elegans* varieties may be sown *in situ* in early autumn and thinned to 22cm (9in) apart for early summer flowering the following season. Provided they are planted in well-drained soil they should survive the winter well. Autumn sowing also produces excellent spring-flowering pot plants for the cool greenhouse.

Seed may also be sown *in situ* in early spring for a late summer display, but to see them at their best, instead of as the poor stunted things on show in many gardens, they should be given a fertile soil enriched with leaf mould – good treatment will be richly rewarded. Water the young plants if necessary in dry weather and stake very early. Clarkias do not transplant well and care should be taken when weeding, as the stems tend to snap off at soil level.

COTTAGE GARDEN VARIETIES

• *Clarkia elegans* 'Apple Blossom'
A favourite from the 1930s, with double flowers in the faintest apple-blossom pink, tinged with salmon. Height 75cm (30in).
• *Clarkia elegans* 'Chieftain'
An old favourite which has been grown since 1931, with double flowers in a beautiful soft, clear mauve, similar to the sweet pea of the same name. A colour picture in a 1931 seed catalogue shows a very desirable plant with blooms almost like small carnations. Height 75cm (30in).
• *Clarkia elegans* Double Brilliant Mixed
A mixture with long sprays of double flowers, freely produced, in a superb colour range. The plants will succeed in sun or partial shade. Height 60cm (24in).
• *Clarkia elegans* 'Salmon Queen'
In cultivation since the early 1930s, this variety has double flowers of a most striking, warm salmon-pink. Height 75cm (30in).

• *Clarkia pulchella* Double Choice Mixed
A choice mixture of this distinctive and very graceful clarkia, with slender spikes of very pretty flowers in various pastel shades, including lilac and pink. Height 30cm (12in).
• *Clarkia pulchella* 'Snowflake'
A new variety with masses of pure white flowers, which will prove invaluable in the garden border and for cutting. Height 30–38cm (12–15in).

Cleome spinosa

Cleomes are large-scale half-hardy annuals. Curious and decorative, they are known as 'spider flowers' because of the long, narrow, pointed seedpods which look like spider's legs and are produced while the plant is still bearing its distinctive pinkish mauve flowers. These substantial plants, often taken to be perennials, have stout, spiny stems and cheerful horse chestnut-like, pungent foliage. They provide a colourful and unusual background massed at the back of a border,

CLEOME SPINOSA COLOUR FOUNTAIN MIXED

the coarse, bushy spikes topped with clusters of single flowers which open upwards in succession. These have conspicuous stamens, often 8–10cm (3–4in) long, protruding from four narrow petals, to give an unusual, airy effect from midsummer until the first hard frosts.

Cleome is a name of uncertain origin, although it is said to have been used by the Greek Theophrastus for some flower – but obviously not this plant which, originating from South and Central America, would have been completely unknown at the time. Exotic-looking plants, cleomes have been grown in gardens since 1810. They are enormously popular in the USA and in continental Europe, where they enjoy the hot summers and are greatly admired. The most common varieties are pinkish mauve in colour, but named forms are available in shades of rose, pink, lavender and white.

Cut for arrangements, the flowers will continue to open for about a week indoors. However, the plants are armed with vicious, hooked thorns which develop where flowering branches join the hairy main stem, and care should be taken when cutting.

CULTIVATION

Seed of these tropical plants is best started under glass, preferably in small peat pots, several weeks before they are planted out in early summer. If grown well, each plant will occupy more than a square metre (square yard) of space. Spider flowers will often self seed, and are frequently found as garden escapes in the southern states of the USA. In warm weather and grown in a rich, well-drained soil, cleomes will leap to 1.2–1.5m (4–5ft), but despite their height they do not require staking. The plants do tend to become leggy and leafless at the bottom, and should be grown in clumps in a posi-

COBAEA SCANDENS 'ALBA'

tion where shorter flowers can grow up and cover their bare knees. Do not dot them individually here and there in the garden, as they will look distinctly gawky. Cleomes enjoy full sun, but will tolerate light shade.

COTTAGE GARDEN VARIETIES

• *Cleome spinosa* Colour Fountain Mixed
A delightful mixture of various shades of pink, rose, lilac, purple and white. Height 60–90cm (24–36in).
• Named varieties include: 'Rose Queen', bright rose; 'Helen Campbell', pure white; 'Violet Queen', deep violet; 'Pink Queen', shell-pink.

Cobaea scandens

Cobaea scandens (Cup-and-saucer vine, Mexican ivy, monastery bells) was named in honour of Father Cobo, a Jesuit naturalist. It is a tropical climbing perennial, usually grown as a half-hardy annual, and will flower in the first year from seed.

It has plenty of oblong leaves, with tendrils clinging to any available support from midsummer to mid-autumn, and large, bell-shaped flowers which open yellow-green and mature to a rather sinister shade of purple (the pale green form masquerades as *C.s.* 'Alba'). These sit on a large calyx or 'saucer', which is bright green.

In the cottage garden, *C. scandens* looks marvellous grown with the Chilean glory flower (*Eccremocarpus scaber*), which has masses of small, tubular orange or yellow flowers and sparse foliage.

COBAEA SCANDENS

The plant is also particularly suitable for growing over an archway or trellis and will do a good job of covering a fence or filling in a large gap on a wall. Given a hot summer and a sheltered spot, it will quickly reach 3–6m (10–20ft).

CULTIVATION

Sow seeds under glass six weeks before the last frost using individual 7cm (3in) peat pots. Place two seeds in each peat pot, sticking them in an upright position. Twenty days after germination remove the weaker seedlings. Plant outside in a good, moist, well-drained soil in full sun or light shade after all danger of frost has passed.

Coleus

Coleus blumei, syn. *C. × hybridus,* is a tender perennial usually treated as an annual which is grown for its extraordinary foliage. The fascinating variety of leaf patterns and vibrant colours completely overshadow the rather small and insignificant pale blue flower spikes, which are best pinched out early to maintain a bushy shape. There are other species such as *C. fredericii* and *C. thyrsoideus,* with quite ornamental panicles of bright blue flowers that appear in winter provided a temperature of 21–24°C (70–75°F) can be maintained, but these do not appear to be available from seed and are seldom grown nowadays.

The arrival of the highly ornamental coleus from Java in 1825 coincided with the Victorian craze for bedding-out, for which it was tailor made. Seeds of this heat-loving tropical plant were germinated in the fashionable glasshouses of the day, pinched and trimmed to a uniform height, and then used to striking effect in formal bedding schemes and 'ribbon' gardening. They would also be trained carefully into various ornamental shapes and used as pot plants to decorate the grandest Victorian conservatories.

Coleus is a member of the mint family and has the square stems which are so characteristic of many Labiatae. In a family of plants which are strongly aromatic – notably thyme, sage, mint, oregano, lavender and rosemary – coleus is only slightly aromatic, but what it lacks in scent it more than makes up for with colour.

The toothed or ruffled, heart-shaped foliage of coleus is blotched, streaked, splashed and stippled in exotic combinations of red, orange, bronze, yellow, gold, purple, chartreuse and white. At one time the only seed-raised strains available were mixtures which would be quite variable, but today there is a wonderful choice of named strains all coming 100 percent true to name and description, with a variety of habits and leaf shapes that are particularly suitable for pots and containers of all sizes.

While coleus are normally associated with formal gardens and bedding displays in municipal parks and gardens, they can also provide colour and accent in the cottage garden. Clumps will enliven a lightly shaded area after spring bulbs and perennials have gone over, and the rich, dark russet and burgundy varieties are particularly effective when grown with silver-leaved plants or at the feet of *Monarda didyma,* the scarlet-flowered bee balm, better known as bergamot.

CULTIVATION

Start coleus seeds indoors eight to ten weeks before the last frost. They will germinate in 10 days at 21–24°C (70–75°F), but need light to do so and should be left uncovered. The first pair of true leaves that emerge after germination shows signs of the colour to come. Should any of the seedlings appear green leaved or distorted, it is best to discard them at this stage. As soon as the young plants are large enough to handle, pot them up individually and grow on in a warm place.

Plantlets purchased from a nursery offer an early start, but growth will be stunted if they are planted out during cool weather. The earliest time you should move the plants outside is when the average night tempera-

COLEUS OLD LACE MIXED

tures remain at least above 5°C (40°F): coleus will not tolerate even a degree of frost.

Set plants 2.5–5cm (1–2in) apart in well drained but moisture-retentive, moderately fertile soil in light shade. Too much shade will cause the colours to become more muted, while strong sunshine will quickly bleach them out.

Cuttings of the most attractive plants can be taken in autumn and will root easily in sand or water. Many gardeners bring their special pot-grown coleus indoors in the winter as houseplants, and take new cuttings in spring to plant out in the garden. Cut back leggy old stems on mature plants to promote bushiness.

COTTAGE GARDEN VARIETIES

• *Coleus* 'Klondyke Brown'
A vigorous plant with cream and green leaves delightfully blotched with brown. Height 25–30cm (10–12in).

COLEUS 'KLONDYKE BROWN'

• *Coleus* 'Milkyway White'
A dwarf, bushy coleus with small, narrow, almost white, finely cut leaves with green margins. Height 15–20cm (6–8in).

• *Coleus* 'Pagoda'
This vigorous plant has yellow leaves which are marked with symmetrical red blotches – a unique two-colour pattern which keeps its beautiful colouring over a long period, even when grown in full sun. Height 25–30cm (10–12in).

• *Coleus* 'Pink Sensation'
A most attractive plant with beautiful, deep salmon-pink leaves narrowly margined with light yellow. Height 25–30cm (10–12in).

• *Coleus* Old Lace Mixed
A dwarf mixture of plants with finely fringed foliage and various lacy coloured markings. Height 15–20cm (6–8in).

• *Coleus* 'Volcano'
A long-lasting, vigorous and profuse grower producing large, almost self-coloured, deep bronze-red leaves with fine picotee edges in pale green. Height 30cm (12in).

• *Coleus* Wizard Series
These plants have foliage in various sizes and a variety of colours, including leaves marked with lime-green, cream and deep bronze, as well as almost self- and bicolours. Height 30cm (12in).

Consolida ambigua

Consolida ambigua, formerly classified as an annual *Delphinium*, is the old-fashioned, hardy larkspur which has been grown in England for centuries. Prized because of their resemblance to the stately perennial delphiniums and for their ease of culture, larkspurs are popular cottage garden flowers, often featured in watercolours of old-world gardens.

Tall rocket or hyacinth-flowered larkspurs are an early-flowering group with finely cut, fern-like foliage and 30–90cm (12–36in) branching spikes, clothed with single or double flowers of white, blue, purple, pink or lavender. The pastel colours blend well together and are set off to great advantage against a dark background of evergreens or a planting of *Perilla*. They make excellent cut flowers.

The stock-flowered and imperial larkspurs are much more widely grown and form tall, sturdy, branching plants, producing noble spikes of flowers 1–1.5m (3–5ft) high in a very wide range of pastel colours. Many colours can be obtained separately and come true from seed. They look particularly attractive massed at the back of a mixed border and are splendid for cutting and drying, retaining their bright colours all winter long.

CULTIVATION

Larkspurs can be sown outdoors in late summer for early flowering the following year, or in the spring for midsummer blooming. Sow thinly, and thin plants to 30cm (12in) apart. They prefer a rich, slightly alkaline soil and a position in full sun. Watch out for slugs, especially when the seeds are germinating, and discourage troublesome birds. Taller varieties may become top heavy with flowers and need to be staked.

COTTAGE GARDEN VARIETIES

Often found under larkspur in seed catalogues, some varieties featured here may also be listed under *Consolida ajacis*.

• *Consolida ambigua* Dwarf Hyacinth Flowered
A dwarf, early-blooming variety with double flowers that are offered in a wide range of colours. Height 30–40cm (12–16in).

SELF-SOWN CONSOLIDA AMBIGUA SEEDLING

• *Consolida ambigua* Exquisite Series
'Blue Bell' – light blue, 'Blue Spire' – dark blue, 'Scarlet Spire' – scarlet-red. Height 1–1.2m (3–4ft).
• *Consolida ambigua* Giant Hyacinth Flowered
An early-flowering mixture of large, fully double flowers in a wide range of colours. Height 1m (3ft).
• *Consolida ambigua* Giant Imperial Mixed
Majestic plants for the back of the border with colours from white to cerise, blue and violet. Excellent for cutting. Height 1m (3ft).

Convolvulus tricolor

Convolvulus tricolor, syn. *C. minor*, commonly known as the 'dwarf' or 'bush' morning glory, is a beautiful annual with brightly coloured, funnel-shaped flowers. It was first discovered growing in Spain and Portugal in 1608 by Guillaume Boel who sent seed to William Coys, an enterprising English gardener with whom he corresponded. At that time the plant was variously known as the 'lesser blue bindweed', 'lesser Spanish bindweed' or 'small blue convolvulus'.

The annual convolvulus was first described by John Goodyer in 1621: 'The seeds hereof were gathered in Spaine by Boelius [Guillaume Boel] and communicated by him to my good friend William Coys, who yerlie doth carefullie sow the same… and hath imparted thereof unto me. It hath not beene hetherto written of that I know'. Parkinson, who also received seed from William Coys, described his convolvulus as 'a most excellent fair skie-coloured blew, so pleasant to behold, that often it amazeth the spectator'. While it would appear to have been unknown to Gerard, Thomas Johnson included it in his revision of the *Herball* in 1633. It is also in the 1658 list of plants growing in John Tradescant's garden at Lambeth, and was offered for sale in William Lucas' catalogue of 1677.

As well as being a popular plant in English gardens, *C. tricolor* was a favourite flower with the seventeenth-century Dutch and Flemish painters. The cool blue and white flowers featured in the works of Jacob van Huysum also appeared in paintings by the English artist James Furber. 'This species especially', wrote the Rev William Hanbury in 1771, 'in many places, goes by the name of the Life of Man; it having flower-buds in the morning, which will be in full blow by noon, and withered up before night'.

C. tricolor is a low-growing, spreading hardy annual, rarely exceeding 30cm (12in) in height and perfect for hanging baskets and containers. The flowers usually open all day and close at night except in very hot weather, when they will shut up shop by early afternoon. Although the flowers are short-lived, they are produced constantly throughout the summer. The blooms are very similar to those of their climbing cousins but, at about 4cm (1½in) across, somewhat smaller. Each flower comes in three colours: the outside edge and most of the petal is mid- or deep blue, pink or purple, then comes a band of white, which in turn descends to a yellow centre. White varieties with stripes and dwarf or more compact forms are also offered by some seed merchants. The elongated leaves of all types are green with light grey-green splotches.

CONVOLVULUS TRICOLOR 'ROYAL ENSIGN'

Mention convolvulus, however, and most gardeners will throw their hands up in horror. The unfortunate antics of the perennial 'bindweeds', with their large, showy white, occasionally pink flowers, a feature of the hedgerows in high summer, has blackened the name of convolvulus. This aversion probably explains why these lovely annuals have never made it to the top of the charts, despite providing flowers that are predominantly a good rich blue, the rarest of summer flower colours.

Apart from its popular use in hanging baskets, containers and window boxes, *C. tricolor* is useful as bedding in an annual border and very attractive when used as a filler in island beds or grown as an edging to the herbaceous border. It is also an excellent choice for planting in the rock garden.

CULTIVATION

Before sowing, scarify the seeds and then soak them overnight. The plants resent transplanting, so seeds should be sown *in situ* in late spring in a moist, well-drained but not over-rich soil, in full sun. Sow thinly and cover lightly. Thin the seedlings to 23–30cm (9–12in) apart.

Earlier flowering can be obtained by making a sowing under glass in peat pots to minimize root dis-turbance when planting out. Sow two seeds per pot, discarding the weaker seedling later. Germinate the seeds at 16–18°C (60–65°F). The plants grow best in warm weather, and thrive in mild coastal regions.

COTTAGE GARDEN VARIETIES

• *Convolvulus tricolor* 'Blue Ensign'
A superb variety with brilliant blue flowers which cover the bushy plants all summer. Height 38cm (15in).
• *Convolvulus tricolor* Mixed
Mixed varieties are available from most seed mer-chants in a range of colours. Height 30cm (12in).

(left to right) ESCHSCHOLZIA, CONVOLVULUS TRICOLOR, LAYIA ELEGANS *with* LINUM GRANDIFLORA VAR. RUBRUM *in background*

• *Convolvulus tricolor* 'Rose Ensign'
This variety gives you four pastel colours – rose, lemon, pink and white – all in one flower. An interesting effect, without being too showy. Height 38cm (15in).
• *Convolvulus tricolor* 'Royal Ensign'
A lovely, eyecatching variety, forming a bushy plant that bears deep vivid blue flowers with a yellow-and-white throat for months on end, from summer to autumn. Height 38cm (15in).
• *Convolvulus tricolor* 'White Ensign'
A new variety with pure white flowers. Height 38cm (15in).

Coreopsis tinctoria

Coreopsis tinctoria, sometimes listed as *Calliopsis bicolor*, is the hardy annual coreopsis with bright yellow and crimson-brown daisy-like flowers on slender wiry stems above finely cut foliage. Its flowers are very similar to those of perennial coreopsis.

The common yellow coreopsis is very pretty planted among cornflowers. Cultivars are available in yellows, mahogany, pinks or purples, either solid or banded. Dwarf and double varieties are also sold. All annual coreopsis are perfect massed in a sunny bed or for edging the border and are good for cutting.

CULTIVATION

Sow seeds *in situ* in early spring. Plant in average soil in full sun and thin to 15–20cm (6–8in) apart. Plants bloom best when crowded together. Stake taller-growing varieties early.

COREOPSIS TINCTORIA 'TOM THUMB BEAUTY'

COTTAGE GARDEN VARIETIES

• *Coreopsis tinctoria* 'Fiery Beam'
A dwarf strain forming compact mounds of foliage covered with masses of small, deep bronze-red flowers – an unusually rich colour. Height 22–38cm (9–15in).
• *Coreopsis tinctoria* Tall Varieties Mixed
This tall-growing mixture of vivid flowers comes in a range of yellow and reddish brown tones. Height 1.1m (3½ft).
• *Coreopsis tinctoria* 'Tom Thumb Beauty'
A lovely strain with golden-yellow, crimson-centred flowers. Height 22–38cm (9–15in).

Cosmos bipinnatus

The name of this plant is derived from the Greek *kosmos*, meaning ornament – a tribute to the beauty of the flower and its use in the garden and home.

Sometimes listed as *Cosmea*, and often referred to as the 'Mexican aster', our present garden forms have originated from three Mexican species. They are without doubt among the most colourful of hardy annuals and one of the few that are really tall, blooming at around 1.5m (5ft).

Seeds of cosmos were collected in Mexico in the late eighteenth century, on one of a series of expeditions commissioned by King Charles III of Spain to investigate the natural resources of his dominions. The expedition, led by Dr Martin Sessé y Lacasta and José Mocino, was beset with problems from the outset. Travelling conditions were nigh on impossible, but a plea to the Spanish government to ship camels to Mexico to help alleviate the problem fell on deaf ears. Dangers lurked around every corner, and before the seeds eventually reached Spain the explorers had endured an earthquake, two volcanic eruptions and an outbreak of leprosy.

The Marchioness of Bute, whose husband was the British ambassador in Madrid at the time of the expedition, received some seed of *Cosmos bipinnatus*, and introduced it to English gardens in 1799, although sadly it was not an instant success. Gardeners tended to be too kind to the plant, growing it in a rich, loamy soil which encouraged lush foliage but few flowers. They also found that it needed real warmth to produce the dahlia-like flowers, which barely managed to bloom at all before the first frosts. Seedsmen in America selected early-maturing plants, which helped, but it was the poorest gardeners – or at least those with the poorest soil – that achieved the greatest success with cosmos, and their superb displays gained popularity for the plant.

C. bipinnatus has delicately cut, lacy foliage and clusters of large flowers, almost 10cm (4in) across, rather like single dahlias, in white, pink, rose or lavender. The serrated flower petals, arranged around a yellow centre,

COSMOS BIPINNATUS

may be daisy-like, crested, doubled, or quilled. The stems are slender and the rapid growth and tall habit of the plant makes it an excellent background for intermediate and dwarf annuals and perennials.

Few plants require so little attention, or self seed as readily as cosmos. In cottage gardens self-sown seedlings are encouraged and can be left to flower at random, billowing over fences and hedges, and flowering non-stop from midsummer until the frosts. Modern varieties are earlier-flowering than the original autumn-blooming Mexican natives.

C. sulphureus is the yellow cosmos, named the Klondike cosmos because of its large gold-centred flowers; its variety 'Sunset' has semi-double orange-red flowers. *C. atrosanguineus* is a half-hardy perennial which is either grown as an annual or treated like a dahlia, the tuberous roots being lifted and stored during the winter months. It has typical cosmos flowers in rich claret, and the scent is rich, too, resembling the aroma of the best Belgian chocolate you can buy. The colour of the flowers is intensified because the centre is exactly the same shade as the petals.

If cosmos flowers are cut when they first open they will last for up to two weeks in water. Take a dozen or more stems, strip off the lower leaves and just plonk them into the nearest vase. It would be almost impossible to arrange them badly.

CULTIVATION

Cosmos are ideal plants for a hot, dry, sunbaked border, and seed should be sown *in situ* in spring after any danger of frost has passed. Thin the plants eventually to 30cm (12in) apart. Taller varieties will need staking to keep them upright, and removing spent flowers will keep the plants blooming until the first frost.

COTTAGE GARDEN VARIETIES

• *Cosmos bipinnatus* Early Sensation Choice Mixed
A mixture of graceful plants with large, colourful flowers in various shades of crimson, pink and white, borne from midsummer well into autumn. Height 90cm (36in).

• *Cosmos bipinnatus* 'Purity'
A beautiful old variety which has been in cultivation for many years, producing large, single, snow-white flowers with a gold centre. Excellent for cutting. Height 90cm (36in).

• *Cosmos bipinnatus* 'Sea Shells Mixed'
A most distinct and delightful new mixture in which the petals are each formed into a perfectly shaped, colourful trumpet. Early and freely flowering, the blooms come in a range of lovely shades of white, crimson and, appropriately, shell-pink, to give an eye-catching, comment-attracting display. Height 90–120cm (36–48in).

• *Cosmos bipinnatus* 'Sonata'
A new cultivar producing whiter-than-white flowers with a small, neat, golden central boss. The flowers are borne on dwarfer, more manageable plants than in most other varieties, making it ideal for the smaller garden. Height 50cm (20in).

Cynoglossum amabile

The Chinese forget-me-not is a hardy biennial with downy foliage and tall, pleasing sprays of small, turquoise-blue flowers in summer. There are also small white- or pink-flowered varieties with either white or blue centres. Growing to 60cm (24in) tall, the plants look particularly attractive grouped together with some of the paler evening primroses (*Oenothera biennis*). Sadly, with the exception of the cultivar  'Blue Showers', Chinese forget-me-nots do not cut well and their beauty must be admired under the open sky.

CULTIVATION

Cynoglossum amabile is usually treated as an annual. Seeds germinate in 2–3 weeks at 20°C (68°F) and seedlings can be planted out in average soil in the spring, distanced 22cm (9in) apart in groups of three or more plants. Deadhead to promote flowering on side branches and to prevent self-sown seedlings from taking over the garden.

COTTAGE GARDEN VARIETIES

• *Cynoglossum amabile* 'Blue Showers'
Multitudes of sky-blue flowers, bred especially to be used as a cut flower. Height 40cm (16in).

• *Cynoglossum amabile* 'Firmament'
A form with indigo-blue flowers produced freely from spring to early summer. Height 40cm (16in).

Dahlia

The tender dahlia is a native of Mexico and numerous varieties were grown in Aztec gardens. The plant was named by the Abbé Canavilles after Dr Andreas Dahl, a Swedish botanist and pupil of Linnaeus, and was originally pronounced dah-le-a, not day-le-a. Dahlia flowers are carried on long stems above erect plants with light green or almost purple foliage. They come in every colour, except blue; their form can be single, round, anemone-like, shaggy mop-like, peony-like, ball-shaped or twisted.

Dahlias were first collected in Mexico in about 1570 by Francisco Hernandez, botanist and physician to King Philip II of Spain, who described and illustrated a dahlia species in his book *Plants of the New World and their medicinal virtues*, which was published posthumously in 1651. It was not until 1789 that the plant was first introduced to Europe, when Vincent Cervantes of the Botanic Gardens in Mexico City sent seeds to the Abbé Canvanilles of the Royal Gardens in Madrid.

Although the early species were nothing to write home about, they moved in most distinguished circles. The first to be seen in England were sent to Kew in 1798 via the greenhouse of the Marchioness of Bute, whose husband was the British ambassador in Madrid at the time. These plants are reported to have died almost immediately, no doubt due to a lack of understanding of their culture. In 1804 Lady Holland sent seeds of three species from Madrid to Mr Buonaiuti, Lord Holland's Italian librarian, who was more successful and succeeded in producing both flowers and seed that same year.

During the Napoleonic Wars, many new varieties were cultivated in France, some of the first tubers being planted at Malmaison by Empress Josephine, reputedly with her own hands. After the peace, many of these French varieties were introduced to England, and by 1817 Lees of Hammersmith were selling fully double ball-flowered hybrids – 'Dahliamania', which became almost as formidable as 'Tulipomania', had begun.

By 1832 the first English hybrid had appeared and by 1836 there were over 1,000 varieties available, some in plain colours, others with edgings or spots and flushes, and some with dramatic stripes. A black-flowered dahlia appeared in 1842, the same year that scarlet and yellow dahlias decorated the triumphal arches in almost every Scottish village on Queen Victoria's route through that country. Newly formed dahlia societies were offering huge cash prizes for the best blooms of the season. Shirley Hibberd, the Victorian author of *Familiar Garden Flowers*, wrote of the dahlia: 'If regarded from the florist's point of view, it is one of the grandest flowers in the garden, and in rank must be second only to the rose'.

The fashion for dahlias the size of mop heads in outlandish psychedelic colours declined during the latter part of the century. By 1880 popular garden newspapers were singing the praises of the new single dahlias, and dwarf-growing sorts began to appear which were popular for bedding-out. The so-called 'orchid-flowered' dahlias appeared on the gardening scene in the 1920s and new hybrids with perfectly shaped flowers continue to be produced to this day.

Many newcomers have boldly carried the word 'blue' in the naming, such as 'Bonny Blue' introduced in 1948, 'Blue Lagoon' in 1951, 'Blue Opal' in 1966,

DAHLIA 'CHILTERN AMBER'

and many more. It would appear, however, that the names reflect the optimism of their introducers more than their actual colours, as the Royal Horticultural Society has identified each and every one as being either lilac, lavender, violet, or just plain purple. While it is highly unlikely that a dahlia as blue as the morning sky or the cornflower is in prospect, there are no doubt plenty who will continue to experiment.

Dahlias will provide an unrivalled display of vibrant colours in the garden, ranging from white and creams, through a whole host of gentle pastel shades, to the deep, thunder-like purples. Flowers range from only 2.5cm (1in) across to the size of footballs, blooming from late summer until the first frosts.

Care should be taken when choosing dahlias to avoid a restless and spotty effect by cramming in plants of every possible hue, to jar hideously with other occupants of the autumn border. Clumps of good shades of pink and lemon-yellow look most attractive growing among blue Michaelmas daisies, while a striking fea-

ture can be created with a well-placed clump of that venerable old gentleman, the 'Bishop of Llandaff', with his bright scarlet flowers and delightful bronze foliage.

The poor dahlia continues to get a bad press and is one of those flowers often despised because of its misuse in garish bedding displays. To dismiss them all, however, is to deny the pleasure of the huge range of subtler shapes and shades.

CLASSIFICATION

There are currently 10 groups of dahlias in cultivation which have been classified by the National Dahlia Society of Great Britain, and popular varieties of all sections are offered in spring catalogues.

SINGLE-FLOWERED – a single row of petals with the central eye clearly visible.
COLLERETTE – single-flowered, but with each bloom bearing an inner collar, not necessarily of the same colour.
WATERLILY – fully double but flatter-flowered varieties, with the central eye completely hidden.
BALL – globular flowerheads about the size of a tennis ball, filled with tightly packed, crisp-looking petals (more correctly called florets).
DECORATIVE – fully double blooms with the central eye completely hidden. Individual petals are broad and may be more or less flat or inward-curving.
CACTUS – double-flowered, with petals that are long, narrow and rolled back to give a spiky, star-like appearance.
POMPON – miniature form of the ball type.

There are also the semi-cactus type, midway in appearance between the cactus and decorative groups, and several unusual forms such as the anemone-flowered, orchid-flowered and peony-flowered types, which fall under the heading of 'miscellaneous'. Dahlia specialists offer a bewildering choice of varieties and gardeners often get carried away.

Cottage gardeners with an eye to the species rather than the garden hybrids will find the fairly hardy *Dahlia merckii* quite charming. It has soft, rose-lilac, single flowers, 5cm (2in) across, borne on long, slender stems, and typical dahlia foliage. Connoisseurs will also appreciate the recently introduced, exceptionally prolific, pure white-flowered *D. m.* 'Hadspen Snowflake' which has curved, slightly longer petals than the species. This cultivar was developed from a pale-coloured seedling discovered some years ago in the, then derelict, garden at Hadspen House in Somerset.

Many types of dahlia make good cut flowers. The most popular are the miniature, small- and medium-flowered varieties, which offer a bewildering choice of both form and colour combinations for arrangers.

CULTIVATION

A sunny, open site and well-drained, rich soil, trenched to a depth of at least 60cm (24in), is the ideal situation for dahlias. A dressing of fine bonemeal forked into the top 5cm (2in) before planting out the tubers in late spring is recommended. Twiggy sticks placed here and there will help to hold up the plants in windy conditions.

In very mild climates the tubers can be left in the ground over winter – but even if frost does not get them, soil pests or fungus diseases probably will. It is therefore advisable to lift the tubers immediately after the first hard frost of winter and allow them to dry out naturally under cover, before trimming them back and storing in trays in a frost-free, damp-proof environment. It is essential to pack or cover the roots in some way so that they do not dry out – by covering them with dry peat or soil, for example. Alternatively, the tubers can be rolled up in clean, dry straw or even old newspapers and packed into large sacks or netting until the spring. Sealing in black plastic, where the exclusion of light and air keeps the tubers in good condition, has recently become a popular method of overwintering.

Bedding dahlias can be raised from seed sown in a heated greenhouse or propagator in late winter. Germination will take one to two weeks. Once the first two leaves have opened, prick out the seedlings into individual 8cm (3in) pots or deep trays. The young plants should be kept shaded for a week or so to avoid wilting, and as soon as they are 12–15cm (5–6in) high, pinch out the growing point to encourage bushy growth. Plant out in late spring when all risk of frost has passed.

The best time to divide dahlias is late spring. A bunch of tubers can be cut into several sections, each with a piece of crown containing one or more 'eyes' and with one or more tubers attached. In very mild areas they can be planted outside straightaway, preferably into soil warmed by cloches for a week or two. Elsewhere, the tubers should be started into growth in deep boxes or large pots of potting compost and protected from frost until planting out.

COTTAGE GARDEN VARIETIES

SINGLE-FLOWERED

• *Dahlia* Coltness Hybrids
Easily raised from seed, these single-flowered dahlias produce a mass of open-centred blooms in a wide range of colours. Perfect for edging, and for cutting for small arrangements. Height 45cm (18in).

• *Dahlia* 'Rigoletto'
Again, this strain is easily raised from seed. The plants are low-growing, with lots of single or semi-double blooms in a variety of colours. Height 30cm (12in).

COLLERETTE

• *Dahlia* 'La Cierva'
This elegant dahlia has rich purple outer petals tipped with white and a contrasting all-white inner 'collar'. Height 90cm (36in).

WATERLILY

• *Dahlia* 'Gerrie Hoek'
A very popular, small-flowered, silvery pink waterlily dahlia that excels as a cut flower. Height 90cm (36in).

BALL

• *Dahlia* 'Moor Place'
An easily grown pompon *par excellence*, with rich, royal-purple blooms of perfectly globular form. Height 90cm (36in).

• *Dahlia* 'Willo's Surprise'
A rather beautiful Australian-raised pompon with masses of small, globular dark red blooms all season long. Height 90cm (36in).

DECORATIVE

• *Dahlia* 'Chiltern Amber'
This small decorative dahlia bears tightly petalled, soft orange flowers and dark green foliage. Height 1.2m (4ft).

• *Dahlia* 'Master Robert'
This small decorative dahlia, popular for thirty years, has purple-blended, yellow flowers 10–15cm (4–6in) across. Height 1–1.2m (3–4ft).

CACTUS

• *Dahlia* 'Biddenham Sunset'
This dahlia bears small blooms in blends of deep orange-red with a yellow base to each petal. Height 1.3m (4½ft).

• *Dahlia* 'Border Princess'
A dwarf bedding type with small, bronze blooms that will light up any border. Height 60cm (24in).

POMPON

• *Dahlia* Pompon Mixed
The flowerheads look like a ball of honeycomb and are in a most delightful mixture of glorious colours. Height

90cm (36in).

• *Dahlia* 'Potgieter'

This prolific dahlia produces honeycomb heads of lemon-yellow. Height 90cm (36in).

MISCELLANEOUS

• *Dahlia* 'Moonfire'

Single amber-orange flowers, 7cm (3in) across, shade darker towards the centre. The foliage is black. Height 75cm (30in).

• *Dahlia* Topmix

These are the tiny 'Lilliput' types, with flowers just 2.5cm (1in) across. They come in pink, white, orange and red, and are perfect for pots on the patio. Height 12in (30cm).

(*clockwise from top left*) *DAHLIA* COLTNESS HYBRIDS, *D.* 'BIDDENHAM SUNSET', *D.* 'MOONFIRE', and *D.* 'MASTER ROBERT'

Dianthus barbatus

'Sweet Williams' belong to the same family as pinks, the *Dianthus* and are known botanically as *Dianthus barbatus*. They have rosettes of lance-shaped leaves and closely packed flowerheads in colours from purple to red, rose and white – in combinations of all or any; as one would expect from members of this genus, these produce a spicy clove fragrance.

A common plant in gardens for centuries, possibly introduced by Carthusian monks in the twelfth century, sweet Williams were used extensively when King Henry VIII had a new garden planted at Hampton Court in 1533, the plants being purchased in bulk by the bushel.

Sweet Williams have collected a string of other names over the years and were known at various times as 'bloomy-downs', 'London tufts', 'velvet Williams' and 'colminiers' (often spelt Col-me-Neers), the latter stemming from the word to 'col', meaning an embrace – a delightfully romantic and appropriate name for the fragrant, bunched flowerheads. According to Parkinson, the speckled kind "is termed by our English Gentlewomen 'London Pride'", although this name later became more closely associated with *Saxifraga umbrosa*.

There are several schools of thought as to the origin of the name 'sweet William'. Some traditionalists believe the flower was named after William the Conqueror, others that it was named by Gerard in honour of William Shakespeare. In her book *Flowers and their Histories* (1956), garden historian Alice Coates suggested that it is much more likely that the plant was originally named 'sweet Saint William' after St William of Aquitaine. On the other hand, there is a legend in Scotland that the flower is named after William Augustus, Duke of Cumberland, the portly third son of King George II. When William led the English army to victory at the battle of Culloden there was rejoicing throughout the land. The Jacobite rebellion was crushed: bonfires were lit in the streets of London and the hero's path was strewn with petals. Handel composed an oratorio in William's honour, inns were renamed The Duke's Head, and a flower was given the name of 'sweet William'.

An unattributed poem summed up the feeling at the time. A passage reads:

Since the Duke's victorious blows
The lily thistle and the rose
All droop and fade, all die away
Sweet William only rules the day.

In dour retaliation, the Scots retorted by christening the obnoxious-smelling common ragwort 'stinking Billy'!

It is rare indeed for a flower grown for so long, and particularly one with saintly connections, not to have been used in medicine or cooking. Gerard made the comment that 'the plants are kept and maintained in gardens more to please the eye, than either the nose or belly… [They] are not used either in meate or medecine, but esteemed for their beautie to decke up gardens, the bosomes of the beautifull, garlands and crownes for pleasure'.

Sweet Williams have never been particularly fashionable in any age, but the plant has always had its admirers. By the early nineteenth century it had joined the ranks as a florist's flower and prizes were offered for the best blooms. Writers at the time spoke of endless variations of colour, from white through pink, crimson and scarlet to purple, with self colours and many variously edged, eyed or spotted blooms. There were also many beautiful double-flowered varieties which were propagated by division or cuttings. The principal sweet William fancier in the 1840s was a Mr Hunt of Buckinghamshire, who raised over 100 varieties bearing flowerheads with 30 or more florets in all colours and variations.

Happily, sweet Williams can still be found in all the old colours. It is also comforting to know that the double varieties, for so long thought to be extinct, are now available from specialist seed merchants. Another survivor is *D. barbatus magnificum*, more affectionately known as King Willie, a dark crimson, double-flowered sweet William which grows no more than 15cm (6in) high. The plant, which is difficult to find and just as difficult to keep, has somehow survived since the seventeenth century. The spreading bronze foliage contrasts well with the dark-coloured, sweet-scented flowers, which positively glow in the sunlight. Cuttings of King Willie should be taken every year, as small plants seem to do better than bigger ones, which tend to rot off at ground level.

Well-grown sweet Williams can reach 60–90cm (24–36in) in height and as much as 45cm (18in) across, depending on variety, and are excellent for cutting, their spicy scent making them all the more welcome in the

DIANTHUS BARBATUS SINGLE-FLOWERED MIXED

home. They are also ideal for planting in small beds near the house, where they will bloom from early spring until autumn, their powerful clove perfume drifting through open windows on a warm summer's evening.

CULTIVATION

Although a true perennial, this old-fashioned cottage garden favourite is invariably treated as a biennial, with seed sown *in situ* in late spring to flower the following year. As soon as the seedlings are large enough to handle, they should be thinned or transplanted to 15cm (6in) apart each way. Once sweet Williams have been introduced to the garden, however, they will self seed with abandon. If plants are required for cutting, simply sow a short row of seeds alongside the vegetable patch.

Sweet Williams are very adaptable plants and have no peculiar fads or fancies. They will grow well in sun or partial shade but, like all members of the *Dianthus*, they do enjoy a fairly chalky soil – a dressing of lime will be appreciated if the soil is very acidic. Plant them, cottage-style, in clumps.

COTTAGE GARDEN VARIETIES

• *Dianthus barbatus* Auricula-eyed Mixed
These are the classic old-fashioned sweet Williams, in a wide range of flower colours from red and pink through to white. Height 45–60cm (18–24in).

• *Dianthus barbatus* Indian Carpet
A dwarf, compact strain with self or bicoloured flowers in the characteristic sweet William colours. Height 15–30cm (6–12in).

• *Dianthus barbatus* New Era Mixed
A flower-the-same-year-as-sown mixture which, if sown under glass in late winter, will be in flower *before* the biennials sown some seven months before. This colourful and strongly fragrant strain has large flowerheads up to 12cm (5in) across in shades of red and pink through to white. Height 60–75cm (24–30in).

• *Dianthus barbatus* Roundabout Series
Sown in early spring, these 'annual' sweet Williams will produce dwarf, compact plants that will flower the same year. The flowers are mostly bicoloured in shades of pink, red and white. They are particularly useful for the front of a border and are covered in summer with a profusion of bloom. Height 15–23cm (6–9in).

• *Dianthus barbatus* Single-flowered Mixed
A lovely range of single-flowered sweet Williams, which include the following self colours:
'Albus' – A pure white. Height 50cm (20in).
'Homeland' – Produces rich, dark red flowers with a white centre. Height up to 60cm (24in).
'Newport Pink' – Good salmon-pink. Height 60cm (24in).
'Scarlet Beauty' – A very striking scarlet sweet William. Height 60cm (24in).

Digitalis

Digitalis purpurea, the beautiful biennial foxglove of the woods and hedgerows, is one of those instantly recognizable plants which scarcely need an introduction. The handsome, spotted purple tubular flowers blooming on 1.5m (5ft) spikes in early summer look equally at home in the wild or in the garden, sowing themselves generously everywhere.

Witch's glove, witch's bell, lady's glove, virgin's glove, glove-wort, thimbles, thimble-flower, finger flower, fox chimes, bloody finger, red finger, dead-man's finger, dead-man's bell – these are just some of the quaint old names for the foxglove. Legend has it that mischievous fairies gave the blossoms to the fox so that he might soften the tread of his toes as he prowled about the chicken coop, but a more likely explanation is that the name foxglove was derived from the Anglo-Saxon *foxes-gleow*, the gleow being an old musical instrument which consisted of an arch that supported a ring of bells of graduated sizes, not unlike the structure of the flower spike itself. The association with fairies and gnomes, gave the plant several other charming names – fairy fingers, fairy-cap, fairy petticoats, fairy thimbles, goblin flower, goblin gloves, flower-of-the-fairies, goblins-and-fairies, and fairy-hat.

To the old herbalists, the foxglove seems to have been a panacea for almost all ailments. The thirteenth-century Welsh 'Physicians of Myddvai' applied the plant externally for scrofulous complaints – hence the family name, Scrophulariaceae. Gerard recommended it as a 'cure for ague, fevers, falling sickness, fresh, suppurating or green wounds, and ailments of the liver, spleen and melt while internally foxgloves were used for cleaning the body of clammy and naughty humours and for cutting phlegm'. By 1629, however, the plant would appear to have fallen into disuse, as Parkinson wrote, 'Foxgloves are not used in Physicke by any judicious man that I know'.

It is not generally appreciated that all parts of the foxglove are poisonous – the plant can either kill or cure. Dr William Withering discovered the foxglove's true beneficial properties in the late eighteenth century and used it to treat patients with dropsy. The drug digitalin, used today in the treatment of heart disease, is extracted from the leaves.

Country folk have long claimed that the storage

DIGITALIS ALBA and ANGELICA

qualities of potatoes, tomatoes and apples are much improved if foxgloves are grown nearby. Cut flowers will also last longer in water if foxgloves are included in the arrangement, or if foxglove tea is added to the water in the vase. The brew is made by pouring boiling water over a handful of leaves and flowers, which is then left to steep overnight.

DIGITALIS ALBA

The only variant of the foxglove that is at all common in the wild is the much sought-after white-flowered form, *D. p. alba*. Much admired in borders since the end of the sixteenth century, this pure white form of the common foxglove will enhance many a shady corner in the cottage garden. The amount of spotting inside the flowers varies, but this plant looks much better when the markings are less prominent. As self-sown seedlings can be purple-flowered, young plants whose leaves have midribs which are brownish or pale purple should be rooted out to keep the white strain going. (An early nineteenth-century authority advised that self-sown seedlings from a white foxglove will come up with purple flowers, whereas seed from the same plant carefully saved and sown in the spring will produce white-flowered plants like the parent.)

Although biennial, foxgloves very often develop a strong constitution which enables them to keep flowering for several years. Cultivated varieties, groomed for stardom, have improved the wild plant out of all recognition, with taller flower spikes, some towering 2–2.2m (6–7ft) high and strong enough to stand on their own without staking; more varied colours, including cream, pink, primrose and apricot; and larger flowers borne all the way around the stem and held horizontally to display the throat markings to better advantage. The true wild plant, however, will always find a home in the cottage garden, possessing as it does an intense, rich purple-red colour lacking in the more sophisticated forms.

DIGITALIS EXCELSIOR HYBRIDS *and HESPERIS MATRONALIS*

CULTIVATION

Cultivation presents few problems. Foxgloves will establish themselves easily in almost any soil in either sun or shade, but are commonly found in the dappled shade at the edge of woodland or groups of trees.

Sow seeds outdoors in late spring to early summer. They should be surface-sown or covered with only a very thin layer of compost so that light can reach them. Once the seedlings are large enough to handle, prick them out into individual pots or seed trays. Plants will be ready for transplanting into their flowering positions, spaced at least 30cm (12in) apart, in late summer and will give a good display the following summer.

After several years, self-sown seedlings of the cultivated varieties deteriorate from the original beauties, and it is advisable to grub them out every four or five years and start again with fresh stock.

COTTAGE GARDEN VARIETIES

• *Digitalis ferruginea*

This is the 'rusty foxglove' from south-eastern Europe and Turkey, with lovely rusty, reddish yellow, almost globular flowers borne on leafy spikes. An eyecatching plant, very much admired. Height up to 2m (6ft).

• *Digitalis grandiflora*, syn. *D. ambigua*

Known as the 'large yellow foxglove', this plant has quite large, open flowers with a slightly pointed lower lip, in an intriguing shade of greenish yellow. The flowers hang thickly on the stems. Fairly perennial, but not too productive of seed. Height 90cm (36in).

• *Digitalis × mertonensis*

A particularly fine hybrid from 1926, which comes true from seed. The large, attractive flowers are a delicious shade of crushed strawberry and appear from early summer until early autumn. Perennial, but easily grown from seed. Height 90cm (36in).

• *Digitalis purpurea* Excelsior Hybrids

The most popular strain, they produce dense spikes of flowers in a wide range of colours including cream, pink, primrose and maroon and make excellent border plants, giving a luxurious air to the garden. Also good for cutting. Height 1.5–2m (5–6ft).

• *Digitalis purpurea* Foxy Hybrids

These 'dwarf' hybrids are a comparatively recent introduction from America. They come in mixed pastel shades and, if treated as half-hardy annuals and sown in late winter under glass, can be in flower in five months. Height 60–90cm (24–36in).

Eccremocarpus scaber

In mild areas this unusual climber is an evergreen, but it is usually treated as an annual. Known as the Chilean glory flower, the plant produces numerous spikes of bright orange, tubular flowers, each 2.5cm (1in) long, and has small, feather-like leaves. It will form a delicate partial screen up to 2m (6ft) high and is suitable for growing over trellis or a pergola. It is also very useful for growing through a hedge or other climbers. Blooming in profusion all summer, it often seeds itself about, with seedlings springing up everywhere in true cottage garden tradition.

CULTIVATION

Seeds started indoors six weeks before the last expected frost, using individual 7cm (3in) peat pots, will flower the same year. Plant out after all frost danger has passed and space the plants 30cm (12in) apart in good, well-drained soil in full sun. The plants will require a trellis or strings to climb up.

ECCREMOCARPUS SCABER and (left) DIGITALIS × MERTONENSIS

Eschscholzia californica

Eschscholzia californica is the tongue-twisting botanical name for the California poppy, the State flower of California, where it grows wild on hillsides and along road verges. It was named in honour of Dr John Friedrich von Eschscholz, a Russian naturalist and physician of German extraction who accompanied Captain Kotzebue on the *Rurik* on an exploratory expedition to north-west America in 1815.

Legend has it that in the late sixteenth century Spanish seamen, sailing along the Californian coast, looked at the hillsides awash with a golden hue and named the country 'La Tierra del Fuego'. The altar-cloth of San Pascual was spread (they said) upon the mountains and, just like Linnaeus when he first saw English gorse, they fell on their knees in prayer. (The Spanish-Californians still make a highly prized hair oil, which is said to promote hair growth, by frying the whole plant in olive oil and adding perfume.)

The story is also told that during the California Gold Rush in the mid-nineteenth century, naïve prospectors seeing the hillsides from afar glowing like burnished gold, ran forward shouting 'Gold! Gold!', imagining for a moment that they were about to scoop the jackpot and that this must surely be Eldorado. It is certainly true that the Men of '49 pressed petals of the flowers to send home to anxious relations as tokens of the wealth that was to come. The California poppy was introduced into Britain in 1826 by David Douglas, who was sponsored by the (not yet Royal) Horticultural Society. He was the first botanist to collect material extensively in California and Oregon, and he sent back several interesting poppies to the old world.

After much lobbying and deliberation, in 1890 the California State Floral Society bowed to pressure from the settlers and chose the California poppy, which spread so lavishly over the countryside, as the State flower, to symbolize their new prosperity. There followed an immediate craze for everything poppied, and poppy souvenirs of every kind were to be found in every store: poppy brooches, embroidered poppies, hideously painted china, as well as poppy buns, poppy butter and poppy baking powder, were all in great demand. Architects replaced the traditional acanthus with the new State flower in their designs, and newspapers and periodicals issued special 'poppy numbers'. Volumes of poppy verse were compiled by anthologists, but poets, it would seem, did not get to grips with the unenviable task of finding a rhyme for *Eschscholzia*.

The California poppy has rich, deep yellow flowers on slender stems and attractive, finely cut, blue-green foliage. The plant grows to about 30cm (12in) and will reward even the most inexperienced gardener with a profusion of silky, cup-shaped flowers up to 8cm (3in) across. There are numerous strains originating from this species which come in a bewildering array of colours, including lemon-yellow, golden yellow, purple-violet, scarlet, rose or white, with single or double blooms (the double forms are sterile).

Eschscholzias look well in the border, in massed plantings, and in containers. Flowers cut for arrangements are short lived and, to use them at all, they need to be cut while still furled.

CULTIVATION

Eschscholzia californica is a perennial or biennial in its native California. Occasionally, after a mild winter, cottage gardeners will find an odd plant surviving in colder climates, but they are nearly always inferior to plants raised from freshly sown seed.

California poppies do not transplant well, so starting seeds under glass is not recommended. Sow seeds at intervals *in situ* in early spring to flower the same year, or in late summer, when they will flower from spring until autumn. Thin to 15cm (6in) apart. They are ideal for a hot, dry, sunny part of the garden, and thrive best in a light, sandy, well-drained soil. Deadhead regularly before they go to seed and the foliage turns the colour of straw.

COTTAGE GARDEN VARIETIES

• *Eschscholzia californica* 'Alba'
A lovely variety with eyecatching, creamy white flowers. Height 35cm (14in).
• *Eschscholzia californica* 'Apricot Chiffon'
An award-winning, dwarf variety bearing double, creamy yellow flowers with an intense coral-orange edging. Height 20cm (8in).
• *Eschscholzia californica* 'Ivory Castle'
A new variety with pure white flowers, possibly the only one of this colour. Height 35cm (14in).

ESCHSCHOLZIA CALIFORNICA and LOBULARIA

• *Eschscholzia californica* 'Mission Bells'
A strain with mostly double flowers, in shades of rose, orange, pink, white, yellow, gold and copper. Height 30cm (12in).
• *Eschscholzia californica* 'Purple Gleam'
This poppy bears lovely flowers in a most delightful shade of lilac-purple. Height 35cm (14in).
• *Eschscholzia californica* 'Red Chief'
Perhaps a little 'over the top' for the average cottage gardener, this variety has brilliant, scarlet-red flowers guaranteed to brighten up the summer border. Height 35cm (14in).

Euphorbia marginata

Euphorbia marginata, or snow-on-the-mountains, is a most unusual hardy annual, grown for its attractive foliage and its small white flowers, with their large, long-lasting petal-like bracts. The oval, light green foliage is striped and margined with white on the upper leaves, with some of the topmost leaves nearly all white. Appearing to be covered with snow, the cool colours contrast well with brightly coloured annuals and provide a complementary background for California poppies (*Eschscholzia californica*) and dwarf zinnias.

Snow-on-the-mountain is often used as a showy cut flower to set off larger flowers. The cut ends should be dipped in boiling water or seared over a flame, then the flowers may be arranged in warm water. Care should be taken when working with this plant, as its milky sap can irritate skin, eyes and open cuts.

CULTIVATION

Not particular as to soil and happy in partial shade as well as in sunny areas, this annual can be sown outdoors in the spring as soon as the ground is friable. It is a quick-grower and dislikes being transplanted; thin plants to 30cm (12in) apart. Be sure to wear gloves when handling it.

COTTAGE GARDEN VARIETIES

• *Euphorbia marginata* 'Summer Icicle'
A dwarf variety with striking foliage. Height 45cm (18in).
• *Euphorbia marginata* 'White Top'
Uniform and erect, 'White Top' is the tallest of the snow-on-the-mountains. Height 90cm (36in).

Gaillardia pulchella

Known as the blanket flower because the flowers rival the brilliant colourings of North American Indian blankets, this attractive hardy annual, 30–60cm (12–24in) tall, blooms in early summer in sunset colours of orange, yellow and red, and combinations. It grows erect with its daisy-like flowers rising above its narrow, deeply cut, downy foliage. In addition to single-flowered varieties, double or quilled flowers are available, and the colour range has been extended to include bronze and cream.

The plants are showy when massed together and because they grow well in dry conditions excellent for containers and window boxes. With their long, curving stems, blanket flowers also make graceful cut flowers.

CULTIVATION

Gaillardias can be sown outdoors after all danger of frost has passed. Choose a position in full sun in well-drained soil and thin the plants to 30cm (12in) apart. Deadhead to encourage continued bloom.

GAILLARDIA PULCHELLA 'LOLLIPOPS'

COTTAGE GARDEN VARIETIES

• *Gaillardia pulchella* 'Lollipops'
A very pretty dwarf variety with yellow, cream and red flowers on a plant with branching stems and grey-green leaves. Height 30cm (12in).
• *Gaillardia pulchella* var. *lorenziana* 'Gaiety'
A most attractive plant with enlarged and quilled petals, giving the red, yellow and purple flowers an almost globular appearance. Height 60cm (24in).

GAZANIA RIGENS 'TALENT'

• *Gaillardia pulchella* 'Red Plume'
A dwarf variety with brick-red double flowers, 5cm (2in) across, held well above the foliage. Ideal for containers as well as the border. Height 30cm (12in).

Gazania rigens

The treasure flower was named after Theodore Gaza, who translated into Latin the botanical writings of the Greek doctor Theophrastus, in the fifteenth century. This showy half-hardy annual has single, bright daisy-like flowers up to 10cm (4in) across, carried on 25cm (10in) stems in summer. The leaves at the plant's base are dark green and felty white underneath.

Many varieties are available either in solid colours, in various shades of yellow, gold, orange, cream, pink or red, rich in sheen, or with contrasting centres of yellow or black. Treasure flowers can be used as groundcover or as edging plants and prefer the hottest, driest, sunniest spot in the garden. They are quite dazzling when massed together, the petals shimmering in the bright sunlight. Because the flowers close at night and on cloudy days, there is little point in cutting them for indoor decoration.

CULTIVATION

Cover the seeds lightly and then shade the trays to exclude all light. They germinate in 15–20 days at 21°C (70°F). Plant out in the garden after the last frosts and space the plants 20–25cm (8–10in) apart. Fertilize at planting time: no further feeding is necessary. Cut the flowers as they fade to encourage more blooms and to keep the plant tidy.

COTTAGE GARDEN VARIETIES

• *Gazania rigens* 'Chansonette'
An early-flowering mixture with exotic, large flowers 7cm (3in) across. The zoned flowers have many contrasting colours between the centres and tips of petals. Height 25cm (10in).

• *Gazania rigens* 'Oranges and Lemons'
A great profusion of flowers in two bright and cheerful colours for summer beds and borders. Blooms borne over a long period. Height 20cm (8in).

• *Gazania rigens* 'Talent'
Compact plants with graceful foliage and generous numbers of long-lasting flowers in shades of yellow, orange, pink and brown. Even after showers, the silvery lustre on the foliage is undimmed. Height 20cm (8in).

Gomphrena globosa

The clover-like flowers of the half-hardy globe amaranth are excellent for fresh and dried arrangements, as well as in the border.

Growing about 30cm (12in) high, it has small, dense flowerheads in red, pink, purple, orange and white, which keep their colour for a long time when dried. The erect, mound-shaped plants are well-branched, with oblong leaves with fuzzy hairs on their edges. The colours of globe amaranth are not particularly harmonious and are best complemented by white flowers such as annual *Gypsophila*.

In cottage gardens the dwarf varieties are frequently seen as an edging plant, while the taller varieties are used for cutting and drying. The plant is also sometimes called bachelor button.

CULTIVATION

Seeds should be soaked overnight before sowing. Sow seed indoors six weeks before the last frost for early flowering. Seeds germinate in 10–14 days at 22°C (72°F). Plant outdoors after all danger of frost has passed and space the plants 20cm (8in) apart. Seed may also be sown *in situ* after the last frost but the plants will flower much later. The only demand these reliable plants make for good performance is sun. They have no particular soil preference.

COTTAGE GARDEN VARIETIES

• *Gomphrena globosa* 'Strawberry Fields'
A new fine strain and the first true red gomphrena, a bed of which looks like a row of long, vertical-stalked, 5cm (2in) strawberries. Blooming in great profusion and brightening any border from summer through until late autumn, the flowers retain this bright red colour indefinitely, either fresh or dried. Height 60cm (24in).
• *Gomphrena globosa* 'Lavender Lady'
Another tall variety with luscious lavender-coloured blooms which are excellent for cutting to use fresh or dried. Height 60cm (24in).
• *Gomphrena globosa* 'Buddy'
A splendid dwarf cultivar with compact, bushy plants, producing long-lasting, royal purple, blooms from mid-summer to late autumn. Height 20–24cm (8–10in).

Gypsophila elegans

Gypsophila elegans, or baby's breath, is a sprawling, but upright hardy annual growing to 60cm (24in) with a multitude of dainty, star-like white or pink flowers that create a misty, effect – an old cottage garden favourite.

GOMPHRENA GLOBOSA   *GYSOPHILA ELEGANS*

Try it as an airy blanket interplanted with tall-growing annuals and summer-flowering bulbs or in the cutting garden where it can be used for arrangements. Because the plants live for only five or six weeks, it is worth making several sowings to prolong the flowering season.

CULTIVATION

Start seeds outdoors in mid-spring. Scatter and press down firmly. The seeds, which will germinate in about ten days, will need to be thinned to 20cm (8in) apart. When making successive sowing, the whole plants may be harvested for indoor arrangements and replaced with fresh seeds. Very often, early plantings will re-seed and flower during the same season. The plants grow well in average soil. However, in areas where soil is acidic, add lime before planting.

COTTAGE GARDEN VARIETIES

• *Gypsophila elegans* 'Covent Garden'
A highly popular strain with larger than average pure white flowers. Height 60cm (24in).
• *Gypsophila elegans* 'Giant White'
Another large-flowered strain with white flowers which are excellent for cutting. Height 60cm (24in).
• *Gypsophila elegans* 'Kermesina'
This delightful variety, not often seen, bears deep rose-coloured blooms. Height 75cm (30in).

Helianthus annuus

And Sunflowers planted for their gilded show
That scale the windows lattice ere they blow,
Then, sweet to habitants within the sheds,
Peep through the diamond panes their golden heads.

JOHN CLARE

The botanical name *Helianthus* means sunflower, by which name this plant is so well known that it scarcely needs an introduction. In brief, however, *Helianthus annuus* has sturdy stems with large, hairy, sticky pointed leaves, and enormous, dark-centred yellow flowers, often 30cm (12in) in diameter, which become top-heavy when seeds are formed. A single flowerhead can, in fact, contain as many as 2,000–3,000 seeds, which are arranged honeycomb fashion. These are rich in protein and are grown commercially in many parts of the world for sunflower oil. In Russia they are eaten like peanuts, prompting garden historian Alice Coates to write that 'the seeds were particularly acceptable to turkeys, parrots, pheasants and Russians' (*Flowers and their Histories*, 1956).

Seeds of *H. annuus* were first sent back to Spanish botanists in the 1560s by European explorers in South America, where the Incas had bred it into a towering stalk topped by spectacular golden flowers. Tales are

HELIANTHUS ANNUUS

HELIANTHUS ANNUUS

told about the sun-worshipping natives of this ancient civilization and of the virgins in the Temples of the Sun who were crowned with helianthus of pure gold, also wearing them on their breasts and carrying them in their hands to reflect the sun. Homage of a sort continues today in the salerooms, with Van Gogh's famous *Sunflowers* selling at Christies in London in 1987 for £24.75million.

Gerard, who called the sunflower the 'golden floure of Peru', succeeded in growing a plant in his garden at Holborn, London, to a height of 4.5m (14ft), where one flower 'was in weight three pounds and two ounces', although he refers to sunflowers attaining heights of 7.5m (24ft) in Spain.

Not to be upstaged, however, the Italians at the time claimed that a plant in Padua reached a height of 12m (40ft), presumably sown by Jacco of beanstalk fame. Today, sunflowers are a favourite with children and a popular item for sponsorship, hardly a summer passing without the local paper showing proud owners dwarfed by massive specimens. If the intention is to grow the tallest sunflower in the neighbourhood, ensure that the sideshoots are pinched out as they appear.

Despite their absurd height, sunflowers somehow look right in the cottage garden, towering above its other inhabitants to peer over high fences, their giant flowerheads following the sun from dawn to sundown. Garden forms have now been bred with much smaller flowers in various shades of yellow, orange, maroon and two-toned combinations. A particularly good strain, *H. a.* 'Autumn Beauty' has an artistic range of colour combinations.

Seedsman today also offer varieties that grow only 30–38cm (12–15in) tall, which provide an impressive display when massed for bedding. These dwarf varieties are also useful for growing in pots and containers.

CULTIVATION

Annual sunflowers should be sown fairly thinly *in situ* in early spring. Choose a sunny situation sheltered from strong winds in moist, well-manured soil, but do not fertilize. The seeds will germinate within two weeks and seedlings should be thinned to about 45cm (18in) apart, as overcrowding will starve the plants and produce poorly developed flowers. They commence flowering when they reach 1.5m (5ft). As the seeds are formed, the flowerheads become heavy and will require staking.

COTTAGE GARDEN VARIETIES

• *Helianthus annuus* 'Giant Yellow'
An impressive plant with huge, golden yellow flowerheads. Height 3m (10ft) or more.

• *Helianthus annuus* 'Holiday'
This variety forms a stately, spherical bush, about 1.3m (4ft) wide, bearing numerous very strong-stemmed, golden-yellow sunflowers 15cm (6in) across. A spectacular garden plant, which is also excellent for cutting to bring sunshine into the house. Height 1.2m (4ft).

• *Helianthus annuus* 'Music Box'
The first dwarf sunflowers are equally at home singly or in groups in a sunny border or in containers on the patio. The showy flowers are up to 12cm (5in) across and come in splendid colours, ranging from cream through yellow and attractive bicolours to mahogany-red. Height 24in (60cm).

• *Helianthus annuus* 'Teddy Bear'
This dwarf sunflower has unusual extra-double, saucer-sized, pompon-like, golden blooms. Easy to grow and quick to flower – a cuddly bear of a plant. Height 24in (60cm).

Helichrysum bracteatum

Helichrysums encompass some of the very best of the 'everlastings' or 'strawflowers'. They are showy half-hardy annuals, chiefly grown as a source of supply of flowers for cutting and drying, but nevertheless decorative plants for both beds and border. The name is derived from two Greek words, *helios*, meaning sun, and *chryso*, meaning gold, a reference to the rich yellow centres of the papery flowers. They have also collected a string of common names along the way: 'immortelles', 'golden flower gentle', 'live longs' and 'eternelle flower' are all quaint names given to helichrysums by past generations of cottage gardeners and still widely used today.

Helichrysum orientale, introduced from Crete in the seventeenth century, is the oldest everlasting in cultivation, although its dried flowers were known much earlier. Gerard, who only saw it as a dried specimen, wrote: 'The golden Mothwort or Cudweed being gathered before they be ripe or withered, remain beautiful long time after, as myself did see in the handes of Mr Wade, one of the Clerks of hir Maiesties Councill, which were sent hime from Padua in Italie'.

During the eighteenth century strawflowers were used by milliners to trim ladies' hats, and to decorate fireplaces in summer and vases in winter.

In *A Complete Body of Planting and Gardening* (1770), Rev William Hanbury described a dwarf variety of *H. orientale* as 'the most beautiful variety belonging to the species, and is one of the most common sorts in Portugal and Spain, where it is propagated to ornament their churches in winter, and from whence we frequently receive it in England to adorn our ladies, who purchase them for these purposes'.

H. bracteatum, the species most widely grown today, was introduced to cultivation in England in 1799 by Messrs Colville of Kings Road Nursery in London, having been collected by Lieutenant Colonel W. Paterson in 'New Holland' (Australia). A Scot who had previously travelled in South Africa, taking the first giraffe skin back to England, he made several unsuccessful attempts in 1793 to cross the Blue Mountains of New South Wales, but named the River Grose, and in 1804 first settled Port Dalrymple in Tasmania with a small party of convicts. Paterson is commemorated by the endemic Australian genus, *Patersonia* (Iradaceae).

In New South Wales there is a common annual, erect form of *H. bracteatum* with lemon- to butter-yellow flowerheads which, given the right conditions, will grow as tall as a man. This is the form which first reached Europe; the eighteenth-century botanist William Aiton noted that it flowered between mid-summer and mid-autumn at Kew as a hardy annual.

Other annual forms with yellow flowerheads, often flushed bronze, and still others with pinkish or white heads borne on stems about 24in (60cm) tall were introduced as seed, also from Australia, by another Scot, James Drummond. The first seedlings raised from this seed were sent to the Caledonian Horticultural Society in 1839 by Lows Nursery, Clapton, where they flowered for the first time in the summer of 1840. Subsequent selection of progeny produced white, scarlet, blood red, and red-flushed single forms, and crimson, terracotta, orange, gold, yellow, salmon, and pink double forms.

These showy Australian everlastings were immensely popular with Victorian ladies, who whiled away their empty hours making winter flower decorations, finicky craftworks and bouquets with the dried flowers. Several species were also used at one time in the making of funeral wreaths.

HELICHRYSUM BRACTEATUM

H. bracteatum is a pretty plant. The daisy-like flowers, 6cm (2½in) across, have bright yellow-orange centres surrounded by stiff, papery bracts in red, orange, pink, yellow or white, often incurving towards the centre, and are borne on narrow, wiry stems. The papery flowers hold their colour indefinitely when dried, and they are also beautiful in fresh floral arrangements.

There are numerous named varieties of the double-flowered *H. b. monstrosum* form with larger flowers in a wide range of colours, borne on smaller plants. There are also mixed and dwarf strains which grow no more than 30–45cm (12–18in) tall.

CULTIVATION

Seed is probably best sown under cloches in the open ground in early spring for a longer period of bloom and harvest, or start seeds indoors four to six weeks before the last frosts. Do not cover the seed as it needs light to germinate, and thin seedlings to 25–30cm (10–12in) apart. The cloche protection will produce plants that flower from early summer. When growing helichrysums in quantity, sow the seed in rows.

Strawflowers are sun-lovers and should be planted in a fairly rich but well-drained soil well away from overhanging shade. The taller varieties, which tend to become leggy, require staking and are best planted at the back of the border.

For winter decoration, cut the flowers before they have expanded fully, making sure they are not wet with dew or rain. Strip off the foliage and wrap fine wire around the stems of small bunches. Hang the plants upside down in a dark, cool, airy shed, attic or basement, and let them dry for two or three weeks. Even the tiny buds will expand, and these will be more attractive than the larger flowers.

COTTAGE GARDEN VARIETIES

• *Helichrysum bracteatum* Bikini Mixed
A mixture of multicoloured dwarf hybrids, which are ideal for drying for smaller arrangements, and excellent for rock gardens, beds and borders. Height 30cm (12in). The named varieties are enormously popular: 'Hot Bikini', a medal winner with red-hot flowers; 'White Bikini'; 'Pink Bikini'; 'Golden Bikini'; and 'Crimson Bikini', with lovely dark red flowers.
• *Helichrysum bracteatum* Pastel Mixed
A development from the popular 'Frosted Sulphur' and 'Silvery Rose' to which has been added white, rose pink and salmon. Height 90–120cm (36–48in).
• *Helichrysum bracteatum monstrosum* Bright Bikini
A new mix, with brilliantly coloured double flowers (including red-hot 'Hot Bikini') on free-flowering dwarf plants. Height 30–45cm (12–18in).
• *Helichrysum bracteatum monstrosum* Tall Choice Mixed Colours
A good mixture of tall-growing varieties which are particularly good for cutting. Height 90cm (36in).

Heliotropium arborescens

Heliotropium arborescens, syn. *H. peruvianum*, is a shrubby tender perennial from Peru, usually grown as a half-hardy annual and commonly known as 'cherry pie'.

The old-fashioned heliotrope has dark green, wrinkled leaves and sprays of large, dense clusters of violet or purple flowers with a rich fragrance – a heady cocktail of vanilla, lemon and a hint of clove, which is sweet but not cloying and once enjoyed, never forgotten. In its native Peru, plants grow 1.2–2m (4–6ft) tall and in parts of Ireland, where the winters are mild, it is widely planted as a hedge, the surrounding air heavy with its fragrance in summer.

Legend has it that heliotrope, the name derived from the Greek *helios*, meaning sun, and *trope*, meaning to turn ('turn to sun'), was once the ocean nymph Clytie, who died for love of the sun god Apollo when he deserted her for her sister. He transformed her into a flower, which always turned its head to watch him.

HELIOTROPIUM ARBORESCENS

Thomas Hood refers to the heliotrope as Clytie in his poem *Flowers*:

> I will not have mad Clytie
> Whoes head is turned by the sun.

The interpretation, however, could equally well apply to dozens of other flowers, but this remained a popular fable for centuries, eventually working its way into discussions of morality, with an eighteenth-century cleric urging his flock to be like the heliotrope: 'Let us all be heliotropes (if I may use the expression) to the Sun of Righteousness'.

H. arborescens was first introduced from Peru by way of France. It was discovered in the Peruvian Andes by French botanist Joseph de Jussieu, who sent seed back to the Jardin du Roi in Paris, where it flowered for the first time in 1740. Phillip Miller, an eighteenth-century writer and gardener, reported that he received the seed 'from the curious garden of the Duc D'Ayen at St Germain which have succeeded in the Chelsea Garden where the Plants have flow-

ered and ripened their seeds for some Years past'. Apart from its use in the perfume industry, some herbalists claimed the flowers would cure warts and gout. The plant was also used to manufacture an astringent tincture 'of great service in clergyman's sort throat'.

Early plants had rather wishy-washy pale blue flowers, which were then much improved by hybridization and selection to produce blooms from deepest violet to rose or white. It was during the nineteenth century that the plant reached the height of its popularity grown in high Victorian gardens in summer and their conservatories in winter, with new varieties appearing almost every year, trumpeted each time as 'new and improved'. Compact forms were produced for use in bedding, and sometimes whole parterres would be filled with them, with good forms then propagated by cuttings and overwintered under glass. Two of the many Victorian varieties raised at that time were characteristically named 'Miss Nightingale' and 'Beauty of the Boudoir'.

Heliotrope makes a decorative display in the border, as well as in cut-flower arrangements. If grown in containers, place the pots where the fragrance of the plant can be best enjoyed. Trained standard plants can be placed on a patio or balcony for the summer, and will scent a large conservatory or sunroom during the long winter months.

CULTIVATION

Start the seeds in gentle heat 10–12 weeks before the last frost, and give the seedlings sufficient time to make strong, sturdy young plants before planting out when the soil and nights have warmed up, spacing them 30cm (12in) apart. They will then provide a good display the same summer.

Heliotrope will grow in any average garden soil, but will do better in one that is rich and well drained. Choose a sunny position, and water frequently to ensure that the soil never dries out.

Some of the modern hybrids have unfortunately lost a degree of their marvellous scent, but the most fragrant plants in the garden may be saved by propagating from autumn cuttings overwintered at a minimum teperature of 10°C (50°F). Training standard plants is relatively simple, but must start as soon as the cutting has rooted. Encourage the long stem by pinching out sideshoots as soon as they appear, until the plant has reached the desired height.

COTTAGE GARDEN VARIETIES

• *Heliotropium arborescens* Finest Mixed

A good mixture with flowers in a range of colours from lavender to purple. Height 60cm (24in).

• *Heliotropium arborescens* 'Marine'

A particularly good variety, with giant heads of deep-violet blue flowers produced all summer and a strong fragrance. Excellent for bedding and pots. Height 60cm (24in).

• *Heliotropium arborescens* 'Mini Marine'

A very fragrant heliotrope, with deep purple flower clusters 20–30cm (8–12in) across. It makes a compact, bushy plant and is a good houseplant for winter. Height 20–25cm (8–10in).

• *Heliotropium arborescens* 'Regale'

A very floriferous variety with darkest blue flowers, and a popular container plant. Height 60cm (24in).

Hesperis matronalis

Sweet rocket, damask violet or dames' violet belongs to the same family as stocks (*Matthiola*) and wallflowers (*Cheiranthus*) and produces large heads of single, chalky white, pale lilac or purple flowers all with a delicious, clove-like fragrance – one of the pleasures of an early summer evening. The toothed, elongated green leaves are rough to the touch.

The single sweet rockets, which are short-lived hardy perennials usually grown as biennials, have been grown in gardens since at least the early seventeenth century and are one of the traditional cottage garden plants, rarely in fact seen outside cottage gardens. They grow to 60–90cm (24–36in) high and flower from early summer through until the autumn. Once introduced to the garden they will self-seed with abandon. Butterflies adore them. They look fine in the wild garden and will often seed into old walls. A few cut flowers mixed with other summer blooms will scent an entire room.

CULTIVATION

Hesperis matronalis enjoys a sunny position, but is not in the least bit fussy about soil. Seed sown outside in the autumn will produce flowering plants in the following summer. Thin plants to 30cm (12in) apart.

HESPERIS MATRONALIS

IBERIS UMBELLATA DWARF FAIRY MIXED

Iberis

Iberis umbellata is the pretty hardy annual candytuft commonly seen in cottage gardens and sometimes referred to as 'globe candytuft'. It was introduced in Elizabethan times from Crete, appearing as 'Candy tufts' or 'tufts of Candie' – 'tufts' refers to the tufted habit of the plant, while 'Candy' or 'Candie' was the old Engish name for Crete. *Iberis* is derived from Iberia, the ancient name of Spain, where several species grow naturally.

Gerard, who called it 'Candie mustard', must have been one of the first to grow the plant and was obviously well pleased with it. Writing of his new find, he records that 'This plant groweth naturally in untoiled places and by high waie sides, in Crete or Candia, in Spaine and Italie, and such like hot regions, from which I received seede, by the liberalities of the Right Honourable Lord Edwarde Zouche at his return into England from those partes, with many other rare seeds for which I think myself much bounde unto his good Lordship'. The plants Gerard grew were 'sometimes blew, often purple, carnation or horseflesh, but seldom white'. The reaction of cottage gardeners today at seeing one of their most popular annuals described in a seed catalogue as having the colour of horseflesh might well be worth recording!

There are apparently no virtues given for candytuft by Gerard or any other herbalist of the seventeenth century; however, a common name used for the plant during the eighteenth century was 'sciatica weed', suggesting that it was probably used as a cure, or at least a treatment, for this ailment.

Candytuft has long been a favourite of cottage gardeners but, because it is one of those plants which even a child can grow, has always been regarded as unfashionable by the gardening elite, who condescendingly dismiss it as a simple plant for novices to grow in their first garden.

I. umbellata has tiny flowers in neat, flattened clusters 5cm (2in) across, borne on stems up to 30cm (12in) tall. They have little or no fragrance, but the colour range is wide, with many named varieties and mixtures available with flowers in pink, crimson, rose, red, lavender and white. The dark green leaves are narrow and lance-shaped. The plants can be used in an annual border, and are very effective for filling gaps left by spring-flowering bulbs in mixed beds. They are best suited to a brief, colourful display, although shearing them after the first blooms fade may encourage a second flush. They also make attractive pot plants that will flower during the winter in a heated greenhouse.

The 'rocket-flowered' or 'hyacinth-flowered' candytufts are strains of *I. amara*, and are frequently listed in catalogues as *I. coronaria*. These are the florists's candytuft, with fragrant white blooms up to 2.5cm (1in) across in dense, hyacinth-like clusters on stems which grow up to 60cm (24in) tall. These are dramatic plants for a border or cut-flower arrangements.

CULTIVATION

The annual candytufts resent disturbance in any shape or form, and seed should be sown *in situ* in early spring. Sow thinly, and then thin severely. They enjoy a position

in full sun in a not-too-rich soil, and should be kept well watered during periods of heat and drought. An autumn sowing will provide early flowers that will be followed by those of plants raised in spring.

COTTAGE GARDEN VARIETIES

• *Iberis amara* Giant Hyacinth-flowered 'Iceberg'
An excellent strain with large, hyacinth-like white blooms on strong stems. Delicately fragrant, and particularly good for cutting. Height 38–45cm (15–18in).

• *Iberis amara* 'Pinnacle'
A reselected form, with a blizzard of the purest white, fragrant flowers encircling the stem for 15cm (6in) or more – a noble annual. Height 38–45cm (15–18in).

• *Iberis umbellata* 'Cream Flash'
A variety with delicious creamy white flowers on compact plants. Excellent for toning down brighter colours in the border. Height 23–30cm (9–12in).

• *Iberis umbellata* Dwarf Fairy Mixed
A delightful miniature strain in an attractive range of pastel colours, ideal for edging. Height: 15cm (6in).

• *Iberis umbellata* Fantasia
A reselected mixture of this popular cottage garden annual with a good, bushy, uniform growing habit and a colour range which includes rose, pink, lavender and creamy white shades, bolstered by good proportions of cherry. Bold colour for the border. Height: 20cm (8in).

• *Iberis umbellata* Flash Mixed
A dwarf, compact strain in a particularly good mixture of colours, ranging from carmine-red, deep red and various shades of pink to lilac, purple and creamy white. Height: 23–30cm (9–12in).

Impatiens

Impatiens, often known as balsams, are popular plants for the greenhouse and garden. The name *Impatiens* is from the Latin, referring to the bursting seedpods, which if touched when ripe, immediately burst, scattering the seed everywhere. They also have the common name of touch-me-not for the same reason. Three main kinds of impatiens are grown in gardens: *Impatiens roylei, I. walleriana* and *I.* New Guinea hybrids.

Impatiens roylei (policeman's helmet, jumping Jack) is a handsome and attractive old-fashioned hardy annual introduced from the Himalayas in 1839. The

IMPATIENS ROYLEI

plant has red stems, lovely bright green foliage and bears a profusion of pendant, rose-pink or purple, helmet-shaped flowers in clusters from midsummer until early autumn. Children never tire of bursting the quaint seedpods which, when ripe, will explode and catapult the seeds a considerable distance at the slightest touch. This plant, reaching 1.2–2.5cm (4–8ft), is not suitable for a small garden as, given the right conditions, it will quickly become an invasive weed. The variety *I. roylei* 'White Queen' is a much sought-after pure white form.

Sow *I. roylei* in spring either in open ground when danger of frost has passed or in a cold frame. Seedlings will develop vigorous plants and should be thinned or planted out 30–38cm (12–15in) apart each way.

I. walleriana or busy lizzy is a tender perennial, originally from Tanzania and Mozambique, and usually treated as an annual in the garden. There are very few plants that can beat busy lizzies for brilliant summer to autumn colour in shady beds, borders, pots and containers. From a humble beginning there are now countless numbers of varieties ranging in height from 15–60cm (6–24in), forming mounded plants covered with 2.5–5cm (1–2in) wide, single or double flowers on short stems, in every colour except true blue and yellow. The dark green colouring of the broad, pointed leaves is a perfect foil for the blossoms.

Excellent for bedding or border, impatiens are also

quite beautiful in hanging baskets and containers because of their mounding habit.

CULTIVATION

Because *I. walleriana* and *I.* New Guinea hybrids are somewhat difficult to grow from seed, most gardeners prefer to choose and purchase plantlets from a nursery or garden centre. They should be transplanted out in a moist soil that is liberally laced with organic matter, and spaced 22–30cm (9–12in) apart. *I. walleriana* will grow taller when set close together.

If grown from seed, they need a minimum temperature of 24°C (75°F) to germinate. Impatiens seed is very small and because of this it is important not to sow too thickly. Press the seed gently on to the compost surface (which has been watered previously and allowed to drain thoroughly). Do not cover the seeds as they require light to germinate, a process which will take 15–20 days. Seeds may be started at any time of the year but should be sown indoors ten weeks before the last frost for garden use. Plants can also be propagated by stem cuttings.

COTTAGE GARDEN VARIETIES

• *Impatiens* 'Bellizzy Colourballs'
A new introduction with fully double blooms in a colour range including pink, scarlet, rose, salmon and white with a few bicolours for good measure. This is good for the garden and will also make a fine pot plant which, on a suitable windowsill, will bloom for months on end. Also use for hanging baskets and window boxes. Height 15–24cm (6–10in).

• *Impatiens* 'Expo Picotee'
This vigorous, compact plant has pale rosy pink flowers with deeper coral shades along the edges. Height 20cm (8in).

• *Impatiens* 'Mega Orange Star'
This compact plant with large 5cm (2in) or more, orange flowers, each with a geometric white star superimposed on top, will succeed outdoors in the border, hanging basket or container, whatever the weather. Height 20–24cm (8–10in).

• *Impatiens* New Guinea F1 hybrids
These are compact plants with glossy dark green, broad, pointed foliage covered with flowers 4cm (1½in) across in many shades of scarlet, rose, flame, cream and bicolours. Some have eye-catching variegated foliage. They are very useful for bedding and make superb pot specimens. They generally require more sun than the common impatiens. Height 20–24cm (8–10in).

• *Impatiens* 'Super Elfin Pearl'
The white flowers of this excellent hybrid F1 are blushed with gentle pink and have a dark rose eye. Height 24cm (10in).

IMPATIENS NEW GUINEA HYBRIDS

Ipomoea

Ipomoea, the 'morning glory', behaves and flowers in the same way as the convolvulus: in fact, the Greek *ipomoea* means 'like bindweed', a reference to the twining stems which bear large heart-shaped leaves, a perfect foil for the profusion of gorgeous trumpet flowers in rich purple, pink, blue or in white and 12cm (5in) or more in diameter.

There has always been some confusion regarding the naming of some of the species. Many in this genus were, and still continue to be, listed as *Convolvulus*, but gardeners should not assume that morning glories are liable to become a nuisance in the way of the more vigorous and invasive wildflower of the hedgerows.

Fleeting though the flowers are, few annuals surpass the morning glory for colour and quick growth. The flowers of older varieties last for just a few hours and generally open in either the morning or the evening, but new hybrids are more tolerant of bright light and heat and often stay open for most of the day.

Morning glories were said to have enchanted Spanish explorers in Mexico and the flowers made their way to Spanish monasteries, where monks adorned manuscripts with morning glory borders. The seeds were once fashioned into bracelets and necklaces, and the roots were pounded and used in medicine, even though all other parts of the plant are poisonous. (Interestingly, *Ipomoea batatas* is the popular sweet potato.) Certain species were used by the Aztecs in religious ceremonials for their hallucinogenic properties, and for this reason made headline news in the during the 1960s. The flower has a place in folklore, too: witches supposedly cast evil spells by wrapping the tendrils around a person nine times, and doing this three days before a full moon made the spell potent.

I. coerulea, syn. *Convolvulus major*, a native of tropical America, was the first ipomoea to be introduced and was described by John Goodyer in 1621: 'Those (flowers) that will open in the morninge making some small shewe overnight, onlie wound together and not of half their growthe, erlie in the morninge they appear in their full length, but ioyned close together with 5 corners, which after a short time open and are round like a little bell, like those of the white Bindweed, but of a delicate Azure or as it were a color of blew and redd mixed together, with five straight strakes or lines

IPOMOEA SEEDLING FROM A MIXTURE (top) and I. TRICOLOR 'HEAVENLY BLUE' (above)

on the inside, like redd darke crimson Velvet. This glorious Shew continueth but awhile, for towards night the same daie that they open, they beginne to vade, and fold themselves in together at the toppe and never open agaiane, and the next day fall quite away.'

Of more than 500 ipomoea species, probably the best-known and the most widely grown variety is *I. tricolor* 'Heavenly Blue'. The large blue flowers which are produced each day mirror the morning sky and have just a touch of white and gold at their centres.

I. alba, the moonflower, climbs to 3–6m (10–20ft) and has deliciously scented, magnificent pure white flowers, 15cm (6in) long and wide, with a faint touch of light green along the floral folds. Moonflowers bloom in early evening, and to see them gradually unfurl as the sun goes down is like watching a slow-motion natural history film. They quickly fold at the first touch of dawn and, but for their beauty, would probably have been named the 'Dracula flower'! *I. alba* will flower in eight weeks from seed, and the heart-shaped leaves, 10–12cm (4–5in) long, and climbing tendrils are excellent for quick screening on an arbour, fence or trellis. The flowers can be cut for an evening table arrangement.

I. nil , syn. *I. imperialis*, has been grown in gardens since the seventeenth century. It has showy flowers 10cm (4in) across in shades of purple, red, blue, pink and white – one of the most famous varieties is 'Scarlet O'Hara', which has very large, bright scarlet flowers and splashes of white on the leaves. The large-flowered Imperial Japanese strains belong to this species. In Japan they are widely grown in pots and continually pruned above the third set of leaves, eventually producing spectacular flowers. *I. nil* will easily climb to 3m (10ft).

I. quamoclit is the 'Cyprus vine' or 'China creeper', a tender annual climber with beautiful, divided leaves, so finely cut that they look like feathers and render the plant attractive even when not in flower. The profusion of pretty but small, scarlet tubular flowers are borne from midsummer to early autumn, but the plant really needs to be grown in a particularly warm, well-drained situation in full sun or in the greenhouse.

CULTIVATION

To get a head start, sow two or three seeds of morning glories in peat pots under glass four to six weeks before the last frost. Before sowing, scarify the hard seed coat with sandpaper and then soak the seeds overnight in tepid water. When the seedlings are 5cm (2in) tall, thin to the strongest and insert a small stake in each pot for it to climb. Place the young plants in a cold frame for a week before planting out, pot and all.

If seeds are to be sown outside, wait until late spring – morning glories will refuse to germinate until the soil temperature warms to 10°C (50°F). Choose a site in full sun, with some shade during the hottest part of the day. Make little mounds of prepared soil about 2cm (¾in) deep and 30cm (12in) apart, and sow two or three seeds in each mound.

Morning glories prefer a moist, well-drained soil, but are tolerant of drought and will grow in the poorest of soils. As the plants grow only 25–30cm (10–12in) wide, it is advisable to set several plants in a row, 30cm (12in) apart, to provide a good show. Deadhead through the summer for a continuous display and avoid overwatering or overfeeding, as this will result in lush foliage but few flowers.

COTTAGE GARDEN VARIETIES

• *Ipomoea hirsuta* 'Mini-Sky-Blue'

A recent introduction, with glorious white-throated, azure-blue blooms, which can be grown in the conservatory or in a warm, sheltered position in the garden. Height 2–2.5m (6–8ft).

• *Ipomoea imperialis* 'Chocolate'

A unique variety, with huge flowers in an unusual and appealing soft shade of chocolate-brown. Height 2.5–3m (8–10ft).

• *Ipomoea nil* Early Call Mixed

An old strain of mixed colours ranging from pink to dark purple. Ideal for cool or short summers, as it is quick and early to flower. Height 2.5–3m (8–10ft).

• *Ipomoea tricolor* 'Pearly Gates', syn. *I. tricolor* 'White Magic'

This variety has large, lustrous white flowers with a creamy throat. Height 2.5–3m (8–10ft).

• *Ipomoea tricolor* 'Super Garland'

A mixture of large-flowered varieties in shades of blue, violet, pink, red and white. Height 2.5–3m (8–10ft).

Kochia scoparia var. *trichophylla*

Kochia scoparia var. *trichophylla*, also known as burning bush or summer cypress, is a popular half-hardy summer bedding plant with feathery, soft green foliage forming a beautiful dense, dome-shaped bush. A hedge of it can reach 90cm (36in) high and may be quite stunning, as the pale green foliage is cool and fresh-looking on the hottest summer day and gradually turns brilliant red at the end of the season. The foliage is also useful in flower arranging.

CULTIVATION

Soak seeds for 24 hours before sowing. Seeds will germinate, uncovered, in 10–15 days at 10°C (50°F). Plant out after all danger of frost has passed in average, well-drained soil and space out 60cm (24in) apart (or 20cm/8in for a hedge). Growth is slow to start with, but increases with the onset of warm weather.

COTTAGE GARDEN VARIETIES

• *Kochia scoparia* var. *trichophylla* 'Acapulco Silver'

Has light green leaves dusted with silver and is particularly attractive. Height 90cm (36in).

Lathyrus odoratus

Well known and loved as the sweet pea, *Lathyrus odoratus* is, as its common name suggests, strongly scented and unquestionably the most prized of all hardy cottage garden annuals. Its airy blossom is made up of a large top petal (banner or standard), two narrow side petals (wings) and two lower petals (keel); they look like old-fashioned sun bonnets. With pea-like tendrils, the plants grow to 1.5m (5ft) tall.

A native of southern Europe, the sweet pea was unknown in British gardens until the first year of the eighteenth century. It blossomed that year in the garden of a Dr Robert Uvedale, a schoolmaster who had received the seed a year earlier from Father Franciscus Cupani, a Sicilian monk, who had first recorded and published its description in his *Hortus Catholicus* of 1697. This original sweet pea was a rather weedy-looking plant, bearing tiny maroon flowers with a deep purple standard. Dr Uvedale, a keen gardener and 'a curious collector and introducer of many rare exotics', was, however, captivated by the scent, and the precious seeds were eagerly shared among gardening friends.

Some 40 years or so after its introduction, two sports appeared: a white variety and a red-and-white bicolor known as 'Painted Lady'. By the end of the eighteenth century seeds were available for sale, and nurseryman Thomas Fairchild recommended them highly to Londoners in his *City Gardiner* of 1772, describing the scent as 'somewhat like Honey and a little tending to the Orange-flower Smell' and noting that 'The sweet-scented Pea makes a beautiful Plant, having Spikes of Flowers of a red and blue Colour'. At the beginning of the nineteenth century there were five colours, and six by 1837 – nothing to compare with the brilliance and size of sweet peas grown today, but all still possessing the same strong, sweet fragrance which so enthralled Dr Uvedale. Ladies at the time were cautioned against admitting sweet peas into their chambers lest the scent should be overpowering.

From these original plants, the real pioneer of the modern sweet pea, Henry Eckford, began to specialize in the flower in 1870. He eliminated the plant's weak points and improved the size, texture and colour of the blooms, but retained the marvellous scent. His sweet peas became known as the 'grandifloras', and of the 264 varieties exhibited at the great Bicentenary Sweet Pea Exhibition in 1900, 115 were of his raising. (As we shall see, however, Eckford's triumph was to be short lived.) In a speech at the exhibition, the Rev W.T. Hutchins spoke of the universal appeal of the sweet pea: 'The sweet pea has a keel that was meant to seek all shores; it has wings that were meant to fly across all continents; it has a standard which is friendly to all nations; and it has a fragrance like the universal gospel, yea, a sweet prophecy of welcome everywhere that has been abundantly fulfilled.'

'The Honourable Mrs Collier', 'Miss Willmott', 'Mrs Walter Wright', 'Henry Eckford', 'Queen Alexandra', 'King Edward VII' – the names recall a time when sweet peas were at the height of their popularity. The flower was a favourite with Queen Alexandra, and in its season no Edwardian dinner table or wedding bouquet would be complete without them. At provincial flower shows the sweet pea entries invariably stole the show and took the prizes; to this day a great deal of energy is expended on growing blooms for exhibition purposes and they still draw the crowds.

The National Sweet Pea Society was founded in Britain in 1901 and it was in this year that Silas Cole, gardener to the Earl of Spencer at Althorp Park, caused something of a sensation when he introduced the variety 'Lady Spencer', the first of the renowned Spencer varieties with their unusual frilled or waved petals, and a new race of sweet pea was born. This variety was, in fact, a sport from Eckford's pink 'Prima Donna', and the break occurred in three different nurseries in the same year.

The arrival of the waved sweet peas was responsible for the rapid decline in the popularity of the grandifloras, which by 1914 had all but disappeared from the gardening scene. But for the work of one or two dedicated enthusiasts, the grandifloras would probably have become extinct – thanks to them, approximately 20 named varieties of grandifloras survive today. Although the flowers are smaller than those of the modern varieties, the colours are more intense and glowing, they are borne in great profusion and the blooms have a strong, heady scent which is sadly missing from the Spencer types and modern varieties.

Sweet peas can be grown against a trellis or fence, or on rough tripods of bean sticks in a border. A hedge of mixed colours in the cutting or kitchen garden will make a delightful feature, and in addition will provide a constant supply of cut flowers for the house. Once flowering starts, sweet peas can be picked every day until autumn, provided, of course, that they are not allowed to set seed.

Although perennial *Lathyrus latifolius* (Everlasting pea) can be grown as an annual. It produces pinky-purple flowers in sprays on stiff stems that are ideal for cutting; there is also a white-flowered form, *L. latifolius* 'Albus'. Both are ideal for growing on wigwams or trellis. Although a relative of the sweet pea, the everlasting pea unfortunately has no scent. Height 2.5–3m (8–10ft).

CULTIVATION

Old-fashioned sweet peas need an open, sunny position and will not tolerate any degree of shade. They are as easy to grow as garden peas, and satisfying results may be achieved by little more than the sow-and-forget technique. What they must have, however, is ample water.

Soak the seeds overnight in warm water before planting and sow them outdoors in the autumn (October 10th in Britain, according cottage gardening ancients).

Sown under glass in late winter, *Lathyrus latifolius* will flower in the first year. Pre-treatments, such as soaking and chipping, are unnecessary for this perennial and may well damage the seed. Plant out in the spring and space 30cm (12in) apart.

COTTAGE GARDEN VARIETIES

• *Lathyrus odoratus* 'Bushby'
It is very difficult to find out much about the background or history of this particular variety. Believed to have originated in Australia and to figure 'Painted Lady' in its pedigree, the two-toned, bright pink flowers have been compared to a flight of butterflies. Deliciously fragrant, 'Bushby' has a long flowering season and can be cut for the house right up until the first frosts. Height 1–1.2m (3–4ft).

• *Lathyrus odoratus* 'Cupani'
This is the variety, cultivar, garden escapee or wild form that was introduced by the Sicilian monk, Father Cupani, in 1699. A compact, robust plant, which has a strong, heady scent and the most beautiful flowers with mauve wings and a maroon standard. The seed is very scarce, but can still be found. Height 1.2m (4ft).

MIXED SWEET PEAS

• *Lathyrus odoratus* 'Painted Lady'
A very old variety in cultivation since the early eighteenth century. The plant is bushy and has highly scented, red-and-white bicoloured flowers, two to a stem. Height 90–120cm (36–48in).

• *Lathyrus odoratus* 'Pink Cupid'
A dwarf, pink-and-white bicoloured variety, which occurred as a sport in the USA in 1895. It was very highly valued, and the original stock of about 1,000 seeds was sold to a leading seed company for a huge sum. This lovely plant is excellent for the front of the border and makes a charming pot plant. Height 15cm (6in).

• *Lathyrus odoratus* Old-fashioned Sweet Peas Mixed
This is a mixture of varieties of the old-fashioned sweet peas which were so popular at the turn of the century. It is not a field-grown mixture, but a combination of several varieties such as 'Mrs Collier', 'Countess Cadogan', 'Cheshire Dark Blue', 'Sicilian Fuchsia' and 'Painted Lady', all grown separately.

• *Lathyrus odoratus* 'Original'
This variety was collected in various places in South America and Europe and is said to resemble the original species. In the nineteenth century it was known as 'Purple Invincible' and is a maroon-and-blue bicolour (the best forms having truly blue wings) with a heavy scent. 'Original' grows slightly taller than 'Painted Lady' and has three flowers to a stem. Height 1.5m (5ft).

Lavatera trimestris

Named in honour of two Swiss plantsmen, the Lavater brothers of Linnaeus' generation, *Lavatera trimestris*, the annual, or tree, mallow, is a hardy old cottage garden favourite. The 90cm (36in) bushy plants, with maple-like leaves, often turning bronze in cool weather, are generously covered with numerous, 10cm (4in) hollyhock-like flowers from midsummer until cut down by the frosts. The flowers have a satin sheen and may be warm rose or glistening pure white.

Because of their habit, looking more like shrubs than annuals, these sturdy, tall-growing plants are truly effective when massed toward the back of a border and rarely need staking. Try them as a fast-growing summer hedge; as cut flowers they are lovely but sadly short-lived.

CULTIVATION

They do well when sown in the autumn where they are to flower and thinned to 60cm (24in) apart. Seedlings may be raised in gentle heat in the spring, but have a very bad habit of damping off when transferred from the seedbed to pots or boxes. Failing an autumn sowing, sow where the plants are to flower, in early spring. Full sun suits them best.

COTTAGE GARDEN VARIETIES

• *Lavatera trimestris* 'Mont Blanc'
A gorgeous mallow with large, pure white flowers. Height 60cm (24in).

• *Lavatera trimestris* 'Ruby Regis'
A fine variety with masses of large, ruby-cerise-pink flowers. Height 60cm (24in).
• *Lavatera trimestris* 'Silver Cup'
A superb, modern (and prize-winning) variety forming sturdy, much-branched plants, completely smothered in flowers in a beautiful shade of bright glowing pink. Height 60–90cm (24–36in).

Limnanthes douglasii

The poached-egg plant, or custard and cream, is a quick-growing hardy annual with a delightful combination of silver and gold saucer-shaped flowers that are delicately scented and beloved of bees. The plant, growing to 15cm (6in) tall, is worth having for its foliage alone, which is neat and fringed in a light, yellowish shade of green, but despite the fact that it is one of the easiest and most free-flowering annuals in cultivation it is rarely seen outside cottage gardens. Every year it will produce a thick carpet of seedlings which will ensure that, once introduced to the garden, it is there to stay.

CULTIVATION

Sowings should be made in the open ground both in the autumn, to flower in early summer the following year, and again in early spring, to flower in midsummer the same year. Thin plants to 10–15cm (4–6in) apart. The poached-egg plant thrives in a moist situation.

LAVATERA TRIMESTRIS (left) and LIMNANTHES DOUGLASII (above)

Limonium sinuatum

Statice, one of the best of the everlasting flowers, is a very popular half-hardy annual for bringing an abundance of colour to the border.

The tiny, funnel-shaped blooms are borne in clusters on stiff stems 45cm (18in) tall. Colours range from white, yellow and apricot to red, deep blue, sky blue and purple, with deeply lobed leaves forming a rosette at the base of the plant. Sea lavenders as they are sometimes known, are ideal in floral arrangements either fresh or dried. These colourful plants are ideal in the cottage garden border and also make an attractive temporary hedge.

CULTIVATION

Seeds germinate in 14–21 days at 24–27°C (75–81°F). Plant out after all danger of frost has passed in well-drained soil in full sun. The plants should be thinned to 30–45cm (12–18in) apart. Fertilize at planting time and water deeply, but infrequently. Statice will tolerate drought, heat, and salt spray.

LIMONIUM SINUATUM

COTTAGE GARDEN VARIETIES

The following are a few of the separate colours available from seed merchants:
• *Limonium sinuatum* 'American Beauty'
Rosy red. Height 50cm (20in).
• *Limonium sinuatum* 'Gold Coast'
A rich yellow. Height 50cm (20in).
• *Limonium sinuatum* 'Iceberg'
White flowers. Height 50cm (20in).

• *Limonium sinuatum* 'Lavender'
A charming strain with lovely shades of lavender. Height 50cm (20in).
• *Limonium sinuatum* 'Rose Light'
Carmine-rose flowers. Height 50cm (20in).
• *Limonium sinuatum* Soft Pastel Mixed
A fine strain producing large, long-stemmed flowers in a quite delightful mixture of soft pastel shades. Height 90cm (36in).

Lobelia erinus

Lobelia erinus has to be one of the most popular plants for containers and window boxes from which its richly coloured flowers can cascade in summer and into autumn. Its compact, spreading habit also makes it useful for groundcover, edging and in rock gardens. It is a perennial, but is far too tender to survive cold winters, although a few will sometimes manage to live over two seasons in milder areas.

Lobelias have small, narrow, green or bronze leaves which grow thickly on well-branched stems, and small bright blue, two-lipped flowers, often with contrasting white or yellow centres. A choice of cultivars is available with red, white or lilac flowers, some with trailing stems. The trailing varieties will reach 30–45cm (12–18in) by the end of the summer; the mounding compact varieties rarely grow more than 15cm (6in) high.

CULTIVATION

As the plants take two months from seed to planting-out size, it is much easier to buy seedlings from a nursery. For those who insist on growing from seed, lobelia seed will germinate, uncovered, in 20 days at 21°C (70°F). Plant them 15cm (6in) apart – they will quickly join together. Pinch to promote bushiness. Provide plenty of water during dry periods, and when grown in containers or hanging baskets. Lobelias like good, moist soil in full sun or partial shade. After the first flowers begin to fade, cut back by half to prolong flowering.

COTTAGE GARDEN VARIETIES

• *Lobelia erinus* 'Crystal Palace'
A superb variety with striking deep cobalt-blue flowers and dark bronze foliage. Height 13cm (5in).

• *Lobelia erinus* 'Riviera Lilac'
A new strain flowering about two weeks earlier than standard varieties, with lovely lilac flowers on vigorous bushy plants. Height 13cm (5in).
• *Lobelia erinus* 'Rosamond'
Carmine-red flowers, with white eyes, and dark green foliage. Height 10cm (4in).
• *Lobelia erinus* 'Sapphire'
This delightful trailing lobelia has myriad deep blue, white-eyed flowers all summer and is excellent for hanging baskets, rockeries, window boxes and the like. Trails 30–45cm (12–18in).
• *Lobelia erinus* 'White Lady'
White flowers and light green foliage. Height 10cm (4in).

Lobularia maritimum

Sweet alyssum has long been the number one favourite for edging flower borders, and there will be few gardeners who are unacquainted with this white-flowered honey-scented plant, so often massed along pathways near the front door, tumbling over rocks in a rock garden or planted in pots on the patio. Its minute, thin, narrow, needle-like foliage is almost entirely hidden by the freely produced flowers.

There are numerous varieties of this hardy annual available today with domed clusters of tiny flowers in shades of rose, lavender or magenta. Like their white counterpart, these are all persistent self seeders and will always find places in the garden to improve. Flowering from midsummer until the frosts, the plant can be sheared to stimulate new growth and a succession of bloom. In mild, sheltered areas, it is rarely out of bloom.

CULTIVATION

Sow seeds *in situ* in average, well-drained soil, fertilized before planting, in full sun, as soon as the ground can be worked. Though so small, the plants spread freely, and should be thinned 15cm (6in) apart. Seeds are invariably listed under 'Alyssum' in seed catalogues.

COTTAGE GARDEN VARIETIES

• *Lobularia maritimum* 'Carpet of Snow'
This excellent white-flowered variety is probably the best known of all, forming a flat mass of white blooms. Height 8–10cm (3–4in).

MIXED LOBELIAS (top) and
LOBULARIA MARITIMUM WITH PETUNIAS

• *Lobularia maritimum* 'Little Dorrit'
An upright little plant with tiny white flowers held aloft. Height 15cm (6in).
• *Lobularia maritimum* 'Rosie Oday'
A very popular variety with heads of scented pink flowers. Height 10cm (4in).
• *Lobularia maritimum* 'Royal Carpet'
As the name would suggest, this alyssum produces mats of regal purple flowers. Height to 7cm (3in).
• *Lobularia maritimum* 'Wonderland Rose'
The deep rose-pink flowers of this variety look lovely with one of the white versions. Height 15cm (6in).

Lunaria annua

Lunaria annua, syn. *L. biennis*, has an astonishing range of vernacular names including 'honesty', 'satin flower' and 'moonwort', surely three of the most attractive common names given to any plant. The four-petalled, stock-like purple flowers are produced in branching sprays and give way to large, flat, oval seedpods which shed their outer coverings to reveal attractive silvery discs, much prized for flower arranging when dried. The genus name *Lunaria* is from the Latin *luna*, meaning moon, and refers to the shape of the seedpods.

Honesty is one of those old-fashioned biennials that are rather difficult to lose once introduced to a garden. The plant seeds freely, although it is not difficult to control, as the seedlings are easily identified and can simply be removed or transplanted away from where they are not wanted.

By the time Gerard wrote his *Herball* in 1597 the plant had already acquired a number of common names, which would suggest that it had been in cultivation in Britain long before 1570, when it was said by William Aiton, in his *Hortus Kewensis* (1789), to have been introduced from Germany. Among the many names mentioned by Gerard, 'lunarie', 'white satin' or 'sattin-flower', 'pennieflower', 'silverplate', 'prick-song-woort', 'Judas pence', 'shillings', 'two-pennies-in-a-purse' and 'money-in-both-pockets' all refer to the unusual seedpods. He notes that 'The stalks are loden with many flowers of a purple colour, which being fallen, the seede cometh foorth conteined in a flat thinne cod, with sharp point or pricke at one end, in fashion of the moone, and somewhat blackish. This cod is com-posed of three filmes or skins, whereof the two outer-most are of an over worne ashe colour, and the inner-most, or that in the middle whereon the seed doth hand or cleave, is thin and cleere shining, like a shred or white satten newly cut from the peece.'

The plant was much used by witches and warlocks in spells, incantations, charms, enchantment and bewitchments during the dark ages. Via the Doctrine of Signatures, which holds that cures may be effected by plants bearing some resemblance to the affected part of its ailment, it was thought to be effective in treating cases of lunacy. According to the Elizabethan poet, Michael Drayton, who describes one such experiment, the process was a rather complex business:

> Then sprinkles she the juice of Rue
> With nine drops of the midnight dew,
> From Lunarie distilling.

Because of the transparency of the pods which hold the seeds, the plant acquired the popular common name of 'honesty', and it has long been thought that wherever the plant grows well, the householder is exceptionally endowed with that characteristic.

Although little attention is paid to the flowers of honesty, they are profusely produced and last for two to three weeks. The plants flower from early to late spring and range from pure white through red to deep purples. The leaves are ovate and toothed; in *L. a.* 'Variegata' they are strikingly margined with creamy white. Honesty has a rather curious habit which can be puzzling at first to the uninitiated: flowers which start off rose-pink or mauve-purple will suddenly appear all white one year and then, by some strange trick of genetics, the next year will be pink or purple again.

The seedpods were used for winter decoration as early as the mid-eighteenth century, and plants are still grown in gardens today for the sole purpose of drying and 'skinning' for dried-flower arrangements.

CULTIVATION

Honesty will grow well in any good soil in sun or partial shade, the seed being sown *in situ* in late summer to produce flowering plants the following spring.

The pods should be gathered before being discoloured by too much rain; once the outer layers of the seedpod are removed the familiar translucent, silvery

SEEDPODS OF LUNARIA ANNUA

lining will be revealed. Dried honesty seedpods are frequently seen for sale in a range of colours. If they are picked green, the pods when peeled will also be green; green stems can be placed in solutions of food dye and, when dried, the seedpods will be coloured.

COTTAGE GARDEN VARIETIES

LUNARIA ANNUA

• *Lunaria annua alba*
This is the much sought-after white-flowered form of honesty, known as the 'white money plant'. Height 75cm (30in).
• *Lunaria annua* 'Alba Variegata'
This is the attractive variegated form with white flowers, which comes true from seed. Height 75cm (30in).

• *Lunaria annua* 'Atro-coccinea'
A delightful crimson-flowered form which is always much admired. Height 75cm (30in).
• *Lunaria annua* 'Munstead Purple'
A fragrant variety with beautiful rich purple flowers and purple seedpods. Height 75cm (30in).

Matthiola incana

Matthiola, or the stock, was known in Elizabethan times as stock-gilliflower, because the spicy fragrance of its flowers was similar to that of the gilloflower (variously spelt), or carnation. Double- and single-flowered stocks were available during the sixteenth and seventeenth century in white, purple, red or striped. The double-flowered plants were much admired at the time and eagerly sought-after. At the time gardeners and botanists happily shared the secrets for successfully producing doubles but much of the advice would, today, be taken with a pinch of salt.

Popular cottage garden plants, stocks are easily grown. They are divided into two broad groups: night-scented stocks (*M. bicornis*) and Brompton stocks (*M. incana*), of which the variety *M. incana* var. *annua* forms the strain known as ten-week or intermediate stock.

The four-petalled lavender and white flowers of the 30cm (12in) high, night-scented stock fold up by day, unfurling only at dusk to release their exquisite perfume

on the warm night air in summer. Sow seeds of this hardy annual in random batches in various parts of the garden, not forgetting outside the bedroom window.

M. incana has long been popular both for bedding and for providing cut flowers. The woolly grey-leaved plant is usually treated as an annual or biennial, although some strains can, in fact, be reasonably perennial. They can also be easily propagated from cuttings although plants raised in this way are usually weaker than those raised from seed. These old-fashioned stocks, growing 7–10cm (18–24in) high, produce heavy spikes of clove-scented white, pink, rose or lavender flowers.

MATTHIOLA INCANA

M. incana var. *annua*, or ten-week stock, is an annual strain, bred by nineteenth-century weavers in northern France where each village grew only one colour or variety of which they were justly proud. Seed of ten-week stocks sown in gentle heat in early spring will flower in ten weeks. The flowers may be either single or double in crimson, pink, lavender, lilac and white. The plant grows approximately 38cm (15in) high and its leaves are long, narrow and grey-green.

CULTIVATION

Seeds of *M. incana* and *M. incana* var. *annua* stocks germinate in 14–18 days at 18–21°C (64–75°F). Do not cover as they need light for germination. Plant out in early summer in beds and borders, preferably near pathways or windows, where their spicy cinnamon and clove scent can be fully appreciated. Space the plants 22–30cm (9–12in) apart. Choose a site in full sun in a moist, moderately rich soil, and water regularly throughout the growing and flowering period.

Some seedlings of ten-week stocks will have dark green leaves, while others are a much lighter green or have a notched leaf. Transplant the latter if you require doubles. The singles that will invariably sneak through, however, are just as strongly scented.

COTTAGE GARDEN VARIETIES

• *Matthiola incana* Dwarf Ten Week Mixed
This bright, sweetly scented mixture with plenty of doubles is excellent for tubs and containers. Height 30cm (12in).
• *Matthiola incana* 'Purple Lady'
This named variety has double, purple flowers. Height 38cm (15in).
• *Matthiola incana* 'White Lady'
A lovely clear-white variety. Height 38cm (15in).
• *Matthiola incana* Tysomic Giant Imperial Mixed
A superb strain with branching plants in a wide range of brilliant colours such as fiery red and canary-yellow with a high number of doubles. The plants can be in bloom in as little as seven weeks from sowing. Height 45cm (18in).

Mimulus

Mimulus, or the monkey flower, is one of the few annual flowers which will do well in shade. The showy, double-lipped flowers with two lobes on the upper lip and three on the lower, come in bright colours that are spotted and blotched in such a way that they are jokingly thought to resemble a smiling monkey face. The succulent, often sticky, serrated leaves which attach to the stems in pairs, are light to medium green.

Tender perennials, grown as half-hardy annuals, monkey flowers form neat, compact mounds, seldom growing more than 30cm (12in) high and, with a long summer flowering period, are ideal in beds, borders and hanging baskets. They thrive in moist soil, even boggy conditions with occasional flooding, and are perfect by a stream or garden pond. They will also bloom beautifully in dappled shade.

CULTIVATION

Monkey flowers can be started from cuttings, which root easily in sand, or purchase plants from your local nursery. Seeds germinate in 5–7 days at 16–21°C (61–70°F) but as the seedlings require 13 hours of light a day to grow, they will need to be started under fluorescent lights. Plant out 15cm (6in) apart in mid-spring in rich, moist, well-drained soil. Feed them with a slow-release fertilizer at planting time and apply a mulch to keep the soil cool and moist. Cut back after the first flush of flowers to promote bushiness and continued flowering.

COTTAGE GARDEN VARIETIES

• *Mimulus* Calypso Hybrids
The Calypso strain has beautiful, early, solid and bicolour blooms of gold, wine and fire-red. Height 30–40cm (12–16in).
• *Mimulus* 'Malibu'
A compact and prostrate variety that is outstanding for bedding, hanging baskets and pots. The flowers come in cream, golden-orange, red and burgundy. Height 15cm (6in).
• *Mimulus* Mystic Hybrids
A lovely strain with solid-coloured blooms in orange, rose and yellow, on compact, spreading plants. Height 20–30cm (8–12in).
• *Mimulus* 'Viva'
Blooming in little more than seven weeks from sowing the seed, 'Viva' produces large, bright and cheerful yellow flowers with large red blotches, on compact plants over a very long period. Height 20–30cm (8–12in).

MIMULUS 'VIVA'

Mirabilis jalapa

Mirabilis jalapa is a tuberous-rooted tender perennial from tropical South America, which is usually grown as a half-hardy annual. A curious and beautiful plant, it is rarely seen in gardens today. The name means 'to be admired' or 'to be wondered at', hence its old name of *Admirabilis*, shortened by Linnaeus to *Mirabilis*. Clusius gave the plant its species name in the mistaken belief that the drug jalap was obtained from the roots.

Seeds of *M. jalapa* were brought from Peru to Spain in the latter half of the sixteenth century, and by the time Gerard wrote his *Herball* in 1597 he had already been growing it in his garden for many years. While other gardeners dubbed it 'marvel of Peru', Gerard went a step further, claiming that it should instead be considered the 'marvel of the world'.

It is hardly surprising that such a fuss was made over this particular flower, as the plants did have a characteristic that appeared to be miraculous – flowers of completely different colours bloomed on a single plant, some of them, moreover, decorated with distinctive stripes. 'This marvellous variety', wrote Gerard, 'doth not without cause bring admiration to all that observe it. For if the floures be gathered and reserved in severall papers, and compared with those floures that will spring and flourish the next day, you shall easily perceive that one is not like another in colour, though you shall compare one hundred which floure one day, and another hundred which you gather the next day, and so from day to day during the time of their flouring.'

Parkinson noted that he often observed that 'one side of the plant will give fairer varieties than another, which is most commonly the Eastern, and the more temperate and shadowie side'. The flowers' habit of opening late in the afternoon on sunny days and closing again when the warmth of the sun strikes them the following morning gained for the plant the further popular name of 'four o'clock flower'. The French call it *belle de nuit* – night beauty. In a summer with overcast skies, however, the flowers will often remain open during much of the day, a cheering sight for the cottage gardener on a dull day. This peculiarity can be exploited delightfully if the plants are grown with *Portulaca grandiflora*, the 'sun plant', a showy plant with large flowers in a very wide range of brilliant colours, which open as soon as they are touched by the morning sun, but are reluctant to open in dull weather and always close at dusk. Between them, the two will provide open blooms 24 hours a day, in day and night shifts!

Marvel of Peru makes a bushy plant 90cm (36in) tall, bearing a profusion of fragrant, funnel-shaped flowers, 5cm (2in) long, in bright red, crimson, purple, pink, rose, lilac or yellow, sometimes striped and sometimes mottled, for most of the summer. Grown for its flowers and evening fragrance, the plant itself is not particularly attractive and is best planted behind others in the middle of a border.

CULTIVATION

A position in full sun and a well-drained soil are essential. Mirabilis will tolerate a poor soil and summer heat and, surprisingly for a tropical plant, it will also do well in cool summers.

Although perennial and producing long, thick black tuberous roots, these tubers rarely survive the winter in frost-prone areas unless lifted in the autumn and stored in the same way as dahlia roots. Gerard would dig up the tubers and store them in a butter fer-

MIRABILIS JALAPA

kin filled with river sand, leaving it to stand in a corner of the house where it 'never receiveth moisture untill all risk of frost had passed'.

While storing the tubers will undoubtedly produce bigger plants and earlier blooms, this can only be achieved successfully for one season, since growth of the root in the second year makes it too unwieldy for storing. Far better to treat them as annuals and raise plants from seed sown under glass in early spring, grown in small pots for planting out in early summer 30cm (12in) apart.

Moluccella laevis

Moluccella laevis, called bells of Ireland, is a half-hardy native to western Asia; the names Molucca balm and Moluccella were given to the plant mistakenly, for at one time it was thought to be a native of the Molucca Islands. Neither, it would seem, has the plant any connection with Ireland, other than being in the favourite colour of the Irish.

Bells of Ireland form dramatic green spires, to 90cm (36in) tall, and are just the sort of curiosity you would expect to find in a cottage garden. Tiny, white or pinkish fragrant flowers are encased in enormous apple-green bells or calyxes that line the stem.

The plants look fine at the back of the border and combine well with sky-blue, pink and lemon-yellow plants. In recent years they have become a favourite subject among flower arrangers and are no longer relegated to the wild garden. They are perfect for both fresh and dried arrangements; simply pull off the small leaves that grow between the bracts, exposing their bell shape.

CULTIVATION

The hardest part of growing bells of Ireland is germinating the seed. They are best chilled for five days in the refrigerator then soaked overnight in lukewarm water to soften and remove the hard seed coat. As they are tap-rooted and will not transplant easily, it is best to sow seed in individual 7cm (3in) peat pots at 16°C (61°F) six weeks before the last frost. Do not cover the seed as they need light to germinate. Plant out in the garden after frost danger has passed and space the plants 30cm (12in) apart. The plant is slow-growing and flowers in late summer.

MOLUCCELLA LAEVIS

Myosotis

The misty, pale blue flowers of *Myosotis*, commonly known as the 'forget-me-not', are a traditional feature of the cottage garden in late spring, and this old-fash-ioned favourite is as popular today as it ever was.

Forget-me-nots have long been associated with true love and, as every gardener who has ever tried to get rid of them will appreciate, constancy. They should be exchanged by friends each leap year on 29 February, or presented to anyone making a journey on that day.

One version of the origin of the plant's popular name appears in a rather touching German legend. A knight and his lady, strolling by the Danube, spied a clump of blue flowers drifting by. The knight, forget-ting the weight of his armour, endeavoured to gather the riverside flowers for his lady and, falling in, cried as he was swept away by the stream, 'Forget me not!'

And the lady fair of the knight so true,
Aye remembered his hapless lot:
And she cherished the flower of brilliant hue,
And braided her hair with the blosoms blue,
And she called it 'Forget-me-not'.

MYOSOTIS ALPESTRIS VICTORIA STRAIN 'ALBA'

Gerard mentioned three species of myosotis in his *Herball*, but these go almost unnoticed, grouped as they are with other plants under the old name of 'scorpion-grass' – the recurving flower stem of the forget-me-not was thought to resemble a scorpion's tail and was expected to cure the scorpion's sting. Rarely, one would assume, was this put to the test in Gerard's homeland!

The many garden forms of forget-me-not come mostly from *Myosotis alpestris*, the alpine forget-me-not, and are best treated as hardy annuals. The species makes dense carpets of gentian-blue flowers with a clear yellow eye that are deliciously fragrant in the evening. As it enjoys a well-drained, gritty soil, it will thrive on the rock garden.

Garden forget-me-nots grow 15–20cm (6–8in) tall and will spread to 25cm (10in) across. *Myosotis* is the Greek equivalent for 'mouse ear', a reference to the soft, hairy leaves. The flowers are tiny but profusely borne, and usually pale or rich blue, although varieties are available with pink or white flowers. The hunt is still on for the striped or variegated sorts which were still being grown at the end of the nineteenth century, but sadly they seem to have disappeared.

Forget-me-nots make an attractive backcloth for spring-flowering tulips and are perfect planted with daffodils, filling every space with a delightful blue haze. A recently introduced brown-leaved forget-me-not with white flowers, *M. raikura*, is ideal for the rock gar-den or troughs.

CULTIVATION

Forget-me-nots will grow freely in most garden soils. They do best, however, in a moist soil in light shade, and invariably produce a finer display from an autumn than a spring sowing. Self seeding can be a bit of a prob-lem, and the plants do occasionally suffer from mildew if under stress, usually through dryness at the roots.

Propagation could not be easier. When the flowers are over, pull up the plants and lay them down in a shady place. The seeds will drop and germinate to give hundreds, if not thousands, of new plants which can be thinned to 15cm (6in) apart and/or transplanted to other parts of the garden.

COTTAGE GARDEN VARIETIES

• *Myosotis alpestris* 'Carmine King'
An erect, compact forget-me-not ideal for bedding, with rosy carmine blooms. Height 20cm (8in).

(right) MYOSOTIS ALPESTRIS and LUNARIA ANNUA

• *Myosotis alpestris* 'Rose'
A particularly attractive and very popular variety with pale rose-pink flowers. Height 40cm (16in).
• *Myosotis alpestris* 'Royal Blue Improved'
A very early and free-flowering forget-me-not, with deep indigo blue flowers providing masses of spring colour. Height 30cm (12in).
• *Myosotis alpestris* Victoria Strain 'Alba'
One of the dwarf Victorian strains, producing dwarf, bushy, ball-shaped plants with a mass of pure white flowers. Height 15cm (6in).
• *Myosotis* 'Blue Ball'
A compact, ball-shaped plant with bright blue flowers. Ideal for edging and bedding. Height 15cm (6in).
• *Myosotis* 'Ultramarine'
One of the finest varieties available, producing dwarf, compact plants with flowers in a glowing, deep indigo blue. Height 15–20cm (6–8in).

Nemophila menziesii

Affectionately known as baby-blue eyes or California bluebells, *Nemophila menziesii* has attractive pale green, hairy, fern-like foliage and bright blue flowers with white centres, which are produced at the tips of the branches. A half-hardy annual, it rarely grows more than 25cm (10in) high and blooms all summer in full sun as long as it is kept well watered. A natural for pots and containers, it is also wonderful in front of borders or as an edging for beds and paths, and can be tucked between paving stones in a patio and planted in rock gardens.

Cultivars are available with solid blue flowers, solid white flowers, or bright blue flowers with white centres.

CULTIVATION
Nemophila menziesii can be sown outdoors in early spring as soon as the soil can be worked. Thin them to 20–30cm (8–12in) apart. They prefer a light, sandy, well-drained soil, sheltered from the wind, and should be fertilized at planting time. Baby-blue eyes will self seed generously.

COTTAGE GARDEN VARIETIES
• *Nemophila menziesii* 'Baby-blue Eyes'
A low-spreading variety with glorious sky-blue blooms.

Excellent for rockeries and edging. Height 15cm (6in), spread 30cm (12in).
• *Nemophila menziesii* 'Penny Black'
An extraordinarily attractive variety bearing deep purple, almost black flowers with a sharply contrasting neat and tidy white edge. Guaranteed to get visitors craning their necks for a closer look. Height 15cm (6in).
• *Nemophila menziesii* 'Snowstorm'
An elegant new variety bearing lovely pure white flowers, heavily, but discreetly, marked with tiny black speckles. Height 15cm (6in).

Nicotiana alata

The half-hardy tobacco plant is right at the top of the list of scented cottage garden annuals. The rich, spicy scent is equal in strength to that of the stocks (*Matthiola*). *Nicotiana alata*, syn. *N. affinis*, known as the 'jasmine tobacco', is the traditional tobacco plant used in bedding and has tubular white flowers and basal leaves like those of a foxglove. Although rather lifeless during the day, the flowers flare into enormous five-pointed star shapes during the evening, emitting a strong fragrance. On the other hand, varieties with pink, red or green flowers appear to be almost devoid of scent.

N. alata reaches a height of 60–150cm (24–60in) and gives much needed height in beds and borders. Group them together for more impact.

CULTIVATION
Seeds will germinate uncovered in 10–15 days at 21–24°C (70–75°F) and should be started indoors 6–8 weeks prior to planting out in early summer. Space the plants 20–30cm (8–12in) apart in humus-rich, moist, well-drained soil in full sun or partial shade. Plantlets of many varieties are widely available at nurseries and garden centres everywhere.

COTTAGE GARDEN VARIETIES
• *Nicotiana alata* Domino Mixed
The fragrant flowers of this neat, bushy *Nicotiana* are open all day. Tolerant of heat and happy in dappled shade, the flowers are scarlet, rose, pink, lime and white with some unusual bicolours. Height 24–30cm (10–12in).
• *Nicotiana alata* Dwarf White Bedder
This variety has large, pure white, strongly scented

NICOTIANA ALATA and COSMOS BIPINNATUS

flowers which remain open during the day, on low bushy plants. Height 38cm (15in).

• *Nicotiana alata* 'Fragrant Cloud'
The large white flowers of this excellent variety have a rich, powerful evening fragrance. Height 90cm (36in).

• *Nicotiana alata* 'Lime Green'
This prolific flowering variety, in an unusual shade of lime-green, is very popular with flower arrangers and an asset to any cottage garden border. (The flowers of *N. alata* 'Lime Green' vary in colour according to their source.) Height 75cm (30in).

Nigella damascena

Nigella damascena, commonly known as 'love-in-a-mist', is a charming cottage garden favourite. The dainty, cornflower-like flowers are set within light green, filigree foliage which veils the flowers, producing a misty show of pastel colours.

The plant has been in cultivation for over four centuries. Over the years, it has acquired a number of other, rather colourful names: 'fennel flower', 'devil-in-the-bush', 'love-in-a-puzzle', 'prick-my-nose', 'love-in-a-hedge', 'lady-in-the-bower', and 'St Catherine's flower' – the flowers suggesting the spokes of her wheel of martyrdom.

Among its virtues, Gerard noted that the dried black seeds of nigella would restore a lost sense of smell 'being often smelled unto from day to day and made warme at the fire when it is used'. His remedy for taking away freckles involved the seed being laid on mixed with vinegar. From its spider-like, rather uncanny appearance, old herbalists also concluded that the plant should prove a good medicine for the bite of the great spider.

N. damascena is said to have been introduced from Damascus in 1570, but it was not the first of its genus to arrive. *N. sativa*, the 'nutmeg flower' or 'Roman coriander', had been cultivated for perhaps 2,000 years or more for its edible and aromatic seeds, which were used in cooking. It was not unknown for gardeners to confuse the two plants, but they quickly found that the seeds of love-in-a-mist were worthless as a flavouring, with Parkinson noting that seed of *N. damascena* could not be substituted for those of *N. sativa* 'as many ignorant persons use to doe'.

The flowers of the species are blue or white, but it is the various garden varieties which are so popular today, notably 'Miss Jekyll' which bears semi-double flowers in a most beautiful shade of soft blue, the result of many years of careful selection, and the strain known as 'Persian Jewels', which takes in a wide range of colours including rose, lavender, pink, purple, white and carmine.

CULTIVATION

Love-in-a-mist is an easy-to-grow hardy annual which should be sown *in situ* in good garden soil in a sunny position and thinned out to at least 30cm (12in) apart each way. The finest plants are usually produced from an autumn sowing, these often reaching as much as 60cm (24in) and forming compact bushes. Good results can also be obtained from an early-spring sowing in the open or under glass; however, the plants resent transplanting, so the seedlings from a sowing under glass should be transferred to individual pots at any early stage and planted out in late spring with the ball of soil around the roots intact.

COTTAGE GARDEN VARIETIES

• *Nigella damascena flore pleno*
A lovely love-in-a-mist, with fully double flowers produced over a long period in various shades of pink, blue and white. Height 30–60cm (12–24in).
• *Nigella damascena* 'Mulberry Rose'
A charming variety with double flowers that open creamy pink and gradually change to a deep rose, only partially hidden in the mist. Height 45cm (18in).
• *Nigella damascena* 'Shorty Blue'
Described by the raiser as 'a real shorty', this splendid new variety grows very quickly, like a miniature hedge, and bears a profusion of dark violet-blue flowers followed by decorative seedpods. It is excellent for bedding, for small gardens and for growing in pots. Height 15cm (6in).

Ocimum basilicum

Sweet basil, which the French refer to as the *herbe royale*, is one of the most decorative and useful of the ornamental hardy annual herbs. It makes a perfect potted plant, providing wonderful fragrance for use on the terrace or patio, and is highly attractive as a garden plant, complementing the other flowers with its colour, texture and aroma. The leaves are varied in colour from deep to light purple and light green, and their texture varies from puckered, to ruffled, to smooth. The flowers are small and creamy in colour and appear from midsummer until the autumn.

Said by Parkinson 'to procure a cheerful and merrie heart', basil was also at one time used as a strewing herb. Nowadays its fragrant leaves are used fresh or dried to give a peppery flavour to food and are indispensable for tomato sauces and salads. Fresh basil leaves are the most tasty, but dried or frozen leaves will work well in cooking.

CULTIVATION
Sow seed outside when the soil is warm and all danger of frost has passed. Germination takes about three weeks. Thin to 20cm (8in) apart. For ornamental purposes, plant sweet basil in rich, well-drained soil in full sun. Apply water-soluble fertilizer monthly, and mulch to keep plants moist during long, hot spells. For culinary purposes, use poor soil as this intensifies the flavouring oils, making the leaves more pungent.

COTTAGE GARDEN VARIETIES

• *Ocimum basilicum* 'Dark Opal'
This form has fragrant purple-black foliage much in demand by flower arrangers. Height 45cm (18in).
• *Ocimum basilicum* 'Green Ruffles'
The serrated, quilted leaves of 'Green Ruffles' are much larger than those of ordinary sweet basil and are very decorative. Try planting it with 'Purple Ruffles' in the middle of a flower border. Height 60cm (24in).

OCIMUM BASILICUM

• *Ocimum basilicum* 'Purple Ruffles'
'Purple Ruffles' has ruffled, fringed, deep purple leaves that are both fragrant and beautiful. The attractive pink flowers should be removed if the plant is to continue growing all summer. Height 60cm (24in).

Oenothera biennis

This familiar cottage garden plant is known as evening primrose because of its lovely clear, primrose-yellow blooms, some 8cm (3in) across. These sleep by day and open at dusk to emit a delicious sweet perfume that is particularly attractive to moths. It has a long flowering season: the uppermost flowers appear in early summer and the stem continues to advance in height, reaching 60–120cm (24–48in) and bearing a constant succession of flowers until well into the autumn.

O. biennis 'Afterglow' is a much sought-after variety with bright-red calyxes that add a touch of brilliant colour to enliven its daytime existence.

CULTIVATION
Sow the seeds *in situ* in early spring in a sunny, well-drained position and thin the seedlings to 15cm (38in)

←⟶

OENOTHERA BIENNIS (above) and HORDEUM JUBATUM (right)

apart. The plants will flower from midsummer the following year. To prevent the plant from becoming a pest, decapitate it before its seeds become fully ripened. Although very attractive, evening primrose can be a troublesome weed if it is allowed to seed itself all over the garden.

Ornamental grasses

Annual grasses have been grown in the cottage garden for centuries to provide cut flowers both fresh and dried for later use in harvest arrangements, door hangings and various other crafts. Their leaf shapes are a pleasing contrast to those of most garden plants; they soften harsh colour schemes, and remain attractive in the garden until heavy snows cover them. Plant grasses in clumps for more impact, with the taller ones in the middle of the border and the short varieties gracefully decorating the front.

CULTIVATION

Sow *in situ* in spring when the soil becomes friable. Plant 12–15 seeds in an area 30cm (12in) square and cover 1cm (½in) deep. Annual grasses thrive in full sun in a well-drained soil. Because they tend to self seed at an alarming rate, the flowers should be picked before the seeds ripen, but save some of the harvested seed for sowing the following year. Beware of buying mixtures of annual ornamental grasses as these can look extremely untidy.

COTTAGE GARDEN VARIETIES

• *Avena sterilis* (Animated oats)
This has awns 6.5cm (2¾in) long which are a lovely feature in the garden, especially as they catch the last rays of the evening sun. The common name refers to their ability to move back and forth as the humidity changes. Height 45cm (18in).
• *Briza maxima, B. minor* (Quaking grass)
Two related species of hardy ornamental annual grass, both with pretty, nodding heads of oval-shaped, pearly white spikelets resembling puffed wheat. Possibly a bit rangy for a formal bed or border, they are excellent in the cutting garden, where the flowers can be used fresh or for dried bouquets. Height *B. maxima* to 30–60cm (24–36in); *B. minor* under 30cm (12in).
• *Hordeum jubatum* (Squirrel-tail grass, Foxtail barley)
This hardy annual grass has flower spikes about 10cm (4in) long and often the same across, which resemble pale green and silver feathers. They eventually turn brown, and individual awns bend in all directions with age. The green leaves are about 15–20cm (6–8in) long and without the flowerheads are easily mistaken for grassy weeds. Height 45cm (18in).
• *Lagurus ovatus* (Hare's-tail grass)
A beautiful hardy annual grass, which is aptly named as the flowerheads look exactly like the soft, fluffy tail of a rabbit. The light green leaves are often 30cm (12in) long and are covered with a soft down. The pale green flowerheads turn off-white with age and are excellent in dried arrangements, while the seedheads will absorb dyes and are often to be found in gift and craft shops dyed in a kaleidoscope of colours. Height 60cm (24in).
• *Setaria italica* (Foxtail millet)
A very striking hardy annual grass that really does look remarkably like a foxtail. The dense panicles are often 30cm (12in) long and bow to the ground with the weight of the seed. The panicles make imposing additions to dried arrangements. Height over 60cm (24in).

Papaver

Papaver is the botanical name for the genus usually referred to as poppies, which includes a very showy and beautiful race of hardy annuals ideally for bringing a vivid splash of colour to the paintbox cottage garden. *Papaver rhoeas*, the common field poppy, with its brilliant scarlet flowers, usually with a black blob at the base of the petals, is a symbol of the tragedy of the First World War and Flanders fields. It has been used to breed numerous garden varieties, both single and double.

The Shirley strain of poppies, raised in 1880 by the Rev Wilkes of Shirley, was descended from one wild red poppy with white-edged petals which he found growing in a field near his home, and was the result of repeated selection and reselection of seedlings over several years. Originally a strain with single flowers, then later doubles as well, in lovely shades of pink, rose, salmon, crimson and white, the Shirley poppies are characterized by their lack of the usual black blotch at the base of the petals and their yellow anthers. The finest are without doubt the picotee types, their silky petals edged with a paler or darker colour.

P. somniferum is the opium poppy, said to have formed part of the garland which crowned Somnus, the god of sleep who, the legend runs, created the poppy to relieve Ceres from her worries and lull her to sleep, since she had been neglecting the growing crops with whose care she was charged. After her refreshing sleep she revived, and so did the crops. This is the reason why Ceres is always represented wearing a crown of both wheat and poppies.

For centuries opium was the only effective painkiller, and opium poppies were grown commercially in the early nineteenth century for the Victorians, who were becoming hooked on patent medicines which relied heavily on opium and other drugs. In fact, Gerard had warned in 1597 that 'It mitigateth all kinds of paines, but it leaveth behinde if oftentimes as mischiefe woorse than the disease it selfe', but it was not until the

(above) PINK PEONY-FLOWERED POPPY and *(right)* POPPY SEEDHEADS

beginning of the present century that its dangers as an addictive drug were generally realized. The solution of opium in spirits of wine, known as laudanum or 'loddy', was frequently used instead of tea by poorer women in the manufacturing towns. The juice of the unripened pod is the source of opium; strangely, the seeds of *P. somniferum* are frequently used for food, since they do not contain a trace of the toxic alkaloids that are present in the sap of the plants. Loaves of bread are sometimes decorated and flavoured with poppy seeds, and opium poppies are the source of poppy seed oil.

RED PEONY-FLOWERED POPPY

P. somniferum has large, cup-shaped, erect flowers up to 18cm (7in) across. The flowers, which are borne on long stalks, range from white to pink or purple, often with a dark blotch at the base of each petal. *P. somniferum* var. *paeoniflorum*, the aptly-named 'peony-flowered' poppy, has gorgeous, fully double flowers in a wide range of colours. During the eighteenth century many garden varieties of *P. somniferum* were grown which are not available to gardeners today, among them a double black and a beautifully striped double with jagged edges. The stiff-stemmed seedpods of the opium poppies are a particular favourite in dried arrangements, and are best gathered when mature but before they become too discoloured.

Varieties of *P. nudicaule*, commonly known as Iceland poppies although they have no connection whatever with that country, have large, colourful flowers, 8cm (3in) or more across, with satin-like petals. The blooms are in bright and enticing shades of white, pink, yellow, orange or red. *P. nudicaule* is one of the few poppies that is useful for cutting, as the flowers last well in water.

CULTIVATION

Poppy seed should be sown *in situ* in a sunny position in well-drained, ordinary garden soil. Sow during autumn for early flowering, followed by spring sowings for midsummer flowering. Mix the tiny seeds with sand before broadcasting on the seedbed, scattering them sparingly. Care should be taken to cover the seed light-

ly, and a fine spray of water will help to settle it. The seeds germinate quickly and are almost certain to come up too thickly. They should be thinned out drastically to at least 30cm (12in) apart as soon as they are large enough to handle. Once established, poppies will self seed with abandon.

COTTAGE GARDEN VARIETIES

• *Papaver commutatum* 'Ladybird'
Selected for the intensity of its flowers, 'Ladybird' is guaranteed to provoke comment from visitors to the garden. It has divided foliage and bears numerous brilliant scarlet flowers with bold black, ladybird-like blotches in the centre of the petals. Height 30–45cm (12–18in).

• *Papaver nudicaule* 'Matador'
As the name would suggest, this long-flowering Iceland poppy has giant-sized flowers up to 12cm (5in) across in a vivid shade of scarlet. Height 40cm (16in).

• *Papaver nudicaule* Meadow Pastels
A truly beautiful strain of Iceland poppies, with large flowers on long, strong stems in a wide range of pastel colours including white, pink and orange, as well as some lovely bicolours. Height 60cm (24in).

• *Papaver rhoeas* Mother of Pearl
A fascinating strain of this popular hardy annual, discovered some 30 years ago in the garden of botanical artist Sir Cedric Morris with flowers in a variety of unusual yet most attractive shades of grey, soft blue, lilac, dusty pink and white, with picotee edges of faint blue. Height 25–35cm (10–14in).

• *Papaver somniferum* 'Hen and Chickens'
A flower arranger's dream, this unusual poppy has large, pale lilac flowers that are followed by a curious arrangement of seedpods, in which the usual central pod has arising from its base several little seedpods, giving the impression of a mother hen surrounded by her brood of chicks. Once dried and dyed, these pods are very decorative, and much sought-after for dried floral arrangements. Height 30–36cm (12–24in).

• *Papaver somniferum* 'Pink Chiffon'
A beautiful peony-flowered poppy with gorgeous double flowers in a lovely shade of bright pink. Height 75cm (30in).

• *Papaver somniferum* 'White Cloud'
A particularly beautiful variety with extra-large, pure white, fully double, paeony-flowered blooms. Height 90cm (36in).

Pelargonium

Pelargonium species include a large number of scented-leaved types, commonly known as scented geraniums – tender, semi-shrubby plants with aromatic, deeply cut, almost ferny leaves and small but comparatively insignificant flowers. The plants were introduced from the Cape of Good Hope during the seventeenth century by English travellers and explorers, inspiring a legion of devotees for over 400 years.

A written description, however, does nothing to prepare the uninitiated for the sheer joy of entering a greenhouse filled with a varied assortment of scented geraniums. The fragrances of roses, oranges, lemons, nutmeg and peppermint hang heavy on the air, the aromatic sweetness everywhere. The leaves also have practical uses, and are frequently used in pot-pourri and in cooking – lemon geranium cake, made with the leaves of *P. capitatum*, and rose geranium jelly are both quite a delicacy.

P. graveolens, the rose geranium, was the first pelargonium to be grown in Britain. Ever since 1690, it has been a popular windowsill plant in old, low-ceilinged cottages. The fragrance – a combination of lemon, rose and balsamic scents – is released when the leaves are touched and helped to relieve the damp and musty smells of these homes.

In Victorian times, scented geraniums were widely grown in greenhouses and conservatories. Dozens of different species, hybrids and sports were widely available, often trained into fan shapes or standards. They later became unfashionable and in fact remained so until quite recently.

Scented geraniums range from small, bushy plants no more than 15cm (6in) high, to quite tall plants up to 2m (6ft). They have a tendency to grow leggy or to scramble if they are not regularly pinched back, but are comparatively easy to grow. The flowers are not nearly as showy as those of other pelargoniums and should be regarded as an added bonus rather than a major feature.

There are dozens of varieties to be had, smelling of different flowers, fruits, spices and herbs, although the scents of *P. quercifolium*, the oak-leaved geranium, which has rather showy purple flowers, and *P. denticulatum*, with large, finely cut leaves that are sticky to the touch, are not at all easy to describe. There are plenty of varieties with finely divided foliage, and a few with white or cream leaf margins which are much admired.

Provided a minimum temperature of 7°C (45°F) can be maintained in winter, scented geraniums will carry on growing all year round. They are ideal for sunny windowsills and conservatories, or for growing in a frost-free greenhouse. During the summer months they can be planted out in the open in a well-drained soil, or in troughs and window boxes. Planted near garden gates or at the edge of paths, they will release their aromatic fragrance whenever they are brushed against. They may also be plunged in beds or borders in their pots, the pots completely covered with soil to give a natural effect. These plants will be much easier to lift in the autumn as the rootballs do not grow too large, which can be a problem when the plants are put potless into the ground.

CULTIVATION

Loam-based potting compost, with one part extra sharp sand to every four parts compost, is ideal for scented geraniums, as it is easier than peat-based compost to re-wet when it dries out. Scented geraniums do not require nearly as much water as other pot plants and will tolerate drying out for short periods. In fact, you should allow the compost to dry out almost completely between waterings, but water thoroughly each time.

Established plants which constantly need repotting into ever larger pots should have their roots trimmed back by one-third and can then be put back in the same pot with some fresh compost. This will help to limit future growth. If growth becomes long and woody, repot the plant in fresh compost and then wait a week or so before cutting back each stem hard to a growing bud.

Plants growing in pots will benefit from a liquid feed every few weeks all year round, given at half the strength recommended for other pot plants. Throughout the year, remove all dead leaves and flowers to keep the plants looking tidy.

If space is a problem, soft or semi-ripe cuttings can be taken in the spring or late summer and the old plants discarded. Soft cuttings will generally root within six weeks if taken in early spring, but later on will take up to three months.

Use a very sharp knife to remove a shoot just above a leaf node. Trim the cutting to 5cm (2in) long (15cm/6in for the oak-leaf geraniums, *P. quercifolium*, just below a node. Remove any flower buds or flowers and all but the top two leaves. Dip the cuttings in rooting hormone and then insert them into loam-based potting compost to a depth of 2.5cm (1in) and firm in. A few cuttings in 8cm (3in) pots will take up very little room on the windowsill or greenhouse bench and can be potted on into progressively larger pots about every six weeks. Avoid overwatering, which can cause stem rot.

It is possible to grow the species pelargoniums from seed, and this is a very good way of obtaining those that can only be found in the seed catalogues. Seeds germinate in 7–10 days at 21–24°C (70–75°F). After the first true leaves appear move the seedlings to individual 5cm (2in) pots and then on into 10cm (4in) pots as they grow larger. Flowers will be produced in about 13–15 weeks.

COTTAGE GARDEN VARIETIES

FRUIT-SCENTED

• *Pelargonium crispum* 'Major'

This variety has rigid stems and small, curled leaves that are crimped at the edges, with a strong scent of lemon rind. The flowers are comparatively large and mauve-pink. Height 60cm (24in). *P. crispum* 'Minor', the 'finger-bowl geranium', grows to only 30–38cm (12–15in).

• *Pelargonium crispum* 'Variegatum'

This variegated form of *P. crispum* is known as French lace or variegated Prince Rubert. The foliage, edged with silver and cream, possesses the same refreshing pungency as that of the species and is excellent for planting out during the summer. It is also ideal for training as a standard and the foliage is much in demand by flower arrangers. Height 60cm (24in).

• *Pelargonium* 'Mabel Grey'

A comparatively recent introduction from Kenya, the foliage of this pelargonium is bold in outline, being palmately divided, and has a very strong lemon-verbena scent. The flowers are mauve. Pinch out regularly to prevent the plant from becoming straggly. Excellent for cooking and in potpourri. Height 30cm (12in).

• *Pelargonium nervosum*

A lime-scented species with a compact, bushy habit and pale mauve flowers. Height 30cm (12in).

• *Pelargonium odoratissimum*

Forming a neat hummock of apple-scented foliage up to 45cm (18in) across, this species sends out long, trailing flowering shoots, which make it a good plant for a hanging pot. The shoots can be trimmed if they become

bare and unattractive. Height 20cm (8in).

• *Pelargonium* 'Prince of Orange'

An upright, bushy, compact plant, with orange-scented leaves and pale mauve flowers. Height 30–45cm (12–18in).

• *Pelargonium* 'Rober's Lemon Rose'

The flowers of this lemon-scented pelargonium are a bright dark pink, and the plant forms a neat bush of small, oak-shaped leaves. Height 30cm (12in).

ROSE-SCENTED

• *Pelargonium* 'Attar of Roses'

Arguably the best of all the scented pelargoniums, with an open habit and a most delightful true rose perfume. The leaves are slightly lobed and the flowers small and pink. Leaves may be dried for use in pot-pourri. Height 45cm (18in).

• *Pelargonium graveolens*

The strongly scented, divided leaves of this species, together with those of *P. capitatum*, are used commercially to produce rose geranium oil. The flowers are pale mauve-pink and the plant is tall growing, although it can be kept to about 90cm (36in) by constantly pinching out the growing tips. Flowers are pale mauve-pink. Height up to 2m (6ft).

SPICE SCENTED

• *Pelargonium fragrans*

The 'nutmeg geranium' has sage-green foliage and small white or cream flowers with red veins on the upper petals. The leaves, which have an aftershave aroma – a mixture of pine and nutmeg – are frequently used in pungent and spicy pot-pourris. Height 23–30cm (9–12in).

• *Pelargonium* 'Lady Plymouth'

Silver-edged, cream-tinged foliage, shaped like that of the oak-leaf geranium and with a peppermint and cinnamon scent, plus pale pink flowers, make this a very decorative plant which is useful for planting out in the summer. Height 60cm (24in).

• *Pelargonium tomentosum*

This species has large, downy, *crème-de-menthe*-coloured leaves, described by Gertrude Jekyll (1843–1932), plantswoman, painter and garden designer, as being 'as thick as a fairy's blanket', which smell

(clockwise from top left): MIXED SCENTED-LEAVED GERANIUMS, PERILLA FRUTESCENS with PELARGONIUM 'ATTAR OF ROSES', PICOTEE PETUNIAS and PHLOX DRUMMONDII

strongly of peppermint as soon as they are touched. In summer a succession of small white flowers add to the beauty. The sprawling plant can easily reach 60cm (24in) across if permitted, and is probably seen at its best hanging downwards over the rim of a large pot. *P.* 'Chocolate Tomentosum' is very similar, but the leaves have a brown centre.

• *Pelargonium* 'Toronto'

To some, the scent of this pelargonium seems more like citrus than ginger, and vice versa. It has a compact habit and the mauve-pink flowers are large for the size of the plant. Height up to 30cm (12in).

Perilla frutescens

The beefsteak plant, *Perilla frutescens* is a tall member of the basil family, frequently used for edging pathways and often seen in cottage gardens grown as a low hedge. This handsome foliage plant has deeply cut, oval, purple-red leaves streaked with metallic overtones and also deeply veined and crinkled. Brilliant burgundy-red stems are an added attraction; the rather inconspicuous flowers appear in late summer. When bruised, the leaves, which can be used for tenderizing meat, give off a strong, spicy aroma that is cinnamon-like.

Growing as tall as 60–90cm (24–36in), *Perilla* should be planted in the middle or at the back of the border. A prolific self seeder, it provides enough seed to attract hungry birds.

CULTIVATION

Sow seed outdoors after the last frost and thin the seedlings to 22cm (9in) when they are 7–10cm (3–4in) tall. It will grow equally well in sun or in shade, but too shady a position will create a lankier plant. Pinch off flowerheads to encourage new bushy growth. The plant can also be propagated from cuttings, which root quickly and easily, even in water.

COTTAGE GARDEN VARIETIES

• *Perilla frutescens* 'Crispa'

This tall-growing variety has attractively curled leaves. Height 60–90cm (24–36in).

• *Perilla frutescens* var. *nankinensis laciniata*

A very attractive variety, bearing deeply cut, dark bronzy-purple leaves and spikes of numerous, charming, pale violet flowers. Height 45cm (18in).

Petunia

Petunias are among the showiest and easiest of garden annuals. They are a particular favourite for window boxes and hanging baskets, their trumpet-shaped flowers cascading over the edges in a riot of colour all summer long.

Petunia nyctaginiflora, a white, sweet-scented, night-blooming flower, was the first recorded petunia. It was discovered in Brazil in 1823 by a French commission and was sent back to Paris for classification, where it was named. *Petunia* is derived from *petun*, the Brazilian name for tobacco, which comes from a closely related genus.

Some seed which was sent home to Glasgow in 1831 by Mr Tweedie, a Scottish merchant in Buenos Aires, produced a violet-coloured flower which, in spite of its obvious resemblance to the white petunia, was at first misidentified by Sir Joseph Hooker and named *Salpiglossis integrifolia*. This was later changed to *Nierembergia phoenicia* – another *faux pas*, as *phoenicia* means crimson and the flower was purple – and finally to *Petunia violacea*. Garden hybrids originally obtained by crossing *P. violacea* with *P. nyctaginiflora* and *P. bicolor* very quickly became fashionable and by the 1840s there were many varieties to choose from, including double bicoloured types which had just been introduced from France.

By the 1880s interest in petunias had begun to wane – bedding pelargoniums were now all the rage and petunias were going out of fashion. Today, however, the plant is enjoying a welcome comeback and is tremendously popular with growers and plant breeders alike, with around 200 named cultivars of the common garden petunia, *P. × hybrida*, listed in wholesale catalogues. The wheel of fashion has turned once more.

Petunias come in every colour of the rainbow. Many have strong, clear self colours, while others are starred, splashed, speckled, striped, veined or edged with a contrasting colour; some have frilled flowers, and many are double. An amazing range of vastly differing types can be found among the plants grown from a single packet of mixed seed, and it is worthwhile looking out for more unusual, way-out sorts with crimped and curled edges or extra-large flowers, and the very

PETUNIAS with BUSY LIZZIES and ARGYRANTHEMUM

dark, velvety blue-black or crimson varieties. These can then be propagated from cuttings taken in the autumn and overwintered in a warm greenhouse. Various strains are listed in seed catalogues, with new varieties introduced annually in an almost bewildering range of colours.

Multifloras are the ordinary petunias with single, funnel-shaped flowers about 5cm (2in) across, and are the best type for massed bedding. With their numerous, relatively small blooms, multifloras can look rather sad in the rain as the flowers close up, but most varieties quickly recover and will bloom well into late summer. Although the F1 hybrids are more expensive, they are without doubt more valuable because of their uniform growth habit, improved colours and ability to stand up to the vagaries of the weather.

Grandiflora single petunias, with flowers up to 10cm (4in) across, require a sheltered spot in order to perform well. They are best grown in pots and containers, where the blooms can be viewed at close range.

Double-flowered forms, in which the blooms are crammed with folded petals to resemble carnations, occur in both multiflora and grandiflora types. They do not enjoy or perform well in wet weather, as the flowers are slow to dry out and tend to rot.

Among the colour variations, 'stars' have five broad white stripes radiating from the centre of the flowers, while 'picotees' have a white edge.

Petunias have always had a delicious scent, particularly the blue and purple varieties, although this quality is scarcely ever mentioned in books and catalogues. They smell strongest at night, their vanilla-like fragrance wafting around the garden on a balmy summer's evening.

CULTIVATION

Seed should be sown under glass 10–12 weeks before the last frost. Sow thinly on the surface of the compost and do not cover the tiny seeds, as they need light to germinate. When the seedlings have developed three or four leaves, prick them out into individual 8cm (3in) peat pots. As soon as the weather warms up, move the pots into a cold frame, and plant out when all danger of frost has passed. Pinch back the plants at planting time to encourage bushiness; space 20–30cm (8–12in) apart.

Petunias must have sunshine for at least half the day and should be planted in a well-drained, moder-

ately rich, cultivated soil. They will benefit from a regular weekly or twice-weekly watering with weak liquid manure. Deadhead regularly to promote continued flowering.

One problem with petunias is that they tend to become rather leggy or straggly by mid-season. Cut them back to encourage new growth; another remedy is to take a long stem about half-way up and roll it gently between your fingers, just to squeeze and soften the tissue, then bend the stem gently backwards so that the upper part is pointing towards the pot or container. Sideshoots will now develop and flower, and the top of the stem will continue to bloom and hide the growing process. Finally, snip off the top for a more compact plant.

COTTAGE GARDEN VARIETIES

• *Petunia × hybrida* Carpet Series
These aptly named petunias have a very dwarf, spreading habit, with medium-sized flowers produced in profusion throughout the summer. The blooms come in pink, red, rose, velvet-blue and white, and show good resistance to bad weather. Excellent for bedding or in tubs, hanging baskets or containers on the patio. Height 23–30cm (9–12in).

• *Petunia × hybrida* Plum Pudding Mixed
A new and striking blend of rich colours, with dark centres and deep, lacy veining on the petals. Colours range from light blue through purple to rose-pink, and include a yellow for contrast. Very weather resistant. Height 20cm (8in).

SINGLE-FLOWERED F1 HYBRIDS

• *Petunia* 'Blue Skies'
An early-flowering hybrid with light blue flowers 8–10cm (3–4in) across. Height 23–30cm (9–12in).

• *Petunia* 'Flame Carpet'
A dwarf, compact hybrid bearing satin-coral flowers with a creamy yellow throat. It can be planted for a mass carpet effect, and is also very effective in baskets and containers. Height 23–30cm (9–12in).

• *Petunia* Grandiflora Bicolour Mixed
A most attractive mixture of striped and star-marked petunias in combinations of wine-red, red, rose, blue and white. Some combinations, however, can be slightly garish. Height 30cm (12in).

• *Petunia* Picotee Ruffled Mixed
A mixture of single petunias with masses of waved and ruffled blooms. Early flowering, compact and very effective for containers or bedding. Height 30cm (12in).

• *Petunia* 'Summer Sun'
A very striking, and rare, true yellow petunia, with
blooms up to 8cm (3in) across. A most attractive plant,
which can be used for bedding, window boxes, hanging baskets, tubs or pots. Height 23cm (9in).
DOUBLE-FLOWERED F1 HYBRIDS
• *Petunia* 'Giant Victorious'
Bred by Sakata in Japan, this superb strain of petunias
has huge, fully double, perfectly formed blooms, each
up to 10cm (4in) across, borne on dwarf, compact plants
which are suitable for the border, pots, hanging baskets
and containers. They come in a wide range of colours
including salmon, rose, scarlet and violet-blue, as well
as some fascinating bicolours. Height 30cm (12in).
• *Petunia* 'White Swan'
This hybrid has perfect double, fringed, lily-white
flowers at least 10cm (4in) across, which are perfect for
bedding. Height 23cm (9in).

Phlox drummondii

The annual phlox are low-growing, spreading plants,
represented almost solely by varieties of *Phlox drummondii*, derived from an American wilding first grown
from seed collected in east Texas by an Englishman,
Thomas Drummond, who sent supplies back to
England in 1835.

The appearance of this rather showy, red-flowered
annual phlox on the gardening scene would seem to
have created something of a stir, although it was apparently still rare in 1837 when botanist John Hindley
(1799–1865) wrote that 'A bed of it has hardly yet been
seen as it is too precious and uncommon to be possessed
by anyone except in small quantities, but I have had
such a bed described to me that I can readily believe
that it produced all the brilliance that my informant
represented'. Just a few years later, however, it was
widely grown – the pride and joy of the garden – and
by the 1840s was re-exported to America where, surprisingly, it was still unknown as a cultivated flower.

The species is straggly in growth and Captain
Symons-Jeune, writing in *The Genus Phlox* (1953) suggested that its popularity waned with that of the hair-
pin used by an older generation to peg down the shoots.
Over the decades *P. drummondii* has been much
improved by cultivation, and nurserymen today offer
a number of named colour forms and dwarf-growing,
compact strains which remove the necessity of pegging
down straggly growth with granny's hairpins.

The annual phlox grows 15–45cm (6–18in) high,
the long, hairy stems and thin leaves topped by colourful, slightly fragrant, circular or star-shaped flowers.
These are only about 2.5cm (1in) across. but are borne
in clusters which remain open for about a week.
Colours include white, pink, red, blue, lavender, purple, salmon and bicolours. They are useful for edging,
borders, rock gardens, window boxes and containers.

CULTIVATION
Sow seed in gentle heat in a greenhouse or cold frame
six to eight weeks before the last frost, preferably in
individual pots as they resent transplanting. It is a good
idea to pinch out the growing point when the plants are
quite young to ensure bushier growth.

Plant them out in late spring 15cm (6in) apart in
full sun in a rich, preferably light, sandy soil with good
drainage. The plants benefit from a monthly feed and
a good watering. Deadhead to keep the display going.

COTTAGE GARDEN VARIETIES
• *Phlox drummondii* 'Brilliant'
An old favourite, at least as old as the century, which
produces dense clusters of bright, dark-eyed, rose-pink
flowers. Good for cutting. Height 50cm (20in).
• *Phlox drummondii* Choice Mixture
A mixture of tall-growing forms, with branching stems
bearing flat-topped clusters of flowers in a wide range
of reds, crimsons and pinks, as well as white. These are
similar to the original species from Texas, which were
so popular with the Victorians but are rarely seen
nowadays – these distinctive plants are due for a comeback. Excellent for cutting. Height 45cm (18in).
• *Phlox drummondii* var.
stellaris
This variety, sometimes called
the 'star phlox', has narrow,
fringed petals in a range of
colours. Height 30cm (12in).
• *Phlox drummondii* Twinkles
This popular strain bears a
profusion of lovely starry
flowers in a wide range of
eyecatching colours. Useful
for bedding. Height 15–20cm
(6–8in).

PHLOX DRUMMONDII
'TWINKLES'

Portulaca grandiflora

With its pretty silky-petalled, rose-like flowers appearing in brilliant red, pink, yellow, gold, orange, cream and white, *Portulaca grandiflora*, or the moss rose, is an old-fashioned favourite. The reddish, well-branched plant stems have a trailing habit and the needle-like, succulent light green leaves enable it to survive in the most inhospitable parched and dry parts of the garden. These half-hardy annuals are perfect for dry slopes, beds and rock gardens where just a few plants cover quite an area of ground – their spread being several times their height. Moss roses can also be used to great effect in containers and hanging baskets. Pot one or two up for a sunny windowsill.

The flowers, which are ruffled and single or double, open on sunny days until late afternoon from summer until early autumn, but they close on cloudy, overcast and rainy days, as well as at night. This is without doubt a perfect annual to plant in that spot in the garden where nothing else will flourish.

CULTIVATION

Sow seed indoors 6–8 weeks before the last frost at 21–27°C (70–80°F). Mix the fine seed with sand for easier sowing but do not cover, as it needs light for germination. Plant out in the garden when frost danger has passed and space the plants 30–38cm (12–15in) apart in full sun and dry, sandy, well-drained soil. Water very sparingly. Moss rose often reseeds itself when happy.

COTTAGE GARDEN VARIETIES

• *Portulaca grandiflora* 'Afternoon Delight'
The double blossoms of this variety stay open well into the evening. Height 15cm (6in).
• *Portulaca grandiflora* Kariba Mixed
Bred in Zimbabwe, this new variety produces strong, spreading plants bearing large double flowers in a brilliant range of colours over a long period. Height 15cm (6in).
• *Portulaca grandiflora* Wildfire Strain
A lovely strain with single flowers which look most attractive cascading from hanging baskets. Height 15cm (6in).

PORTULACA GRANDIFLORA

Reseda odorata

Reseda odorata, or mignonette, the sweet-scented, fragrant weed of Egypt, was introduced to Britain from Egypt, via France, in the mid-nineteenth century. It appeared first in London florists' windows and quickly found a niche in the window boxes of London balconies, where the inconspicuous flowers would release their distinctive fragrance on warm, sunny days. The poet Cowper, who came of age in the year when the flower first reached these shores, gave it a name which stuck at the time – Frenchman's darling, hence mignonette.

Mignonette was a plant to be found in every cottage garden before the Second World War, where its delicious scent could be detected by anyone leaning over the garden gate. Sadly, it is rarely grown today although it is one of the most delightfully fragrant of flowers.

Although referred to as an annual, mignonette is actually a half-hardy perennial. It has a spreading habit, with leafy stems, many small brownish-yellow flowers, which are excellent for cutting, and grows to 30cm (12in) high. Sprays cut in late autumn, placed in water and kept indoors in a cool room will retain their delicate and pronounced fragrance well into winter.

There are a number of modern seed strains available with red, yellow, sulphur, golden yellow and orange flowers, as well as several named varieties. Unfortunately, none of these seem to have the same fragrance of the unimproved mignonette.

CULTIVATION

Mignonette should not be regarded as an easy-to-grow annual as it is, in fact, quite temperamental. Sow the seed thinly in a well-prepared, well-limed, sunny position in early spring where the plants are to bloom and thin out the seedlings to 10–15cm (4–6in) apart. Mignonette sown in the autumn and protected by cloches will flower earlier than plants sown in spring.

Tree mignonettes, popular in Edwardian times, were often put out in the fragrant garden during the summer, their pots buried in the ground. They are fun to grow: sow seeds in a pot and retain the strongest plant, which should be supported with a stick. Pinch out sideshoots at the second joint to create a tall stem, and allow a standard head to form at the top.

COTTAGE GARDEN VARIETIES

• *Reseda odorata* 'Fragrant Beauty'
Haunting sweet fragrance and red-tinged, lime coloured flowers are this plant's attractions. It is excellent for a spring-flowering pot plant if sown in the autumn. Height 30cm (12in).

• *Reseda odorata grandiflora*
Another old favourite with large flowerheads and a heavy scent. Height 40cm (16in).

• *Reseda odorata* 'Machet'
A Dutch strain listed as long ago as 1931, with large, solid spikes of fringed flowers tinged red. Height 30cm (12in).

• *Reseda odorata* 'Red Monarch'
As the name would suggest, this variety has more red in the flowers. Height 30cm (12in).

RESEDA ODORATA 'MACHET'

Rhodochiton

A tender perennial, generally grown in the conservatory, purple bell vine (*Rhodochiton atrosanguineum*) is also well worth trying as an annual in a sheltered spot in the garden. It can look very beautiful when growing well and in full bloom: the leaves are heart shaped and tinged red at the margin, and the tubular flowers, produced from summer to autumn, look like tiny parachutists, with their purple petals hanging beneath a large red calyx – an intriguing sight in any cottage garden.

CULTIVATION

Sowing times can be critical; it seems to do best when started indoors in early spring and planted outdoors in early summer, about 30cm (12in) apart.

It needs a warm aspect, well-drained but moisture-retentive soil and a long, sunny summer to thrive outside. Provide unobtrusive but strong support.

RHODOCHITON ATROSANGUINEUM

Rudbeckia hirta

Rudbeckia hirta, the so-called gloriosa daisies, have single or double daisy-like flowers with deep yellow outer petals and domed, silky, deep brown centres in summer and into autumn. The plants are short-lived perennials, usually grown as hardy annuals, and grow 20–90cm (8–36in) tall.

The name gloriosa daisy has been applied to the multitude of varieties that have been developed from a prairie weed; flowers are available in many warm shades of yellow, gold, orange, russet and mahogany; many of them have bands of colour intermixed. There are single or double varieties with flowers to 15cm (6in) across; the single flowers all have a large black or brown centre, contrasting with the colour surrounding it. They can be used in beds or borders, and look well planted with ornamental grasses in a wildflower setting. The flowers are good for cutting.

RUDBECKIA HIRTA 'BRIDAL ROBE'

CULTIVATION

Seeds can be sown *in situ* after frost danger has passed. Sow in average soil in full sun or light shade and thin the plants to 30–60cm (12–24in) apart. Incorporate fertilizer at the time of planting, but do not feed them again. Although they thrive best in full sun, they will tolerate poor soil and erratic waterings; however, they do flourish better with care. Taller varieties may need some protection from strong winds, or stake them to prevent them toppling over. Cut the flowers off as they fade to encourage further blooms; they will self sow easily.

COTTAGE GARDEN VARIETIES

• *Rudbeckia hirta* 'Bridal Robe'
A most unusual strain with flowers streaked orange-red and with dark eyes. Height 60cm (24in).
• *Rudbeckia hirta* 'Double Gold'
Bright golden-yellow and semi-double flowers, up to 11cm (4½in) across, with deep brown eyes. Height 90cm (36in).

• *Rudbeckia hirta* 'Goldilocks'
A dwarf variety with double and semi-double blooms of bright gold on compact plants. Height 20–25cm (8–10in).
• *Rudbeckia hirta* 'Irish Eyes'
A lovely variety producing strong, base-branching plants and bearing large, golden-yellow flowers with distinctive olive-green centres. Excellent in the border and for cutting. Height 60cm (24in).

Salvia

Salvia is a very large genus and includes many varied and choice plants, of which several species are annual and certain others, while perennial, are easily flowered during their first year from seed. Annual salvias have tubular, two-lipped flowers in blue, rich violet-blue, red, salmon or white, borne on narrow spikes all summer.

From the Latin *salvo*, meaning I heal or save, salvias were at one time grown more for their medicinal properties than for any decorative effect – a very old country saying, 'Eat sage in May and you'll live for aye', is a jingle that has been around in a number of forms for centuries. Apart from being used to treat colds, headaches, aching muscles and sore throats, sage leaves were once rubbed on the gums and teeth to remove stains and sweeten the breath, a practice which continued well after the introduction of toothpaste and toothpowders.

Salvia sclarea, or 'clary', a handsome old-fashioned biennial which grows wild in southern Europe, had many uses, and a diffusion of its seeds or its aromatic leaves has been used as an eyewash for tired and inflamed eyes since medieval days, hence its old name of 'clear-eyes', later shortened to 'clary'. According to Culpeper, placing a whole seed under the eyelid until it dropped out and repeating the performance several times would 'take off a film which covereth the sight; a handsome and safe remedy, it is a great deal easier than to tear it off with a needle' – ouch! In Tudor times the leaves were regarded as something of a delicacy, dipped in batter and fried, to be brought to the table as a second course, a sort of clary-leaf fritter, which presumably would have been washed down with sage beer, a popular beverage of the day.

S. sclarea forms attractive rosettes of grey-green, hairy leaves, 23cm (9in) long, in the first year. It is an attractive enough garden plant even at this stage, but is followed in the second year by impressive 90–150cm (3–5ft) loose spikes of small, pale violet-flushed flowers encased in conspicuous broad, papery, pale rose or blue bracts. Plantswoman and garden designer, Gertrude Jekyll (1843–1932) expressed a particular liking for the plant when she wrote that the whole effect of the large, branching spikes of mixed and broken colours was extremely delightful to any eye trained to colour. As an added bonus, bees are frequent visitors to the flowers.

S. viridis, the 'purple-topped clary' which is often still listed as *S. horminum*, has been grown since the early sixteenth century, but surprisingly has no medicinal properties. The plant, which seldom tops 45cm (18in), is grown not for the tiny, pale lavender flowers but for the showy, petal-like bracts which enclose them. While *viridis* would indicate that the bracts are green, cultivated forms are in fact brightly coloured. The deep purple, carmine-red and white varieties are striking plants and bring a splash of instant colour to the border. They are particularly useful for planting where spring bulbs have gone over, and are very attractive in fresh or dried arrangements.

SALVIA PATENS

S. farinacea, the 'mealy-cup sage', is a tender perennial introduced from Texas in 1847 and usually grown as an annual. This lovely species will produce 60cm (24in) tall, slender, lavender-like spikes of violet-blue flowers in its first year from seed. The stems appear to be dusted with flour and the blooms are held in calyces covered with short, whitish hairs, giving the plant its distinctive mealy appearance. The plants are excellent for cutting, and dry well for winter floral arrangements.

There are a number of good forms of this ornamental sage, such as 'Blue Bedder', which is more compact than the species, and the free-flowering 'Royal Blue', both with deep blue flowers. 'Victoria', which has medium-blue flowers, is larger and more branching, while 'Alba' is the lovely white-flowered garden variety.

The exotic sages, half-hardy species introduced from Mexico during the early nineteenth century, were particularly popular among gardeners of the time for their bright, pure colours. *S. splendens*, the brilliant 'scarlet sage', is the parent of the modern-day bedding hybrids. The one that many gardeners think of whenever 'salvia' is mentioned, it is a showy plant that has been misused to the point of abuse in many gardens, especially when grown near purple or pink petunias. Placed with care, however, the scarlet sage can be a very effective garden plant.

S. patens, the 'gentian sage', is a half-hardy perennial which will flower in the first year of its life and die when subjected to frost. Easily grown as an annual, it reaches 60cm (24in) high and has deep green foliage covered with short, sticky hairs, and large flowers of brilliant gentian-blue.

S. grahamii, a tender, deciduous shrub, is usually treated as an annual but will survive the winter in mild areas, attaining a height of 1.5m (5ft) or more if grown against a warm wall. More often than not, however, it is grown in 23cm (9in) pots under glass and plunged outside for the summer, or in a movable tub, where it will throw out a succession of glowing, carmine-scarlet flowers, with a broad, wavy lower lip, for months on end. When crushed, the leaves smell strongly of blackcurrants.

CULTIVATION

Seeds of the majority of salvias need sowing under glass six weeks before the last frost on a moistened planting medium (soak those of *S. splendens* to speed germination). Germination is best at 18–19°C (64–66°F). Prick seedlings into trays then individual pots, increasing the size of these according to growth. After danger of frost has passed, plant them out at 30cm (12in) apart. Water frequently and feed monthly to keep the plants vigorous. They will grow in any soil but enjoy a position in full sun where they will often self seed, forming large patches over the years.

Seed of *S. viridis* can be sown *in situ* in early spring; they are best in full sun and well-drained soil. Thin to 30cm (12in) apart.

S. patens, a half-hardy perennial, evergreen in mild climates, will flower the same year from a sowing under glass as above. The tubers of *S. patens* can be lifted, shaken free of soil and stored over the winter in the same way as gladioli and dahlias.

S. grahamii can be propagated from soft cuttings taken during the summer, or by severing rooted pieces from an established plant. Plants which have survived the winter outside should be pruned in early spring, simply cutting back some of the older shoots to their new basal growths.

COTTAGE GARDEN VARIETIES

• *Salvia farinacea* 'Silver'
As the name suggests, this plant bears an abundance of spikes of silvery white flowers. Height 60cm (24in).
• *Salvia farinacea* 'Victoria'
A great border plant, producing numerous long-lasting spikes of vivid blue flowers in less than four months from seed. Height 60cm (24in).
• *Salvia sclarea* var. *turkestanica*
An excellent variety of clary sage with pinkish white flowers, and bracts with a powerful aromatic odour so strong that a hand or sleeve lightly brushed against the plant will retain the scent for several hours afterwards. Height 75cm (30in).
• *Salvia viridis* 'Oxford Blue', syn. *S. horminum* 'Oxford Blue'
A much sought-after variety particularly appreciated by flower arrangers, with really bright, Oxford-blue papery bracts. Height 50cm (20in).
• *Salvia viridis* 'Pink Sundae', syn. *S. horminum* 'Pink Sundae'
This charming old variety has highly coloured, rosy carmine bracts with veins in a deeper shade. Height 50cm (20in).

Scabiosa

Scabiosa, from the Latin *scabies*, meaning itch, is not a disease, but a genus of very pretty plants, including the old-fashioned hardy annual *S. atropurpurea*, which Parkinson tells us was common in gardens before 1629. The genus does have medicinal qualities, however, and indeed was used extensively by herbalists to treat scabies and other skin ailments. It was even thought at one time to be a cure for leprosy.

S. atropurpurea was among hundreds of plants introduced by John Tradescant the Elder who, along with his son, also named John, sought 'slipes, seedes and rootes' of unusual plants through a network of friends, horticultural enthusiasts and ambassadors throughout the world. At first the plant was mistakenly called 'Indian scabious', although it is a native of southern Europe. In fact it has several common names, and it is not surprising that one of them should be 'pincushion flower', as the light-coloured stamens that protrude from each of the many tiny flowers clustered together in a mound look like pins stuck into a Victorian pincushion.

Because of its sombre purple colouring – like the dark colouring of the veil traditionally worn by widows in deep mourning – which is particularly pronounced in the wild scabious and the variety known as 'King of the Blacks', one of the darkest colours in garden flowers, it acquired the names 'mourning brides' and 'mournful widows'.

In France it was known as *fleur de veuve*, widow's flower, and the Italians called it the same – *fior della vedova*. This morbid fascination with the plant extended even further in Portugal, where *S. atropurpurea* was woven into funeral wreaths. Also known, more pleasantly, as 'sweet scabious', the flowers had at one time a musky fragrance which is sadly missing from most varieties today.

S. atropurpurea bears its pincushion-like flowerheads on wiry stems that rise up to 90cm (36in) from basal rosettes of well-divided leaves. It is excellent for cutting and a boon to flower arrangers, as the flowers last for 10 days or more in water without dropping their petals. Bees and butterflies love the blooms, which are followed by pale green, cupped seedpods covered with bristly, reddish hairs and resemble a bottle brush.

There are many strains and named varieties available, including double-flowered and both tall and dwarf forms, in a wide range of shades of red, pink, rose, maroon, purple, deep purple, almost black, lavender, cream and white.

S. *stellata*, or 'paper moons', is an annual from southern Europe that is grown for its unusual seedheads. It, too, is a flower arranger's dream: soft lavender blooms on long, firm stems are produced

SCABIOSA STELLATA

throughout the summer and then ripen into bronze-coloured, spherical seedheads that look more like coral fossils than flowers. The stems can reach 90cm (36in) and are much in demand for dried arrangements.

CULTIVATION

Sow thinly *in situ* in early spring into finely raked, moist, warm soil at a depth of 1.5cm (½in). Seedlings should be thinned to 30cm (12in) apart.

Any soil is suitable but they do best in full sun; a mulch will help keep the roots cool. Fertilize at planting out time and again each month. Water when the soil is dry, preferably in the morning, as foliage that is wet all night is prone to disease. To obviate the need for staking, avoid planting in open, exposed positions. If deadheaded, the plants will bloom until cut down by the first frost.

COTTAGE GARDEN VARIETIES

• *Scabiosa atropurpurea* Cockade Series

Popular double-flowered plants in a mixture of pink, red, lavender, blue, maroon and white. A tall plant, which requires light staking. The seedheads remain intact when dried and make good solid cone shapes for

winter arrangements. 'Rose Cockade' is a named variety with rose-pink flowers. Height 90cm (36in).

• *Scabiosa atropurpurea* The Imperial Giants

A lovely strain that includes a deep maroon-purple colour as well as pink, white, scarlet, deep rose, red, lavender, blue and white. Height 90cm (36in).

• *Scabiosa stellata* 'Sternkugel'

A most attractive and useful plant with spherical heads, 8–10cm (3–4in) in diameter, composed of 20 or so pale blue flowers, each about 2.5cm (1in) across, which are tightly packed together. These globular heads turn into creamy white, spherical seedhead posies resembling parchment flowers: in fact, admirers will take some convincing that they are natural and not artificial flowers. Height up to 60cm (24in).

Schizanthus × wisetonensis

Schizanthus × wisetonensis is a hybrid derived from the crossing of two species, *S. grahamii* and *S. pinnatus*, which were introduced to gardens from Chile over 150 years ago, and named after Wiseton, where the first interbreeding was accomplished. The generic name comes from the Greek *schizo*, meaning to divide, and *anthos*, meaning a flower, and alludes to the delicately fringed flowers which resemble the edging of old Irish lace. More familiar names are 'butterfly flower' and 'poor man's orchid'. The Victorians called it 'fringe-flower'.

S. × *wisetonensis* forms dense bushes of finely cut, distinctly ferny foliage which are smothered in beautifully marked, butterfly-like flowers which are produced in profusion during the spring and summer months.

Colours include apricot, salmon, light pink, crimson, lilac, violet and yellow, all vying in their efforts to predominate. Clustered on slender, cascading stems, the flowers have prominent gold veins and exotic markings in the throat.

Schizanthus are normally grown as greenhouse annuals or for large pots and containers, as the brittle stems need protection from strong winds and beating rain – tubs of specimens measuring 90cm (36in) in diameter and bearing thousands of flowers will reward patient gardeners. However, nearly all may be successfully raised as half-hardy annuals and planted out

SCHIZANTHUS × WISETONENSIS 'HIT PARADE'

in the open border. Protection with cloches in the early stages will enable the plants to steal a march on nature and reward the gardener with a brilliant, orchid-like display in early to midsummer.

CULTIVATION

Sow seed in gentle heat (16–18°C/61–64°F) in early spring. Alternatively, for spring-flowering plants under glass, a sowing can be made in late summer. The seeds are very fine and should not be covered with compost; however, they need darkness to germinate, so cover the trays or pots with a sheet of black plastic. Prick out the seedlings individually into 8cm (3in) pots as soon as they are large enough to handle. Keep them cool in a cool greenhouse and provide abundant light and air: they don't mind hot days as long as the nights stay below 18°C (64°F). As soon as the roots begin to break through the sides of the soilball, pot on into 11cm (4½in) pots, and finally into 20–25cm (8–10in) pots, in which the plants will flower. Pinch out the growing tips as soon as the shoots are 10–15cm (4–6in) long to encourage bushiness.

The young plants may be transplanted or moved into the garden after all danger of frost has passed. Choose a sheltered position in full sun or light shade and a rich, moist soil with good drainage. Space 30cm (12in) apart.

Early staking is advisable, although grown in tubs and large pots with stiffer-stemmed plants such as marguerites and geraniums, the plants will receive natural and inconspicuous support. In a window box or other containers, schizanthus appear to perform best when root-bound. When the pots are full of roots, the plants will benefit from gentle feeding with liquid manure. The flowering season is short, lasting only three or four weeks, but can be extended by successional sowings.

COTTAGE GARDEN VARIETIES

• *Schizanthus × wisetonensis* Angel Wings Mixed
A colourful strain which forms compact, conical plants with light pink, salmon, carmine, scarlet, lilac and purple flowers, so freely produced that they almost hide the foliage. Height 30–45cm (12–18in).
• *Schizanthus × wisetonensis* Disco
An improved strain and one of the best for garden use, although it was originally bred for pot culture. The plants are neat and compact, with flowers in various shades of red and maroon, all with a yellow centre. Height 30–38cm (12–15in).

• *Schizanthus × wisetonensis* Dwarf Bouquet Mixed
This dwarf mixture is excellent for pots and containers. The plants are smothered in crimson, rose, amber, pink and salmon flowers. Height 30cm (12in).
• *Schizanthus × wisetonensis* Giant Hybrids Mixed
A mixture of giant, branching plants, producing large flowers with gold markings. Requires early staking. Height 60–120cm (24–48in).
• *Schizanthus × wisetonensis* Hit Parade
A particularly fine strain with large, well-marked flowers in extraordinarily rich and brilliant colours. Height 25–30cm (10–12in).
• *Schizanthus × wisetonensis* Star Parade
A mixture of very dwarf schizanthus which make outstanding pot plants for early summer. The compact, ball-shaped plants bear masses of blooms in a wide range of colours. Height 15–23cm (6–9in).
• *Schizanthus × wisetonensis* Sweet Lips
A range with picotee-edged, striped and veined, orchid-like blooms in deep, strong shades of red and pink. Height 30–38cm (12–15in).

Senecio cineraria

Senecio cineraria is one of several grey-leaved plants that have been known to cottage gardeners since Victorian times as dusty miller. Grown for its highly ornamental downy, silver-white foliage, dusty miller is a truly adaptable half-hardy perennial, used as edgings, buffers between strong colours in beds and borders, and as a pretty feature in window boxes and containers combined with trailing lobelias, petunias, begonias and impatiens.

The plants which grow up to 75cm (30in) high, have neat clusters or deeply cut leaves covered with dense, white-woolly hairs, and yellow mop-head flowers, which many gardeners never see, for when grown as an annual, dusty miller rarely blooms.

CULTIVATION

Start seeds indoors 8–10 weeks before moving seedlings outside after the last frost. Plant in full sun or light shade and in a light, sandy, well-drained soil. Incorporate fertilizer into the soil before planting, and space the plants 20–30cm (10–12in) apart. No further feeding is necessary. Dusty miller can be cut back if it becomes leggy.

COTTAGE GARDEN VARIETIES

• *Senecio cineraria* 'Cirrhus'
A dwarf variety with bright silver, rounded foliage and exceptional rain resistance. Excellent for pots and containers. Height 45cm (18in).

SENECIO CINERARIA

• *Senecio cineraria* 'Silverdust'
A very dwarf variety with finely-lobed, silver-white foliage which is ideal for growing among brightly coloured summer bedding plants. Height 20cm (8in).

Tagetes

Tagetes erecta, the tall African marigold, and the similar but smaller *T. patula*, or French marigold, are both annuals of Mexican origin but arrived here by way of North Africa and France, acquiring their misleading names *en route*. The generic name *Tagetes* is said to be after Tages, son of Genius and grandson of Jupiter, a celebrated beauty who taught the art of divination to the Etruscans.

Tagetes are half-hardy annuals with a recorded history stretching back to the Aztec Indians, who used the plants for various purposes including the treatment of hiccups. Early in the sixteenth century seed of *T. erecta* was sent to Spain by explorers and was soon to be seen in every monastery garden, grown under the name 'rose of the Indies'.

After the sacking of Tunis and the liberation by Emperor Charles V in 1535 of the thousands held captive there by the Moors, *T. erecta*, which had become naturalized on the North African coast and was thought to be a local flower, was reintroduced into Europe under the name of *flos Africanus*, in honour of the Emperor's victory, and continued to be known by this name until well into the eighteenth century. Although the date of its introduction to England is uncertain, Gerard had a single and a double yellow, and Parkinson had doubles in many shades of yellow, as well as single and quilled-petal types.

T. erecta is a vigorous plant with large, showy flowers 8–11cm (3–4½in) across in brilliant orange, lemon, gold and sulphur-yellow. Hybridization has produced chrysanthemum-flowered varieties with globe-shaped double blooms, and densely double carnation-flowered varieties, in which the petals are waved and rolled. After many years of searching, Burpees in the USA, who have raised hundreds of cultivars since 1915, succeeded in introducing white marigolds, the best of which is undoubtedly 'Snowdrift'.

Some strains of African marigold are about 45cm (18in) high, but the majority of the better forms grow to 90cm (36in) or more and are usually placed at the rear of the bed or border. In fact, they can be grown to an enormous size by means of disbudding and judicious feeding. For exhibition purposes, some growers limit the number of blooms to only one per plant.

In 1754 James Justice an enterprising eighteenth century Scots gardener wrote in *Scots Gardeners' Director* of plants 'five Feet high, which rather appeared like flowering Shrubs, than annual Plants'. He also grew them in pots as houseplants for the winter.

The rather unpleasant smell of both foliage and flowers – something akin to stale urine – unfortunately prevents the use of *T. erecta* as a cut flower. Parkinson would appear to have been fortunate in having secured one of the less offensive varieties, as he described the plant as 'This goodly double flower, which is the grace and glory of a Garden in the time of his beautie... The flower of this, as well as the single, is of the verie smell of new waxe, or of an honie combe, and not of that poisonful sent of the smaller kindes'.

T. patula followed a similar route to that of its cousin from Mexico to Spain, but from there it was sent to France, again some time during the early sixteenth century, where it was distributed among the curious in Europe. It is believed to have been introduced into

England by the Huguenots fleeing from the Massacre of St Bartholomew in 1572, and flowered for the first time a year later.

French marigolds are smaller than African marigolds, ranging in height from 15–35cm (6–14in), with single and double flowers 2.5–5cm (1–2in) across in many shades of yellow, orange, copper, mahogany, red, and combinations. Unfortunately, it too is saddled with an unpleasant odour, which led many of the early writers to believe it was poisonous. Parkinson wrote that 'but for the beautiful colour, and doublenesse of the flower, pleasant to the eye, and not to any other sense, this kind would find room in few gardens'. Writing much later in 1770, the Rev William Hanbury also confessed that the plant is 'possessed of a strong disagreeable smell, which occassions it being so far abhorred, that few care to handle it, and most chuse to admire its charms at a distance only'. Despite its smell, the plant went on to achieve great popularity and during Victorian times became an exhibitors' favourite, the perfect symmetry and markings of the blooms perfected to vie with the auricula and ranunculus as a florist's flower.

Today, modern French hybrids are available that make tiny, compact bushes 15–20cm (6–8in) tall, with beautifully cut foliage and a refreshingly aromatic smell. They are ideal for bedding and edging, as well as being particularly useful for window boxes and other containers. They are as near as you can get to an instant flower, the buds appearing in a very few weeks from sowing.

CULTIVATION

Sow seed of African marigolds in gentle heat in early spring and plant out after all danger of frost has passed. Give them ample space for development – 24–45cm (10–18in) – and ensure that taller varieties are staked.

These are hungry plants, and are only seen at their best in a rich and thoroughly prepared soil. Particular care must be exercised in watering, as the roots are liable to mat on the surface and prevent moisture from soaking down into the soil. Removing spent blooms regularly will encourage continuous flowering.

Sow and raise French marigolds as suggested for *T. erecta*, but space 15–24cm (6–10in) apart. However, these marigolds flower best in a comparatively poor, dry conditions, as they have a tendency to make excesive leafy growth if planted in rich soil.

COTTAGE GARDEN VARIETIES

• *Tagetes erecta* Cupid Formula Mixed
These neat, globular plants almost hide themselves under their chrysanthemum-like gold and yellow double blooms, each up to 8cm (3in) across. Perfect for the small garden, ideal for the border and for edging, and excellent for growing in tubs and pots. Height 20cm (8in).

• *Tagetes erecta* Inca Series

A quite outstanding range of F1 hybrids, which can flower in only a couple of months from seed. They have huge, brilliantly coloured, fully double flowers, up to 10cm (4in) across, in gold, orange and yellow. Height 30cm (12in).

• *Tagetes erecta* Sunset Giants

This strain bears large, long-stemmed flowers in a range of colours from pale yellow to deep orange. Height 90cm (36in).

• *Tagetes patula* Bonita Mixed

These carnation-flowered French marigolds produce lots and lots of flowers, lots of petals and lots of colour combinations. Treat as a half-hardy annual, or a sow-and-forget. Height 30cm (12in).

• *Tagetes patula* 'High Dune'

Introduced in 1994, to create this variety the breeders returned almost to the original Mexican species for their inspiration and arrived at this new yet almost archetypal French marigold. 'High Dune' produces mounds of attractive, delicate, fine foliage, over which are scattered single velvety, red-maroon flowers all summer until the frosts. Rain- and drought-proof. Height 35cm (14in).

• *Tagetes patula* 'Legion of Honour'

A pretty, single-flowered variety bearing golden yellow flowers with dark brown markings. An old favourite, now much in demand. Height 23cm (9in).

Thunbergia alata

This plant's common name, black-eyed Susan, says it all. A tender, twining tropical perennial that is grown as a half-hardy annual, it is studded with striking yellow, cream, orange or white flowers, 4cm (1½in) across, each with a purple to black eye. It will reach a height of 3m (10ft) in a good summer, and flowers over a period of three or four months. It has light green, arrow-shaped leaves. Plants are often seen trailing from hanging baskets and window boxes.

CULTIVATION

Seeds germinate in 14–21 days at 21–24°C (70–75°F). Plant out 30cm (12in) apart in moist, fertile soil in early summer.

Tithonia rotundifolia

Tithonia rotundifolia, syn. *T. speciosa*, the Mexican sunflower, is one of the fastest-growing and certainly one of the biggest annuals, easily topping 1.2m (4ft) during a moist summer. The genus is named after Tithonius, the king of Troy, beloved of Aurora, the goddess of the dawn, who asked Zeus for immortality for her handsome lover but forgot to ask for eternal youth!

Tithonia, a half-hardy annual, was introduced early in the nineteenth century and, like its relative the zinnia, hails from Mexico and Central America. It no doubt had a place in the gardens of the ancient Inca civilization, since it is also known as the 'golden flower of the Incas'. The deeply veined, somewhat coarse leaves look very much like those of sunflowers; in fact, the biggest and only distinction between *Helianthus* and *Tithonia* as far as most gardeners are concerned is that sunflowers are yellow and the Mexican sunflower is orange – a fiery orange-scarlet as brilliant as the pottery of its native land.

T. rotundifolia is a spectacular plant, very variable in height, according both to the season and where it grows, but generally it can be relied on to exceed 90cm (36in). The 5–8cm (2–3in) showy, daisy-like flowerheads, with orange or scarlet petals encircling

GOOD RESULTS FROM UNNAMED MIXTURES OF TAGETES

a golden yellow centre, are freely produced from mid-summer until mid-autumn.

The Mexican sunflower likes it hot and sunny. It will quickly make a temporary hedge or screen, but should be well staked. A colourful display can be had with very few plants by growing tithonias and cleomes together in a large border. Individual specimens are very effective, but they must have plenty of room to be appreciated – this rules out the small garden, where their impressive stature would be overpowering and claustrophobic.

The long-stemmed flowers of tithonia are excellent for cutting, but remember to seal the hollow stem in boiling water or over a flame. The blooms are faintly fragrant, and are attractive to butterflies.

Tithonias deserve to be better known. They are guaranteed to cause comment wherever they are grown and are well worth trying.

CULTIVATION

Sow seed under glass eight to ten weeks before the last frost. Pot up the seedlings into 12cm (5in) peat pots as soon as they are large enough to handle and plant out, pot and all, in midsummer. Space the plants 60–90cm (24–36in) apart in an ordinary, well-drained garden soil in full sun. Mexican sunflowers are very tolerant of heat and drought and should not be overwatered, otherwise they will grow lush leaves and stems at the expense of flowers.

COTTAGE GARDEN VARIETIES

• *Tithonia rotundifolia* 'Goldfinger'
This form, with vivid orange-scarlet flowers, is much dwarfer than the species. Excellent for cutting. Height 60–75cm (24–30in).
• *Tithonia rotundifolia* 'Torch'
A good cultivar with orange-scarlet flowers. Height 1.2m (4ft).
• *Tithonia rotundifolia* 'Yellow Torch'
A colour break in tithonias, with exceptionally bright, chrome-yellow flowers 8cm (3in) across. A fine plant for cutting and for the back of the border. Height 90–120cm (36–48in).

THUNBERGIA ALATA (top)
and TITHONIA ROTUNDIFOLIA

Torenia fournieri

The trumpet-shaped flowers of the wishbone flower are like small gloxinias. They are sky-blue, with violet lips and a yellow throat, and cover the plant, nearly hiding the bronzy-green, pointed leaves in summer and early autumn. The common name comes from the wishbone shape of the stamen in the centre of the flower. From a distance they look like pansies, but on closer examination they are very different.

These compact, colourful half-hardy annuals are used as edging or border plants or in massed plantings or containers. They bloom well in semi-shade, but will not tolerate being dry.

CULTIVATION
Sow seeds indoors 10–12 weeks prior to planting out in the garden after all danger of frost has passed. The seeds are tiny, and are more easily sown evenly if mixed with a pinch of sugar before sowing. Germination takes 10–15 days at 21°C (70°F). They prefer fertile, moist soil in partial or full shade. Space them 15–20cm (6–8in) apart.

COTTAGE GARDEN VARIETIES
• *Torenia fournieri* Clown Mixed
A beautiful strain producing very compact plants with large, velvety flowers in a wide range of shades of blue, light blue, rose-pink and white. Height 15cm (6in).
• *Torenia fournieri* 'Compacta'
This old-fashioned variety has lavender blooms with dark, velvety blue markings and a bright yellow blotch inside the trumpet-shaped flowers. Height 20cm (8in).
• *Torenia fournieri* Panda Series
An early flowering selection with white, pink and yellow flowers. Good for containers or as a bedding plant. Height 10–20cm (4–8in).

Tropaeolum majus

Tropaeolum majus, the homely, old-fashioned garden nasturtium, has long enjoyed popularity as an easy-to-grow cottage garden plant with its vividly coloured, spurred, single or double flowers on slender stems growing from the axils of the leaves; some newer varieties hold the flowers well above the foliage. A perennial in its native South America, it is usually grown from seed as a hardy annual.

To confuse matters, the nasturtium of the garden is *Tropaeolum*, while *Nasturtium* is the botanical name for the unrelated watercress: the familiar common name of 'nasturtium' signifies 'that which twists the nose', merely, it would seem, because the leaves have the pungency of cress leaves.

Tropaeolum, from the Greek, means 'trophy', alluding to the shield-like appearance of the leaves. Linnaeus describes the flowers rather imaginatively as resembling spear-pierced, bloodstained helmets.

All parts of the plant – seed, leaves, flowers and buds – are edible and are used to garnish salads, but do be sure only to use pesticides suitable for vegetable crops if you are planning to use nasturtiums as food. The spicy, peppery leaves are rich in vitamin C, and seeds gathered while still green can be used as a substitute for capers. Pickled nasturtium seeds are hot and bitter – excellent with bread and cheese, washed down with a glass of elderberry wine. *T. majus* has been credited by the old writers as having the power, in certain atmospheric conditions, of actually emitting electric sparks or flashes from the leaves and flowers; however, without any factual evidence to refer to, one wonders whether this strange phenomenon was observed before or after eating pickled nasturtium seeds, or whether perhaps a glass or two of elderberry wine had something to do with it!

Nasturtium seed which was first sent to Europe by explorers from the expanding Spanish Empire during the late sixteenth century excited and enthralled the botanists, who eagerly sought more seed and information from travellers and missionaries. Gerard was said to have received his seed in 1597 from his dear friend Jean Robin, the keeper of the King's Garden in Paris. In his *Herball* he described the leaves as 'round like wall peniwort, with a smell and taste like the garden Cresses', and 'The flours are dispersed throughout the whole plant, of colour yellow, with a crossed star overthwart the inside, of a deepe Orange colour: unto the backe-part of the same doth hang a taile or spurre'.

T. majus and its varieties are vigorous growers. They are either bushy, growing to 30–45cm (12–18in), or trailing, with stems that can reach 2.5m (8ft) or more in length. The flowers of both types are 5–6cm (2–2½in) across and may be either single or double. Blooms come in a wide range of colours including red, pink, mahogany, yellow, scarlet, orange, tangerine and bicolours. Some are spotted or blotched, and a few are fragrant. The round leaves are a rather dull green and 5–18cm (2–7in) across, although there are several variegated varieties which are most attractive.

Nasturtiums make excellent temporary climbers, rapidly covering trellises or fences. They are also useful for trailing over tree stumps and for carpeting dry, sunny banks where little else will grow. The dwarf or bush varieties can be used as bedding or edging plants, and are the excellent for growing in pots or containers and hanging baskets.

T. peregrinum, syn. *T. canariensis*, the popular 'Canary creeper', is another species which is often to be found in cottage gardens. Growing up to 4m (12ft) in a season, *T. peregrinum* has slender stems, small pale green fig-like leaves and a profusion of prettily fringed, canary-yellow flowers. It grows well in sun or semi-shade, rapidly making a splendid dense screen for the summer, and boasts the longest flowering display of any of the annual climbers. Some plants will grow so vigorously that their weight may well cause weaker supports to collapse.

TROPAEOLUM PEREGRINUM

CULTIVATION

As nasturtiums do not transplant well, the seed, which is large and easy to handle, should be sown *in situ* after all danger of frost has passed. Thin them to 20–30cm (8–12in) apart according to variety. Choose a position in full sun or light shade; unless the leaves are required in quantity, it is a mistake to plant nasturtiums in a rich soil, as this will produce an abundance of foliage but very few flowers. However, they also loathe drought and in these conditions will fade away in mid-season just when they should be at their best. On the other hand, if conditions are too wet the foliage will conceal the flowers completely. Do not fertilize, and water sparingly and only when the soil is dry.

Nasturtiums are a magnet for blackfly and the problem should be dealt with before it gains a hold – a derris-based insecticide will usually do the trick.

Unlike the common nasturtium, *T. peregrinum* responds well to the good life and can be grown quite successfully in a good, rich soil without the growth becoming coarse. Sowings of the Canary creeper made

TROPAEOLUM MAJUS 'ALASKA' (left) and T. MAJUS GLEAM SERIES

eventually covered with a mass of double, delightfully scented flowers, more flowery and less spicy than in other nasturtiums, in a range of brilliant colours. Height 38cm (15in).

• *Tropaeolum majus* 'Strawberries and Cream'
A new and showy variety with light yellow, semi-double flowers, boldly blotched with scarlet in a delightful combination. It also makes an interesting summer-flowering pot plant for a cool, well-lit windowsill. Height 22cm (9in).

• *Tropaeolum majus* Whirlybird Series
These unique, large-flowered nasturtiums produce single, spurless flowers in a bright colour range. The upward-facing blooms are held above the compact yet vigorous mounds of foliage. Ideal for beds, borders and all kinds of containers. Height 30cm (12in).

Verbena

The vast majority of verbenas are hardy or half-hardy perennials, natives of the New World but also grown quite successfully as half-hardy annuals in Britain and Europe and flowering freely during the first year from seed. Annual verbenas come in a range of colours and have dark green lightly cut leaves in basal rosettes. The individually small flowers make flat clusters up to 7cm (3in) across.

The first of the New World verbenas to reach Britain was *V. bonariensis* in 1726. Dr James Sherard, a keen botanist, first grew the plant from seeds which

under glass will get away quicker and start to flower earlier than those made outside, but will begin to fade in late summer, while outdoor sowings will continue to look good, with lots of flowers and healthy leaves up until mid-autumn.

COTTAGE GARDEN VARIETIES

• *Tropaeolum majus* 'Alaska'
This is an absolute must for those who like variegated plants. 'Alaska' carries brightly coloured, semi-double flowers above foliage that is attractively marbled with pale cream in a variety of abstract patterns, so that some leaves are almost devoid of green. One of the few variegated plants that comes almost completely true from seed. Height 20cm (8in).

• *Tropaeolum majus* 'Empress of India':
An old named favourite with dark, almost black foliage and single, deep crimson flowers. Height 22cm (9in).

• *Tropaeolum majus* Gleam Series
The Gleam hybrids have long been a favourite with cottage gardeners, their vigorous bushes of foliage

were taken from a dried specimen sent from Buenos Aires. *V. bonariensis* is quite unlike the bedding plant we call verbena: in fact, growing 1.2–1.5m (4–5ft) tall, most cottage gardeners need some convincing that it is a member of the same genus.

This eyecatching plant has tiny, pale purple flowerheads held in dense clusters and pairs of narrow, pointed leaves on rigid stems which are rather brittle, so staking is recommended. It looks particularly effective when grown in a mass, or towering above smaller plants in a mixed border. Sown early, it will flower the same year, and will usually provide a few self-sown seedlings. Although often described as a hardy perennial, the plant will rarely survive a cold winter.

V. rigida, syn. *V. venosa*, the 'lilac verbena', is also a native of Argentina and was discovered in 1830. It resembles *V. bonariensis* closely but is shorter, growing to 30–60cm (12–24in), and bears its clusters of small, dense, deep lilac-blue flowers on stiffly branched plants from midsummer until the end of the season.

Ever since a writer in the *Cottage Garden* in 1850 recommended that *V. rigida* be combined with scarlet pelargoniums to give a 'shot-silk effect', new plants have been raised each year for use as bedding plants. Because of these bedding associations, choosy gardeners are often rather sniffy about growing *V. rigida*. All too often it is grown in association with rich orange tagetes, a combination which gets the plant a bad name for poor gardening taste; however, used in harmony with a soft pink, ivory, or even cherry colour, it can be very effective. It is ideal for edging a stone path or paving or for planting in a bold group.

Parents of *V. × hybrida*, the common garden verbena, or 'rose vervain', were all introduced from South America between 1826 and 1837. Hybridists used at least three species, *V. chamaedrifolia, V. incisa* and *V. tweedii*, in the breeding of this bedding verbena, with spectacular results. *V. × hybrida* quickly became a popular plant and was soon to be seen in every Victorian parterre. By the 1880s there were around 100 named varieties from which to choose, and for a time the plant was taken up by the florists, with fine blooms raised for exhibition purposes.

Named cultivars available to cottage gardeners today include the deep purple 'Hidcote', the soft pink and scented 'Silver Anne' and the striking scarlet 'Huntsman', all closely resembling their Victorian ancestors but with a much stronger constitution. The

shrubby, unscented 'Sissinghurst', with small bright pink flowerheads, it has been decided, is a species, and is now sold as *V. tenera* 'Sissinghurst'.

V. × hybrida is usually divided into three categories: small-flowered, which include auricula-eyed varieties, the flowers all possessing a prominent white eye; giant-flowered; and the *compacta* or dwarf, bushy forms. The plants make a stunning show of colour, the range including shades of scarlet, crimson, rose, pink, lavender, lilac, purple and white. Depending on the variety, they may be either upright or spreading, growing 15–30cm (6–12in) high, with deeply quilted or textured foliage.

The shrubby lemon verbena is from the same tribe, although thumbing through plant lists it will be found under *Aloysia citriodora* or *Lippia citriodora*.

VERBENA X HYBRIDA 'SILVER ANN'

Lemon verbena must surely rank as one of the most delightful of all scented plants. It is frequently confused with lemon balm (*Melissa officinalis*), but has a richer, sharper lemon scent and, of course, looks nothing like it. The leaves are long, pointed and crinkled, and the small mauve flowers are produced in scattered spikes. Grown against a sheltered sunny wall in a favourable climate it can reach 2–2.5m (6–8ft), but in less favoured regions the plant is more often grown in tubs, which can be stood outside in the summer and moved under glass for the winter.

Lemon verbena leaves are harvested during midsummer, or whenever they are mature. They dry well and retain their inimitable scent and flavour. If warmed up until crisp, they can easily be rubbed down to a fine powder and used for culinary purposes.

Lemon verbena is also used in pot-pourri, and makes a change from lavender in sachets. The scent is brought out by occasionally crushing the leaves.

CULTIVATION

As plants of *Verbena × hybrida* are so variable from seed most gardeners prefer to grow them on from purchased plants. However, for seed cultivation follow this process: chill the seeds of one week before sowing, surface sow on moistened soilless or loam-based potting compost, cover with black plastic until germination begins – 3–4 weeks at 10–24°C (50–75°F). After the first true leaves appear, transplant into trays. When they are established (after about 10 days) harden off then plant out when all danger of frost is passed. Space 25–30cm (10–12in) apart.

V. rigida flowers in the first year from seed. Follow directions as for *V. × hybrida*. The tuberous roots of *V. rigida* can be lifted for the winter and stored in the same way as dahlias.

V. bonariensis, sown as above will also flower in the first year. It will often self-seed but will not make a big clump.

Named varieties like *V. tenera* 'Sissinghust' and good forms can be increased by cuttings taken from the old shoots and inserted in a cold frame in high summer. These cuttings can be lifted when rooted and overwintered in boxes in the greenhouse.

COTTAGE GARDEN VARIETIES

• *Verbena × hybrida* 'Amethyst'
An extremely eyecatching variety, bearing vivid cobalt-blue flowers with a distinct white eye. Height 23–30cm (9–12in).

• *Verbena × hybrida* 'Aphrodite'
A spreading variety with small, deep lilac flowers striped with white. Excellent for pots and containers. Height 15–20cm (6–8in).

• *Verbena × hybrida* 'Blue Lagoon'
The best true-blue verbena, with clusters of rich blue flowers that look spectacular when planted *en masse* and edged with white alyssum. Height 23cm (9in).

• *Verbena × hybrida* Olympia Mixed
An early-flowering strain with dwarf, compact growth and a wide colour range. These well-known verbenas produce their brightly coloured flowers almost continuously from midsummer until autumn. Height 25cm (10in).

• *Verbena × hybrida* 'Peaches and Cream'
A comparatively new variety which has created something of a sensation, picking up numerous awards and medals along the way. The colour is truly lovely, showing shades of apricot, cream, orange and yellow all rolled into one; sometimes these colours are present separately on the same plant. An ideal bedding plant, and wonderful for containers and hanging baskets. Height 23cm (9in).
• *Verbena × hybrida* 'Silver Ann'
A very pretty pastel verbena with abundant rose-pink heads and fine-cut dark green leaves on a spreading bush. Height 45cm (18in).

Viola × wittrockiana

The happy-faced garden pansies are borne on sprawling plants that provide these brilliantly coloured flowers continuously as they grow. Although perennial, pansies are best grown as annuals since they will lose vitality by the second year. The velvety blooms, from 5–13cm (2–5in) across, may be yellow, purple, blue,

VIOLA 'JACKANAPES'

pink, red, white, bronze, lavender or orange. Some have solid, clear colours, but many others have contrasting splotches, brightly coloured centres and markings that create the unique pansy faces. The leaves are heart-shaped or oval, and very often deeply lobed.

Pansies are popular for massing with spring-blooming bulbs, in cottage garden plantings, and are suitable for containers, hanging baskets and window boxes. Cut flowers make charming arrangements.

Most pansies are bought from garden centres, but they may be grown from seeds sown in a cool place (about 10°C/50°F) 12 weeks before the last frost. Seeds will germinate in ten days. When the weather improves, seedlings should be moved out to a cold frame as they really dislike heat. Plant out in a moist, fertile soil in full sun or partial shade, spacing 22–30cm (9–12in) apart. Deadhead and cut back leggy plants to prolong flowering.

COTTAGE GARDEN VARIETIES
• *Viola* Crystal Bowl Series
A pansy strain for those who like flowers with solid colours. These dwarf, compact plants have 11 different, distinct colours including deep blue, purple, white and rose. Height 15cm (6in).
• *Viola* 'Jackanapes'
A very old cultivar with crimson-brown upper petals and bright yellow lower ones. It is not sprawling and has a compact dwarf habit with erect flower stems. Height 13cm (5in).
• *Viola* Majestic Giants
This superb strain has flowers as much as 10cm (4in) across and, in spite of their immense size, they are produced freely and profusely. The mixture contains an extensive range of bright colours, including red, yellow, deep rose-purple – most with cheeky blotches. Height 15cm (6in).

Xeranthemum annuum

Xeranthemum annuum is one of the oldest of the *immortelles* or everlastings in cultivation. An attractive and easily grown hardy annual, to 50cm (20in) high, it has white, woolly leaves and white, purple, magenta or pink flowers, each 4cm (1½in) across. They are borne freely all summer. The true flower in the centre of the flowerhead is surrounded by papery bracts of the same colour. Grow them in the cottage garden or in a cutting bed and use cut flowers both in fresh or dried arrangements.

CULTIVATION

As seedlings resent transplanting, sow seeds directly outdoors in late spring in sandy soil and full sun. They should be thinned to 20cm (8in) apart. Plants bloom about 11 weeks after sowing.

Zinnia

At the end of the alphabetical list, but definitely not at the bottom of the popularity stakes, are the zinnias, half-hardy annuals with daisy-like flowers and thick olive-green leaves. They are available in many Heights, flower forms and colours.

Although the majority of the zinnias are natives of Mexico, where they have been grown for centuries, the genus was named in honour of Johann Gottfried Zinn, an eighteenth-century professor of botany and physics at Göttingen University and author of *Hortus Goettingensis*.

When the Spanish first invaded the Aztec empire in 1520, the gardens of Montezuma were said to equal if not surpass anything to be seen in Europe. Besides the zinnia, the ruler grew dahlias, sunflowers and morning glories. He dispatched his gardeners to all four corners of his realm to track down and introduce new plants and trees, instructing them to prick their ears and sprinkle blood on the leaves of any new species when planting!

It was some time before zinnias first reached Britain. The first, *Z. pauciflora*, was sent to Phillip Miller, nurseryman and writer, from the Royal Gardens of Paris in 1753. It was followed by *Z. elegans*, a rather dowdy, purplish red wildflower that became the parent of our present-day varieties, which was supplied by Professor Ortego of Madrid, who sent seed to the Marchioness of Bute in 1796. It took the genius of nineteenth-century hybridizers to work their magic and turn this rather uninspiring plant, which the Aztecs calles 'eysore', into one of the most popular of bedding plants. It is perhaps because one often sees partially faded flowers on the same plant as half-developed blooms that the plant was given one of its common names, 'youth and old age'.

The first double forms were raised by the French nurseryman, Grazau, in 1856 and in less than a decade a race of colourful, hardier strains were produced, eagerly sought after for the formal gardens of the day. Although most of the breeding during the nineteenth century appears to have been directed to the production of dwarfer and more compact forms, the giant zinnia had already made its debut. In 1865 Mrs Beeton,

ZINNIA 'PETER PAN'

in her book *about Gardening*, quoted a British firm, Messrs Barr & Sugden, as writing 'Our Sardinian correspondent in the autumn forwarded to us a photographed group of double Zinnia flowers, the smallest of which was 3 threequarters inches deep and eleven inches in circumference; another had 586 petals'.

ZINNIA MULTIFLORA

Both the giant and dwarf-flowered forms of *Z. elegans* come in a remarkable range of colours including white, yellow, orange, scarlet, crimson – in fact, almost every conceivable shade except blue, with either single or double flowers, some the size of buttons and others relatively large. The smallest zinnias grow only 15cm (6in) tall, but the tallest can reach up to 1.2m (4ft). Depending on their size, zinnias can be used for edging, background, borders, mixed beds or containers. The rigid stems, and the fact that the flowers do not drop their petals, make them ideal for cutting.

Different flower shapes have been developed and appear in most seedsmen's catalogues under classifications such as dahlia-flowered, scabious-flowered, California and Burpee giants, cactus-flowered, Lilliput and pompon strains. Some new and interesting novelties include 'Envy', with appropriately chartreuse-green flowers, and 'Carved Ivory', an F1 hybrid with unusual creamy white flowers.

CULTIVATION

Zinnias enjoy good living and adore the sun, so should only be grown in a rich, well-prepared soil and a warm, sunny position. Forget all you have read about them being difficult to raise, and treat them more as sow-and-forget annuals by sowing seed *in situ* in late spring when the soil is warming up. Pinch out the growing points of young plants to make them bushy, and space them 15–30cm (6–12in) apart, according to the variety.

The plants appreciate a good watering during hot, dry weather and when they commence flowering, but to prevent mildew – to which zinnias are susceptible – ground-level watering is recommended. The plants should also be fed monthly with a liquid manure to encourage vigorous growth.

COTTAGE GARDEN VARIETIES

• *Zinnia angustifolia* 'Old Mexico'
This variety of *Z. angustifolia*, the so-called 'classic zinnia', has chunky double blooms borne on compact, rounded plants, in a range of bright marmalade shades. Height 30–40cm (12–16in).

• *Zinnia elegans* Dahlia-flowered Mixed
These very decorative zinnias have large, double flowers with lots of rounded petals. 'Canary Bird' has primrose-yellow flowers, 'Scarlet Flame' vivid-scarlet, and 'Polar Bear' white. Height 60cm (24in).

• *Zinnia elegans* Giant Cactus-flowered Mixed
A strain with large, semi-double, cactus-style flowers with lots of long, narrow, quilled petals in a wide range of colours. Height 60–90cm (24–36in).

• *Zinnia elegans* Scabious-flowered Mixed
A rather strange, distinctive and beautiful strain bearing blooms with a tight, double, quilled centre and a collar of broad, flat rays. Usually sold in a mixture of bright colours. Height 60–90cm (24–36in).

• *Zinnia elegans* Whirlygig Mixed
This mixture produces very attractive, bicoloured blooms in a wide range of colours. The petals tips are a different colour from the rest of the flower, creating its unique appearance. Ideal for late-summer bedding. Height 60cm (24in).

• *Zinnia haageana* 'Persian Carpet'
Unlike other garden zinnias, *Z. haageana* varieties have predominantly red, yellow and mahogany flowers. The old-fashioned variety 'Persian Carpet' has very attractive, small, semi-double and double flowers in bicolours and tricolours. The plants are free flowering and weather resistant. Height 25–30cm (10–12in).

• *Zinnia multiflora*
Rarely seen in gardens, this unusual zinnia has single, red flowers with dark centres. Height 60cm (24in).

• *Zinnia* 'Peter Pan'
Splendid dwarf mixture including scarlet, plum, pink, pale pink, yellow, cream and white flowers. Use in bold patches in beds and borders. Height 25cm (10in).

WHO'S WHO?

JOHN GERARD (1545–1612)

Herbalist and gardener to Lord Burghley in the Strand, London, and at Theobalds in Hertfordshire, John Gerard also had a famous garden of his own in Holborn, London, where he *laboured with the soile to make it fit for plants, and with the plants, that they might delight in the soile.*

Gerard was a passionate collector of new plants, many of which he obtained via merchant friends who travelled abroad. Large numbers of these new plants find their first description either in the two lists, or *Catalogues* of flowers grown in his own garden in 1596 and 1599, or in his famous *Herball or Historie of Plantes* (1597). Despite numerous inaccuracies and shortcomings, these publications are major landmarks in the history of gardening and are of great value in establishing what plants were actually in cultivation in England at the time.

JOHN PARKINSON (1567–1650)

John Parkinson was apprenticed as an apothecary but was also a passionate collector of flowers. His garden, situated in Long Acre, Covent Garden, London, was well stocked with rarities. He wrote *Paradisi in Sole, Paradisus Terrestris* (1629) – the title a Latin pun on his own name, Park-in-sun – the first English illustrated book devoted primarily to ornamental plants. It offers a delightful picture of early seventeenth century gardens, despite the poor quality of the woodcuts. After its publication, Parkinson was appointed King's Botanist to Charles I. In 1640, his *Theatrum Botanicum, A Herball of a Large Extent*, the culmination of his life's work, was published. Listing 3,800 plants and drawing its information from many sources, the plants are grouped, somewhat oddly, according to their medical properties – *venemous, sleepy, or hurtful plants, cooling or succory-like plants, hot and sharpe-biting plants,* and so on. The large number of species which did not fit into any of the categories were gathered together into what he called *The Unordered Tribe.*

NICHOLAS CULPEPPER (1616–1654)

Nicholas Culpeper was apprenticed to an apothecary of St. Helens, Bishopsgate, London, and in about 1640 set himself up as an astrologer and physician in Red Lion Street, Spitalfields, London. His strong conviction in astrological medicine – that every disease was governed by a planet and could be cured by herbs under the domination of that planet – would, nowadays, single him out as a quack, but he was perfectly sincere in his peculiar beliefs and, though poor himself, never grudged free medical assistance to those in need.

In 1649 he published an unauthorized English translation of the Latin *Pharmacopoeia* of the College of Physicians and, in so doing, brought down upon himself the wrath of the medical profession. A revised and augmented edition, *The English Pysician Enlarged* (1653), in which he describes the good and bad qualities of plants, became enormously popular, and versions of it continued to be published up to and including the present century. He died from consumption at the early age of 38, leaving a wife, seven children and 79 manuscript books and translations on astrology and medicine, some of which were published posthumously.

REVEREND WILLIAM HANBURY (1725–1778)

One of the most notable of that well-known breed of distinguished writers, the gardening churchmen, William Hanbury became rector of Church Langton in Leicestershire in 1753. Having a natural genius for planting and gardening he had, two years previously, begun to make extensive plantations and gardens in the parish and two other adjoining parishes. Five years later these were valued at £10,000. In an *Essay on Planting* in 1758, he proposed a scheme whereby these gardens were to be vested in a body of trustees, the produce sold, and any profits put to good use in various charitable causes. However, his daydreams of providing a village hospital, a public library, a picture gallery, a college with various professorships and, last but not least, a choral college at Oxford, from the accumulated funds were sadly unrealized, as the income from the trust at the time of his death was just over £190. Eighty-six years later, when it had got as high as £900, the scheme was wound up.

William Hanbury obtained seeds and plants for his garden from all quarters, including many from North America. His *Complete Body of Planting and Gardening*, published fortnightly from 1769–1773, in sixpenny parts, is a thoroughly comprehensive and knowledgeable work, amounting to two large folio volumes.

SEED MERCHANTS & SOCIETIES

UK SEED MERCHANTS

Chiltern Seeds
Bortree Stile, Ulverston,
Cumbria LA12 7PB

J.W. Boyce
67 Station Road, Soham, Ely,
Cambridgeshire CB7 5ED

Samuel Dobie & Son Ltd
PO Box 90, Paignton,
Devon TQ3 1XY

Mr Fothergill's Seeds
Gazeley Road, Kentford,
Newmarket, Suffolk CB8 7QB

Sutton Seeds Ltd
Hele Road, Torquay,
Devon TQ2 7QJ

Thompson & Morgan (Ipswich) Ltd
London Road, Ipswich,
Suffolk IP2 0BA

Unwins Seeds Ltd
Histon, Cambridge,
Cambs CB4 4LE

WILDFLOWERS AND HERBS

John Chambers
15 Westleigh Road, Barton,
Seagrave, Kettering
Northants NN15 5AJ

SWEET PEA SPECIALISTS

Robert Bolton & Son
Birdbrook, Halstead,
Essex CO9 4BQ

Les Marchant Sweet Peas
17 Old Road, North Petherton,
Bridgwater, Somerset TA6 6PF

US SEED MERCHANTS

W. Atlee Burpee Co
300 Park Avenue, Warminster,
PA 18974

Gurney's Seed & Nursery Co
110 Capital Street, Yankton,
SD 57079

Johnny's Selected Seeds
Foss Hill Road, Albion,
ME 04910–9731

Park Seed Co
Cokesbury Road, Greenwood,
SC 29647

DeGiorgi Seed Company
6011 N Street, Omaha,
NE 68117–1634

R.H. Shumway Seeds
PO Box 1, 571 Whaley Pond Road,
Graniteville, SC 29829

SPECIALIST SOCIETIES

Cottage Garden Society
(Clive Lane)
Brandon, Ravenshall, Betley,
Cheshire CW3 9BH

The American Cottage Gardener
131 East Michigan St, Marquette,
MI 49855

National Dahlia Society
(E.H. Collins)
19 Sunnybank, Marlow,
Bucks SL7 3BL

British Fuchsia Society
(R. Williams)
20 Brodawel, Llannon, Llanelli,
Dyfed SA14 6BJ

British Pelargonium & Geranium
Society (Carol & Ron Helyar)
134 Montrose Avenue, Welling,
Kent DA16 2QY

National Sweet Pea Society
(J.R.F. Bishop)
3 Chalk Farm Road,
Stokenchurch, High Wycombe,
Bucks HP14 3TB

National Viola & Pansy Society
(Mrs P. Tipping)
24 Baldwin Street, Smethwick,
Warley, West Midlands B66 3RQ

FURTHER READING

Some of the recommended books in the list below are out of print but are well worth searching for.

Balfour, A.P. *Annual and Biennial Flowers* (Geoffrey Bless Ltd, London 1959)

Christensen, Carol Landa, & Marston, Ted. *Annuals* (Publications International Ltd, Lincolnwood, Illinois)

Coates, Alice M. *Flowers and their Histories* (Hulton Press, 1956)

Fish, Margery. *Cottage Garden Flowers* (Faber Paperbacks, 1980)

Frutig Bales, Suzanne. *Container Gardening* (Burpee American Gardening Series, New York, 1993)

Garden Way Publishing, Eds. *Annuals* (Doubleday Book & Music Clubs Inc, USA, 1989)

Gardening from Which? magazine (Subscription, Hertford, England)

Gray, Rob, & Proctor, Rob. *Annuals* (Harper Collins, New York, 1991)

Halliwell, Brian. *Old Garden Flowers* (Bishopsgate Press, 1987)

Hay, Roy. *Annuals* (The Bodley Head, London, 1937)

Hessayon, Dr D.G. *The Bio Friendly Gardening Guide* (pbi Publications, 1990)

Lane, Clive. *The Cottage Gardener's Companion* (David & Charles, Newton Abbot, 1993)

Loewer, Peter. *Annuals* (Better Homes and Gardens Books, Des Moines, 1994)

Loewer, Peter. *Organic Gardener's Annuals* (Van Patten Publishing, Portland, Oregon, 1993)

Mansfield, T.C. *Annuals* (Collins, 1949)

Reilly, Ann. *Annuals* (Houghton Mifflin Company, Boston, 1990)

Sunset Books and Sunset Magazine, Eds. *Annuals* (Menlo Park, 1994)

Weaver, Pat. *Annuals and Bedding Plants* (HarperCollins, 1989)

INDEX

Abutilon × *hybridum* 42;
  maximum 42; *variegata* 16, 42
*Ageratum houstonianum/
  mexicanum* 23, 26, 38, 42–3
Agrostemma githago 25, 33, 43
Aiton, William 97, 112
Alcea/Althaea rosea 20, 26, 38,
  43–5
Amaranthus caudatus 15, 16,
  20, 27, 46–7; *tricolor* 46, 47
Ammobium alatum 16, 47
Anethum graveolens 20
Antirrhinum majus 15, 17, 20,
  23, 26, 33, 38, 40, 48–9
Argyranthemum 23, 50–1;
  frutescens 50, 51
Aster, Chinese 26, 38, 60–2
Atriplex hortensis 16, 52
Avina sterilis 26, 124

Baby-blue eyes 19, 120
Baby's breath 26, 28, 94–5
Basil 16, 17, 123
Baskets, hanging 21, 23, 31
Beans, runner 17, 31
Beefsteak plant 16, 132
Beeton, Mrs 155–6
Begonia, tuberous 19, 23, 52–4;
  wax 16, 19, 23, 52, 54
Begonia semperflorens 16, 19,
  23, 33, 52, 54;
  × *tuberhybrida* 19, 23, 52–4
Bellis perennis 26, 54–5;
  prolifera 54
Bells of Ireland 20, 26–8, 32,
  33, 117
Bergamot 72
Black-eyed Susan 15, 19, 23,
  31, 147
Blanket flower 15, 92–3
Borage 25, 28, 55–6
Borago officinalis 25, 55–6
Bourne, Hermon 46
Brachycome iberidifolia 23,
  56–7
Brassica oleracea 16, 32, 57–8
Briza maxima 20, 26, 28, 124
Broccoli, purple/white 17
Browall, John 58
Browallia speciosa 19, 23, 58
Buonaiuti, Mr 80
Burning bush 16, 105
Busy lizzie 15, 19, 23, 33, 39,

102–3; New Guinea 16, 23,
  102–3
Bute, Marchioness of 78, 80, 155
Butterfly flower 19, 33

Cabbage, ornamental 16, 32,
  39, 57–8
Calendula officinalis 10, 15, 17,
  23, 25, 26, 33, 38, 58–60
California bluebells 120; poppy
  15, 25, 26, 33, 38, 90–2
Callistephus chinensis 26, 38,
  60–2
Campanula medium 25, 62
Canary creeper 31, 150
Canavilles, Abbé 80
Candytuft 15, 25, 33, 38, 101–2
Canterbury bells 25, 62
Cardiospermum halicacabum
  31, 62
Celosia argentea cristata 20, 28,
  63–4; *plumosa* 26, 63–4
Centaurea cyanus 26, 33, 64–5;
  imperialis 65; *moschata* 26,
  64, 65
Chamomile, corn 24
Chater, W. 44
Cheek, Roy 50
Cheiranthus 15, 19, 25, 29, 65–7
Cherry pie 15, 23, 26, 29,
  98–100
Chilean glory flower 31, 89
Cineraria 19
Clarkia 15, 20, 25, 26, 33, 68–9
Clary 139
Cleome spinosa 19, 20, 26, 38,
  69–71
Climbers 30–1
Clusius 116
Coates, Alice 84, 95
Cobaea scandens 31, 71
Cobo, Father 71
Cockscomb 20, 26, 28, 63–4
Cole, Silas 106
Coleus blumei 19, 33, 72–3
Colour 14–15
Consolida ambigua 15, 19, 20,
  25, 26, 33, 38, 74–5
Containers 21–3, 31, 37
Convolvulus 23, 26, 38, 75–7
Convolvulus tricolor 23, 38,
  75–7
Coreopsis 15, 77

Coreopsis tinctoria 15, 77
Corn cockle 24, 25, 33, 43
Cornflower 24, 25, 26, 33, 64
Cosmos 20, 25, 26, 38, 78–9
Coys, William 75
Culpeper, Nicholas 44, 139
Custard and cream 109
Cutting, plants for 25–6
Cynoglossum amabile 19, 79
Cypress, summer 16, 105

Dahl, Dr Andreas 80
Dahlia 15, 19, 20, 26, 27, 38–40,
  80–3; *merckii* 81–2
Daisy, 54–5; double 26;
  Gloriosa 15, 138–9; hen-and-
  chicken 54; Paris 50; Swan
  River 23, 56–7
Damping off 35
Deadheading 25, 38, 42
Dianthus barbatus 29, 38, 84–5
Digitalis 20, 25, 86–9; *alba* 87;
  grandiflora 18–19, 89;
  purpurea 18, 19, 86, 87, 89
Dill 20
Dioscorides 49, 64
Diseases 40
Douglas, David 68, 90
Drainage 21, 23
Dried flowers 11, 27–8
Drummond, James 97; Thomas
  135
Drying out 21, 23
Dusty miller 144–5

Eccremocarpus scaber 31, 89
Eckford, Henry 106
Erysimum 15, 19, 25, 29, 66–7
Eschscholz, Dr J.F. von 90
Eschscholzia californica 15, 25,
  26, 33, 38, 90–2
Euphorbia marginata 16, 92
Evening primrose 19, 29, 79,
  123–4
'Everlasting' flowers 11, 27, 28,
  47, 97–8, 154; pea 31;
  Winged 16, 47

Fairchild, Thomas 106
Fennel 20
Fertilizer 18, 22, 25, 37
Fish, Margery 67
Floss flower 23, 26, 38, 42–3

Foeniculum vulgare 20
Foliage 16–17
Forget-me-not 15, 19, 24–6,
  118–20; Chinese 19, 79
Four-o'clock flower 23, 29
Foxglove 19, 24, 25, 38, 86–9
Foxtail barley 28, 124
Fragrance, flowers for 28–9

Gaillardia pulchella 15, 92–3
Gaza, Theodore 93
Gazania rigens 15, 93
Geranium 15, 16, 19, 21, 26, 28,
  29, 129–32; oak-leaf 129–30;
  rose 129, 130
Gerard, John 44, 46, 48, 49, 55,
  59, 64, 65, 84, 86, 96, 97, 101,
  112, 116, 118, 121, 126, 145,
  149
Globe amaranth 26, 28, 94
Gomphrena globosa 26, 28, 94
Goodyer, John 75, 104
Grasses 11, 27, 124; hare's
  tail/squirrel-tail 28, 124
Gypsophila elegans 26, 28,
  94–5

Halliwell, Brian 50
Hanbury, Rev. William 46, 56,
  75, 97, 146
Hardening off 36
Helianthus annuus 15, 19, 20,
  25, 38, 95–6
Helichrysum bracteatum 28, 33,
  38, 97–8; *orientale* 97
Heliotrope 15, 98–100
Heliotropium arborescens 15,
  23, 26, 29, 39, 98–100
Hernandez, Francisco 80
Hesperis matronalis 25, 29, 100
Hibberd, Shirley 80
Hill, John 48
Hindley, John 135
Hollyhock 20, 26, 38, 40, 43–5
Honesty 11, 19, 24, 25, 28,
  112–14
Hop, variegated 31
Hordeum jubatum 28, 124
Humulus japonicus variegatus
  31
Hunt, Mr 84
Iberis amara 101–2; *umbellata*
  25, 33, 38, 101–2

Impatiens 16, 19, 23, 26, 33, 102–3; *roylei* 25, 38, 102; *walleriana* 15, 19, 23, 102–3
d'Incarville, Father 60
Ipomoea 15, 31, 33, 38, 39, 104–5; *alba* 104–5; *quamoclit* 105
Jekyll, Gertrude 130, 140
Johnson, Thomas 75
Justice, James 60, 145
de Jussieu, Joseph 99

Kale, ornamental 16, 32, 57–8
Kochia scoparia 16, 105

Lagurus ovatus 28, 124
Larkspur 15, 19, 20, 25, 26, 28, 33, 38, 74–5
Lathyrus latifolius 31, 107; *odoratus* 15, 26, 29, 31–3, 38, 106–7
Lavatera trimestris 20, 109
Lettuce 17
Lewis, Captain Meriwether 68
Limnanthes douglasii 24–5, 33, 109
Limonium sinuatum 28, 110
Lippia citriodora 29, 152–3
Lobelia 19, 23, 110–11
Lobelia erinus 19, 23, 110–11
Lobularia maritima 10, 15, 19, 23, 25, 26, 29, 33, 38, 111–12
Loudon, J.C. 50
Love-in-a-mist 11, 15, 26, 28, 33, 121–3
Love-lies-bleeding 15, 16, 20, 27, 46–7
Love-in-a-puff 31, 62
Lucas, William 75
Lunaria annua 11, 19, 25, 28, 112–14

Madwort 10
Mallow, jagged 44; tree 20, 109
Maple, flowering 16, 42
Marguerite 23, 50–1
Marigold 15, 20, 23, 24, 27, 28, 38; African 26, 145–7; corn 24; French 26, 33, 145–7; Pot 10, 15, 23, 25, 26, 28, 33, 38, 39, 58–60
Marvel of Peru 15, 29, 116–17
Matthiola bicornis 29, 114; *incana* 15, 23, 29, 33, 114–15
Meconopsis cambrica 25
Melissa officinalis 153
Mexican ivy 31, 71
Mignonette 11, 15, 29, 137
Miller, Phillip 99, 155
Millet, foxtail 28, 124
Mimulus 19, 23, 115

Mirabilis jalapa 15, 23, 29, 116–17
Mocino, José 78
Moluccella laevis 20, 26–8, 32, 33, 117
Monarda didyma 72
Monastery bells 31, 71
Monkey flower 19, 23, 115
Moonflower 104–5
Moonwort *see* Honesty
Morning glory 15, 31, 33, 38, 39, 104–5
Moss/sun rose 23, 136
Mountain spinach 52
Myosotis alpestris 15, 19, 25, 26, 118–20; *raikura* 118

Nasturtium 15, 16, 19, 20, 23, 25, 31, 33, 39, 149–51
Naturalizing 24–5
Nemophylla menziesii 19, 120
Nicotiana 11, 15, 19, 20, 23, 33, 34, 38, 39, 120–1; *alata* 29, 120–1; *sylvestris* 29
Nigella damascena 11, 15, 26, 28, 33, 121–3

Oats, animated 26, 124
Ocimum basilicum 16, 123
Oenothera biennis 19, 29, 79, 123–4
Orach, garden 16, 52

Pansy 15, 16, 19, 23–5, 32, 38, 154
Papaver 15, 25, 26, 38, 126–8; *nudicaule* 128; *rhoeas* 33, 126; *somniferum* 126, 128
Paper moon 11, 142
Parkinson, John 44, 46, 48, 64, 65, 75, 84, 86, 116, 123, 141, 145
Paterson, Lt Col 97
Pelargonium 15–17, 19, 23, 26, 28, 29, 129–32, 152; *denticulatum* 129; *graveolens* 129, 130; *quercifolium* 129-30
Perilla frutescens 16, 74, 132
Pests 21, 39–40
Petunia 15, 19, 23, 26, 29, 33, 38, 39, 132–5
Phlox 32, 38, 135
Phlox drummondii 32, 38, 135
Pinching out 37
Pliny 43
Poached egg plant 24–5, 33, 109
Policeman's helmet 38, 102
Poppy 15, 20, 24–6, 33, 38, 126–8; Iceland 128; Welsh 25

Portulaca grandiflora 23, 116, 136
Pot-pourri 28
Pressing, flower 27–8
Pricking out 12, 33, 35–6
Pruning 39

Quaking grass 26, 28, 124

Reseda odorata 15, 29, 137
Rhodochiton atrosanguineum 31, 138
Rudbeckia hirta 15, 138–9
Rust 40, 44, 49

Sage 23, 26, 139–41
Salpiglossis 19
Salvia 19, 23, 139–41
Salvia 139–41; *farinacea* 26, 140; *patens* 141; *sclarea* 139–40; *splendens* 33, 140; *viridis* 140, 141
Saxifraga umbrosa 84
Scabiosa atropurpurea 26, 29, 33, 38, 141–2; *stellata* 11, 142
Scarification 32
Schizanthus pinnatus 15, 143; × *wisetonensis* 19, 33, 143–4
Seed, collecting 10, 38; growing from 10, 32–8, under glass 11, 34–5; self- 10, 12, 24; storage 32
Senecio cineraria 19, 144–5
Sessé y Lacasta, Dr Martin 78
Setaria italica 28, 124
Shade, plants for 15, 18–19
Sherard, Dr James 151
Snapdragon 15, 20, 23, 26, 33, 38, 48–9
Snow-on-the-mountain 16, 92
Spider flower 19, 20, 26, 38, 69–71
Spraying 26, 40
Staking 20, 37–8
Statice 28, 110
Stock 11, 15, 21, 23, 28, 29, 33, 34, 114–15; night-scented 29, 114
Stratification 32
Strawflower 28, 33, 38, 97–8
Sunflower 14–15, 19, 20, 25, 38, 95–6; Mexican 15, 19–20, 33, 147–8
Sweet alyssum 10, 15, 19, 23, 25, 26, 29, 33, 38, 111–12;
Sweet pea 11, 15, 20, 21, 26, 28, 29, 31–3, 38, 39, 106–7
Sweet rocket 24, 25, 29, 100
Sweet scabious 26, 29, 33, 38
Sweet sultan 26, 64
Sweet William 29, 38, 84–5

Swiss chard 17
Symons-Jeune, Captain 135

Tagetes 15, 23, 38, 145–7, 152; *erecta* 20, 26, 146–7; *patula* 26, 145–6
Theophrastus 69, 93
Thinning 34
Thunbergia alata 15, 19, 23, 31, 147
Tithonia rotundifolia 15, 19–20, 26, 33, 147–8
Tobacco plant 11, 15, 19, 20, 23, 29, 33, 38, 120–1
Torenia fournieri 19, 149
Tradescant, John 75, 141
Transplanting 12, 33, 36, 37
Treasure flower 15, 93
Tropaeolum majus 15, 16, 23, 25, 31, 33, 149–51; *peregrinum* 31, 150–1
Turner, William 44, 49

Uvedale, Dr Robert 106

Vegetables 7, 17
Verbena 15, 26, 32, 33, 38, 151–4; lemon 28, 29, 152–3; lilac 152
Verbena bonariensis 26, 32, 151–2; × *hybrida* 33, 152–4; *rigida* 152, 153
Vine, balloon 31, 62; cup and saucer 31, 71; Cyprus 105; purple bell 31, 138
Viola 19, 24, 154
Viola 15, 19, 25; × *wittrockiana* 23, 32, 38, 154
Violet, damask/dame's 29, 100

Wallflower 15, 19, 25, 28, 29, 65–7
Watering 21–3, 25, 31, 34–7
Weeding 39
Wigwams 30–1
Wildflowers 24–5
Windowboxes 21–3, 31
Wishbone flower 19, 149
Withering, Dr William 86

Xeranthemum annuum 28, 154

Zinn, Johann Gottfried 155
Zinnia 15, 20, 23, 26–8, 38, 40, 155–6
Zinnia angustifolia 156; *elegans* 15, 20, 23, 26, 38, 156; *haageana* 156; *pauciflora* 155